WORLD HERITAGE, TOURISM AND IDENTITY

The remarkable success of the 1972 UNESCO Convention Concerning the Protection of World Cultural and Natural Heritage is borne out by the fact that more than 1,000 properties have now been designated as possessing Outstanding Universal Value and recognition given to the imperative for their protection. However, the success of the Convention is not without its challenges and a key issue for many sites relates to the touristic legacies of inscription. For many sites inscription on the World Heritage List acts as a promotional device and the management challenge is one of protection, conservation and dealing with increased numbers of tourists. For other sites, designation has not brought anticipated expansion in tourist numbers and associated investments. What is clear is that tourism is now a central concern to the wide array of stakeholders involved with World Heritage sites. It is a motivation for regions, states and communities to be put on the World Heritage List and it is certainly an outcome of being on the List.

This volume, through a diverse range of international cases covering cultural, natural and mixed World Heritage sites, covering both the developed and the developing world, examines the ways in which sites have been inscribed on the World Heritage List and what this has meant in terms of tourism relating to practical issues of management, carrying capacity and the experiences of tourists and local communities. It also looks at the way 'being on the list' shapes, and is shaped by, shifting values and politics at the macro and micro level.

T0361240

Heritage, Culture and Identity

Series Editor: Brian Graham,
School of Environmental Sciences, University of Ulster, UK

Other titles in this series

Bosnia and the Destruction of Cultural Heritage
Helen Walasek with contributions by Richard Carlton,
Amra Hadžimuhamedović, Valery Perry and Tina Wik
ISBN 978 1 4094 3704 8

World Heritage in Iran
Perspectives on Pasargadae
Edited by Ali Mozaffari
ISBN 978 1 4094 4844 0

Edible Identities: Food as Cultural Heritage
Edited by Ronda L. Brulotte and Michael A. Di Giovine
ISBN 978 1 4094 4263 9

Who Needs Experts?
Counter-mapping Cultural Heritage
Edited by John Schofield
ISBN 978 1 4094 3934 9

The Making of a Cultural Landscape
The English Lake District as Tourist Destination, 1750–2010
Edited by John K. Walton and Jason Wood
ISBN 978 1 4094 2368 3

Cultural Heritage of the Great War in Britain
Ross J. Wilson
ISBN 978 1 4094 4573 9

Many Voices, One Vision: The Early Years of the World Heritage Convention
Christina Cameron and Mechtild Rössler
ISBN 978 1 4094 3765 9

Partitioned Lives: The Irish Borderlands
Catherine Nash, Bryonie Reid and Brian Graham
ISBN 978 1 4094 6672 7

World Heritage, Tourism and Identity
Inscription and Co-production

Edited by

LAURENT BOURDEAU
University of Laval, Canada

MARIA GRAVARI-BARBAS
University of Paris 1 Pantheon-Sorbonne, France

MIKE ROBINSON
University of Birmingham, UK

LONDON AND NEW YORK

First published 2015 by Ashgate Publishing

2 Park Square, Milton Park, Abingdon, Oxfordshire OX14 4RN
711 Third Avenue, New York, NY 10017

Routledge is an imprint of the Taylor & Francis Group, an informa business

First issued in paperback 2018

British Library Cataloguing in Publication Data
A catalogue record for this book is available from the British Library

The Library of Congress has cataloged the printed edition as follows:
World heritage, tourism, and identity : inscription and co-production / [edited by] by Laurent Bourdeau, Maria Gravari-Barbas, and Mike Robinson.
     pages cm. -- (Heritage, culture, and identity)
  Includes bibliographical references and index.
  ISBN 978-1-4094-7058-8 (hardback)
1. World Heritage areas. 2. Heritage tourism. I. Bourdeau, Laurent, editor.

  G140.5. W678 2015
  910--dc23

2014046524

ISBN 978-1-4094-7058-8 (hbk)
ISBN 978-1-138-54656-1 (pbk)

Contents

List of Figures

List of Tables

List of Contributors

Arellano, Alexandra, School of Human Kinetics, University of Ottawa, Canada.

Bourdeau, Laurent, Department of Geography, Université Laval, Canada.

Brantom, Jane, Heritage and Tourism Research, UK.

Cardeira da Silva, Maria, Faculty of Social Sciences and Humanities, Universidade Nova de Lisboa, Portugal.

Carmichael, Barbara, Department of Geography and Environmental Studies, Wilfrid Laurier University, Canada.

Crawford, Kevin R., Department of Geography, Liverpool Hope University, UK.

Doherty, Sean, Department of Geography and Environmental Studies, Wilfrid Laurier University, Canada.

Fukushima, Ayako, Department of Environment Design, Kyushu University, Japan.

Gravari-Barbas, Maria, Institut de Recherche et d'Études Supérieures du Tourisme, Université Paris Sorbonne-Paris 1, France.

Halpenny, Elizabeth A., Faculty of Physical Education and Recreation, University of Alberta, Canada.

Hurnath, Chaya, Faculty of Geography and Planning, Université de Toulouse, le Mirail, France.

Jimura, Takamitsu, Business School, York St John University, UK.

Keshodkar, Akbar, Department of Humanities and Social Sciences, Zayed University, United Arab Emirates.

Khirfan, Luna, School of Planning, Faculty of Environment, University of Waterloo, Canada.

McClanahan, Angela, University of Edinburgh/Edinburgh College of Art, UK.

Quinlan Cutler, Sarah, Department of Geography and Environmental Studies, Wilfrid Laurier University, Canada.

Reed, Ann, Department of Anthropology, University of North Dakota, USA.

Robinson, Mike, Ironbridge International Institute for Cultural Heritage, University of Birmingham, UK.

Salazar, Noel B., Faculty of Social Sciences, University of Leuven, Belgium.

Sambadoo, Priscilla, Institut de Recherche et d'Études Supérieures du Tourisme, Université Paris Sorbonne-Paris 1, France.

Shieldhouse, Richard, University of Florida, USA.

Shortliffe, Sarah Ellen, International Association of World Heritage Professionals, Brandenburg University of Technology, Germany.

Stuart, Stephen A., Faculty of Human Sciences, Saint Paul University, Ottawa, Canada.

Torres Martínez, Isabel Maria, Institute for Tourism Research, University of Bedfordshire, UK.

Wall, Geoffrey, Department of Geography, Faculty of Environment, University of Waterloo, Canada.

Xiang, Yixiao, Department of Tourism Management, School of Management, Shandong University, China.

Chapter 1

World Heritage and Tourism: From Opposition to Co-production

Maria Gravari-Barbas, Laurent Bourdeau and Mike Robinson

The relationship between World Heritage and tourism is a long standing and complex one. Despite tourism being mentioned only once amongst the 38 articles of the 1972 "Convention Concerning the Protection of the World Cultural and Natural Heritage"[1] (UNESCO 1972) it has been a constant reality in the day-to-day practices of site management and has long underpinned how World Heritage Sites are perceived, encountered and experienced in the wider social and political realm. Over 40 years and more since the Convention, consideration of tourism as an active variable in the production and consumption of World Heritage has shifted from being implicit, to being ever-more explicit in both policy and practice.

There are of course numerous sites on the World Heritage List which, for reasons of protection, daily management, or issues of physical and perceptual access, do not attract significant numbers of tourists. In addition, the designation of World Heritage status may fall upon sites, particularly urban sites, which already have some degree of tourist activity. However, in the main it is difficult to think of World Heritage Sites without imagining swarms of tourists taking photographs, lines of parked tour buses and attendant souvenir stalls. Anyone arriving at a World Heritage Site is confronted by the realities of tourism; significant numbers of tourists, along with a service sector which has developed in scale and scope to meet the needs of the temporary but recurrent tourist population. Aside from some signs of the long term attrition of physical fabric and litter, there are seldom markers of excess tourists immediately visible. Negative impacts tend to be cumulative and hidden, revealing themselves rather more subtly through price inflation, community displacement and acculturation.

---

1   In the 1972 Convention, the term "tourism" appears only once, in Article 11.4 which defines the property that may appear on the List of World Heritage in Danger "may not appear on this list of the cultural and natural heritage which is threatened by serious and specific dangers, such as the threat of disappearance caused by accelerated deterioration, large-scale public or private works, rapid urban or tourist development, destruction due to changes in the use or ownership of the land changes deep due to unknown causes; abandonment for any reason, armed conflict or threat of burst, calamities and disasters, large fires, earthquakes, landslides, volcanic eruptions, changes in water level, floods and tidal waves."

More direct and visible is the process of infrastructure developments associated with tourism development, and while not necessarily within the boundaries of World Heritage Sites it has been argued that they can impact on the quality of the site (Leask and Fyall 2006). Certainly within the academic literature considerable attention has been given to studies which exemplify the problems that tourism can, and does, pose to the physical fabric of cultural and natural heritage sites and to the socio-cultural well-being of nearby local communities. Such studies have fed, and are fed by, a pervasive discourse which suggests that tourism is *de facto*, a threat to World Heritage. But while the impacts of tourism—whatever their extent—are assessed, measured and managed, wider geo-political questions are raised regarding the category of World Heritage itself and whether there is indeed some degree of a causality between site designation and the ability to attract tourists. However, it goes without saying that World Heritage Sites are not homogeneous and their management is not monolithic (Bourdeau, Gravari-Barbas and Robinson 2011; Di Giovine 2009). They differ considerably in terms of their reputation, the extent of the tourism flows around them and the extent to which the State and related actors contribute (Ashworth and van der Aa 2006). It is this diversity in the face of the uniformity of production, and production at the nexus between the global and the local, which creates an interesting "heritagescape" (Di Giovine 2009) and an interesting field of research (Djament-Tran, Fagnoni and Jacquot 2012).

The entanglements existing between tourism and World Heritage are in evidence across the marketing and communication networks that pervade the developed and developing world. Many destinations, whether at the national or regional scale, privilege "World" heritage amongst their inventories of attractions to visit, in actions of genuine pride but also in the knowledge that they carry an additional appeal for the tourist market. Tour operators devise their routes and itineraries to include World Heritage Sites as "highlights" and there are operators that specialize in packaging World Heritage centered itineraries. The British-based company Hurlingham Travel offers what it presents as the "World's Most Expensive Vacation" (at $1.5 million) to see all of the World Heritage Sites in "luxury," cutting through some 157 countries (http://hurlinghamtravel.co.uk/). While it appears that no one, at the time of writing, has undertaken the tour it demonstrates in the extreme the prestige that is loaded onto the World Heritage label. The United Nations Educational, Scientific and Cultural Organisation (UNESCO) itself plays to the realities of the iconic role of World Heritage Sites in national tourism marketing campaigns and frequently carries advertisements for country destinations in its *World Heritage Magazine* that frame heritage sites and landscapes, not only as having particular values and that require protection, but as places for tourists to visit. More indirectly too UNESCO is caught up in the dilemma of promoting World Heritage Sites whilst at the same time seeking their protection from the excesses of tourism. In 2008 for instance UNESCO collaborated in the publication of the popular promotional guide *1001 Historic Sites You Must See Before You Die* (Cavendish 2008), which while offering a

Preface by the then Director-General of UNESCO, Koichiro Matsuura warning of the dangers of poorly managed tourism, nevertheless provided a highly visible promotional message.

Guide-books similarly give prominence to World Heritage in their prescriptive narratives of destinations. Visual texts directed to prospective tourists by way of national advertising campaigns and filmic montages that aim to provide a scopic overview of place in a limited time, again, strongly feature images of World Heritage Sites and, in a similar vein, creative works of film, literature and commercial advertising, have, knowingly and unknowingly, increasingly employed World Heritage Sites as both background and foreground for story purposes. In the vernacular recollections of journeys and holidays that now litter cyberspace in the form of blogs and personal diaries, replete as they are with copious photographs, visits to World Heritage Sites are accorded a degree of detail and reverence and a visit to them has become a kind of social marker of achievement. What is important to note about these various representations of World Heritage and their intersections with the realms of tourism is that they speak of a process of both conscious and unconscious appropriation whereby the sites, structures and landscapes that have been accorded "outstanding universal value" (OUV) through the UNESCO procedure, are then projected and promoted for possessing this value by agents that normally have had no direct input into the processes of valuation and assessment. Such appropriation is an entirely rational action on a number of grounds.

First, for a tour operator or destination marketing organization, it is common sense to draw upon those resources that will attract tourists by virtue of their strong aesthetic appeal or some other feature that will "promise" the tourist a note-worthy experience. What we may term the "attractiveness" of World Heritage requires deeper interrogation and we will return to this later. The consistent and longstanding highlighting of World Heritage in tourism marketing campaigns acts to further embed sites in public consciousness and accentuates their value. They accrue their own social capital by virtue of their very presence in the public sphere. The overlap of World Heritage Sites with the iconic markers of international travel and tourism that pre-date the 1972 Convention—the Pyramids of Giza, Statue of Liberty, Coliseum of Rome, Taj Mahal, etc.—points to a recognized value *outside* of the UNESCO process and that resonates with a wider system of representation and recognition that tourism taps into and which Barthes (1972) recognized in his well-known critique of the guidebook as a form of reductionism. Many World Heritage Sites map directly onto well established "must-see" tourist attractions.

Second, the ways by which the tourism sector draws on World Heritage speaks to an accepted authority of UNESCO and the inter-active processes of nomination and inscription between Nation state and the transnational influence of this United Nations body. Implicitly this is an acceptance of the 10 criteria used to evaluate World Heritage and the over-arching concept of "outstanding universal value." Though not articulated as such, those elements within the vast, diverse and fragmented tourism sector that readily adopt the images and stories of World Heritage, are effectively validating the power of UNESCO in deciding that some aspects of tangible cultural heritage is more important/significant/ outstanding than other aspects. Within the discourse of marketing, UNESCO provides the ultimate endorsement of a product, taking it from the self-appointed processes of national interest and parochial concern and into the apparent realms of something "objectively verified" and of "trans-national" importance. This allows a tour operator, or a destination, to move away from saying that tourists should visit a site because the national or regional authority suggests we *should*, but rather implies there is a higher and more pervasive/persuasive voice that can direct the tourist to something special.

Third, and related to the above, the layers of value that accumulate through the label of World Heritage and the additional pulling power this implies, are perceived to bestow a potential economic premium in the form of an increased volume of tourists, plus, additional tourist-related development, mainly in the form of retail and accommodation. In terms of attracting increased numbers of tourists Fundamental economic rationality entails that the category of World Heritage presents a market opportunity to those engaged in tourism. While we can recognize the diversity of sites, the dissemination of norms, discourse through the international conventions (Cousin 2008), together with the role played by international institutions and the mass media in the promotion and diffusion of World Heritage values and, what Marcotte and Bourdeau (2006, 2012) note as the reputation of the World Heritage label, all points to the power and pervasiveness of a *universalist* perspective (Benhamou 2010) and to the UNESCO meta-narrative claim of unity in diversity (Di Giovine 2009), with the World Heritage List as the emblematic expression of this.

Being "Part of the World" and the "World Brand"

The rationale that gave rise to the 1972 Convention and the category of World Heritage fundamentally remains as one of protection and preservation of sites, monuments, cultural and natural landscapes, for the benefit of wider humanity. Through the State signatories to the Convention (190 member states have ratified the Convention as of September 2013) UNESCO fulfils a paternalistic role as a guardian of cultural and natural heritage "under threat" and recognized to be "unique and irreplaceable" and whose "deterioration or disappearance" would constitute a "harmful impoverishment of the heritage of all the nations of the world," presumably including the handful of nations that have not signed up to the Convention. At one level it could be argued that to be included in the World Heritage List was to acknowledge the fragility and uniqueness of a particular site and an awareness that it is under particular threat. At another level this could be seen to suggest the weakness of governance for heritage on the part of the member states and their inability to protect their own sites. In cases relating to developing countries where the principles and practices of heritage management and appropriate legislation for site protection may not have fully evolved, intervention through the efforts of UNESCO as a response could be welcome. Reading the sheer number of sites now designated as World Heritage and taking into account the unaltered text of the Convention, it would seem that there have never been so many heritage sites in need of protection.

To *be* a World Heritage Site is to have participated in a process of evaluation. At one level this is a kind of accreditation; an outcome or reward for matching up to a set of criteria, widely accepted. A heritage site, property or landscape is "tested" against the over-arching concept of Outstanding Universal Value. This itself has been long debated inside and outside of the UNESCO sphere and whilst firmly embedded in the 1972 Convention and remaining the fundamental condition for the inscription of World Heritage, since the Convention and particularly since the first 12 sites were inscribed in 1978, there have been numerous attempts to examine and refine the concept and the way it is mobilized in selecting Sites for the World Heritage List. Over the years the criteria have been refined and since a review of Operational Guidelines in 2005 there are now 10 criteria; the first six dealing in the main with cultural heritage and the remaining four dealing with natural heritage.[2] The Operational Guidelines themselves have undergone several reviews in the normative course of their on-going 'testing' against sites submitted for inclusion on the List and though the principle of OUV has remained sacrosanct in the listing of World Heritage, we can identify shifts in the ways it has been interpreted. Christina Cameron (2005) in a keynote paper to a Special Expert Meeting on the World Heritage Convention held in Kazan identified that in the mid-1980s the interpretation of the term Outstanding Universal Value had shifted from something which equated to 'best of the best' and was in effect applied to sites which were already widely recognized as being "iconic," to an interpretation of sites being "representative of the best."[3] In the Operational Guidelines which came into being in 2005, Outstanding Universal Value was defined as being "*so* exceptional as to transcend national boundaries and to be of common importance for present and future generations of all humanity" (UNESCO 2005).

This is a powerful claim and it begs so many questions: In *what* ways do World Heritage Sites transcend national boundaries? How does this transcendental value manifest itself? And what is actually meant by the term *common* importance for present and future generations and, important in what sense? Despite elaborate

---

2   The Operational Guidelines (for the Implementation of the World Heritage Convention) are periodically revisited and revised in response to wider debate and emergent knowledge born out of practice. Within the Guidelines, concepts central to the production of World Heritage, such as "authenticity" and "integrity" are examined along with management and planning concepts such as "buffer zones."

3   Cameron noted the growing Tentative List almost as an indicator that the World Heritage List was moving inevitably to an enactment of the definition of "representative of the best."

and nuanced discussions which have taken place over the years around the concept of OUV and the attendant World Heritage Criteria it is noticeable that adjustments have been slight and even re-enforcing (Parent 1979).[4] Value is largely defined as relating to the material being of the Site with emphasis upon issues such as integrity and authenticity. Historical values, along with artistic or aesthetic values, are given primacy in what Michael Petzet (2005: 9) refers to as "classical values." We can see the lineage tracing itself back to Kant with this emphasis upon non-instrumental values almost in a self-generating and self-sustaining way to produce, via a rational and objective process, World Heritage. But whatever intellectual challenges the concept generates, the key point is that it has accepted *authority* through the signatories to the Convention; an authority that has also been accentuated through accumulated practice.

Accepting the parameters of World Heritage is to recognize a *category* of heritage. Understanding World Heritage as a category is useful in that it allows us to consider not just what is included in the category but also what is excluded. This in turn encourages us to focus on the implications of belonging to a particular category or not. Most categories are recognized as being constructed according to the shared properties that their members share. However, this classical, objectivist view of categories is dependent upon the external hand of the people doing the categorizing and is not solely dependent upon "real world" similarities (Lakoff 1990). While it is important that we recognize the subjectivist, relativist realities of the World Heritage category, this does not necessarily challenge its value. The observation of the steadily climbing total of sites that belong to this category attests to its functionality as well as to its success. With or without knowing how a site measures up to the concept of OUV, there is a desire to be part of the category. The key to understanding this lies in way in which sites are projected to a level of "world" recognition. At the same time in creating and embellishing the "World Heritage" category a distance of separation is created with the rest of what we term heritage. This "other" heritage is *de facto* de-valued in relation to its more extra-ordinary, "significant" counterpart. Public meaning and attachment to ordinary heritage may or may not be altered but in terms of prioritizing resources to maintain and manage heritage it would seem that there is displacement in favor of designated World Heritage.

The term "world" is laden with expectations and assumptions that are made manifest when it is widely accepted and applied. It carries within it several meanings. It implies universal acknowledgment akin to the notion of a "world" championship where, out of the processes of contestation between several, a winner emerges. It implies ranking and reward, whereby "world" heritage receives a metaphorical gold medal and as a consequence other heritage sites do not. In principle a claim as to what constitutes OUV needs to be clear and unambiguous.

---

4   For instance, Michael Parent in 1979 attempted to refine the criteria and at a Global Strategy Meeting in Amsterdam in 1998, focus was on emphasizing the universalism inherent in the concept.

In practice OUV is a matter of judgment, collectively arrived at and based in experience that is inevitably relative and subjective where the line between World Heritage winners and losers is a fine one. This is not to denigrate the subjectivity of the approach but merely to recognize it.

Locating World Heritage within a wider understanding of global sociology is helpful in allowing us to understand the desire to be part of what Elliot and Schmutz (2012) term the "Universal Cultural Order." The "world" as a holistic entity, as something greater than the sum of its parts and which implies action and conduct as "global" in scope, is a distinctly modernist idea born in the period between the two world wars and picked up institutionally in the fervor of post-World War Two optimism. As Pemberton (2001) has argued, the idea of the global is a seductive one with a rhetoric that pervades the cultural sphere as well as economic and technological interests. The meta—message of World Heritage is a courageous, positive and powerful one—that there are tangible reminders of the past—which have the capacity to remind us all, now and in the future, of the successes and failures of humanity. We should remind ourselves that World Heritage is project of UNESCO in the context of the United Nations emerging out of twentieth-century turmoil, war, ignorance and the ongoing threat of physical and intellectual destruction. The Hague Convention for the Protection of Cultural Property in the Event of Armed Conflict, adopted by UNESCO in 1954, was symbolic of an emerging ideal of a "culture of the world" and of a concern for "mankind" that transcended the nationalisms of conflict. The Hague Convention focused on of protection of heritage (Sandholtz 2007) and much paved the way for the 1972 World Heritage Convention (Carducci 2008).

To believe in, and speak of concepts such as "mankind," the "international community," "common humanity" and critically, OUV, in 1972, was a bold venture and very much part of a decidedly modern vision of the world. It also reveals an interesting intellectual continuity with enlightenment-thinking, particularly in its evocation of Kantian notions of moral value and universal aesthetic taste applied to both the works of man and nature and capable of being arrived at through a rationality that was also seen to be universal. In picking through the text of the Convention and indeed through the various iterations of the Operational Guidelines for the Implementation of the Convention and within the vast numbers of reports which lie behind the inscription of each World Heritage Site, there are the footprints of the philosophy which adheres to a belief in a universalism which of course is only reflecting the UNESCO rationale of "intellectual and moral solidarity of mankind."

Hitchcock (2002), in discussing the process of inscribing Zanzibar Stone Town in Tanzania on the World Heritage List in the year 2000 evokes Benedict Anderson's (1983) notion of "imagined communities," constituted in this case by World Heritage Sites, as if collectively belonging to an international world order and subject to agreed laws and policies. Certainly in the processes of assembling a case for, and the narratives of, inscription, it is easy to see how state parties can comprehend the discourses of UNESCO as being somehow representative of a transnational governing power. The language, not only of the World Heritage Convention but of the declarations, recommendations and day-to-day communiqués surrounding it, project an air of transnational authority which is in counterpoint to the realities of policies and finances being firmly embedded in individual states; what Galla (2012: 3) refers to as the difference between soft and hard law. This brings a national reality to the concept (ideal) of transnational policy and is a key source of dissonance in the production and management of World Heritage.

To *have* a World Heritage Site within a region or nation state carries considerable symbolic value. The value of having some mark of global status is part of the process of identity construction. In the same way that world champions in sport are appropriated by nation states, region, cities and even more localized communities, being acknowledged as "having" a World Heritage site is a way of participating in the world. To be able to display the World Heritage badge is to be a member of the "being part of the world club" and in part, it helps to explain the desire for nations to keep proffering candidates for inscription. What is telling about the World Heritage List as it approaches 1,000 sites is not only the burgeoning number of properties already inscribed but the longer list of properties which have been submitted on the Tentative List. Two interesting issues emerge. The first relates to the notion of "having," for while World Heritage status can and is widely proclaimed by a member state it is also signaling the movement to the realms of global ownership—for the world, on behalf of the world. In legal terms this of course is only metaphorical ownership. Moreover, legal ownership is not the same as moral ownership and brings up issues around the ways by which member states seek to inscribe sites and the level to which communities of interest are, or are not, involved in the process.

The second issue returns to the potency of the "world" concept. The privately instigated campaign of the New Seven "World Wonders," the brainchild of mobile phone millionaire Bernard Weber was designed to create a category of important heritage sites. The campaign which began in 2002 and culminated in 2007 when the "new"' Seven World Wonders were announced clearly differed in its approach from UNESCO and the public voted for their favorite heritage site in open-competition style. The website for the campaign proudly proclaimed that "the Official New 7 Wonders of the World have been elected by more than 100 million votes to represent global heritage throughout history" (http://world. new7wonders.com). After initial liaison UNESCO distanced itself from the initiative. What could loosely be termed an "alternative," if shorter list, of World Heritage was compiled over a short period of time and without any scientific scrutiny or detailed consideration. The list of seven sites were voted into existence and all had already been inscribed on the "official" World Heritage List. What was interesting about this campaign, despite the criticisms of UNESCO, was the way it was enthusiastically embraced by the governments of the 20 finalists. It pointed to a need for "world"' recognition and also to the exposure it gave such sites which correlated in the minds of the supporting nations to increased number of visitors. While significant research is lacking with regard to the impact of this campaign, there is evidence that some sites did generate increased volumes of tourists through the exposure brought about by the campaign.

Inscription on the World Heritage List is not normally accompanied by additional resources for site protection. A World Heritage Fund does exist to allow UNESCO to support remedial work for urgently threatened sites but this is extremely limited totaling approximately $(US) four million in 2013; this being derived from contributions and donations from the majority of member states. Rather, being on the World Heritage List implies a long term resource commitment with finances required for the management of site. In a sense, the promise of finances having to be committed to the maintenance and management of a site could be seen to be a disincentive to states. Two related issues materialize. The first is that while a site foremost needs to demonstrate *Outstanding Universal Value* and a management plan in place, there is no precise requirement for member states seeking to have properties on the list to make explicit budgetary commitments to the site. Deterioration of a property due to lack of resource would however show up through Periodic Reporting and the UNESCO World Heritage Committee retains the overall sanctions of flagging the site as being in danger and ultimately, "de-listing" the site. The second issue relates not to the perceived financial costs of listing a site but to the perceived financial benefits of this. The conventional argument is to point to the raised profile of being a World Heritage Site and the symbolic capital this represents. This is essentially an argument of leverage based upon a premise that the site will attract financial resources because of the public and political recognition attained. But this would appear to be more of a working assumption rather than a scientific argument and requires further research. Anecdotally, World Heritage Sites seem to struggle with models of financial sustainability and in line with many other heritage sites are located in the realm of public subsidy by virtue of their more intangibly expressed "non-use"' values (existence value, bequest value etc.) within the public policy domain.

Here is one of the key paradoxical issues related to being on the World Heritage List. Designating a site as World Heritage is founded upon a particular notion of value, collectively expressed and endorsed through the signatories to the 1972 Convention. The concept of Outstanding Universal Value, is accepted as being a common measure of value to demarcate "World Heritage" from "other" heritage however, this is largely considered as a form of intrinsic value and as such it treats sites and properties as essentially non-market "goods." And yet, once a site has been accorded this value—in material terms it bears the World Heritage symbol—it becomes marketable. It is this "branding" process which appears to facilitate touristic interest, or *increased* touristic interest to the site. Symbolic value is bestowed upon a site by virtue of the processes, narratives and discourses drawn from the 1972 Convention and played out by designated individuals and organizations. This "brand value" can stimulate visits to the site and in various forms and formats be transformed into economic value. This transformation can be dramatic as in the case of the Iwami Ginzan silver mine complex on Honshu

Island in Japan when before it was inscribed on the World Heritage List in 2007 it attracted around 15,000 visitors a year. As a World Heritage Site in 2008 it attracted nearly one million visitors (Russell 2011).

There are of course less dramatic examples and others where the label of World Heritage has produced little or no effect. However, empirical research on the role of World Heritage in stimulating an increased volume of tourists is largely absent and studies that exist are complex and show considerable variation (Arezki et al. 2009; Cellini 2011). Yang, Lin and Han (2010) for instance indicated that in China, the cache of World Heritage Sites was significant in explaining the increased numbers of international tourists to certain destinations. In counter-point, in a study looking at the World Heritage Site of the Portuguese Quarter in Macau, Huang, Tsaur and Yang (2012) indicated no significant effects of World Heritage Listing on tourism, aside from a short-term increase in tourist interest. Such studies, though increasingly needed, do point to the problems of de-limiting the World Heritage "effect"' from a wider range of active variables and also direct our attention to the time taken to establish the World Heritage brand (Poria, Reichel and Cohen 2011), as well as the time taken to forget it.

Heritage and Tourism as Concomitant Phenomena

Although the relationship between heritage and tourism is often difficult to quantify and has evolved from the intersections between different 'philosophies' involving actors with divergent and even opposing approaches (Lazzarotti 2003), over the past two centuries both phenomena have exhibited similar trends. The category of heritage has undergone a thematic expansion through chronological space while tourism has also undergone expansion in volume and variety. Tourism through its production of images and narratives has long played an integral role in the construction of heritage. Guide books, for instance have frequently had the effect of privileging and sanctioning heritage for tourist audiences, even when local communities have remained less convinced of their relevance. Even Goethe was struck by the surprise of residents in Italy to the enthusiasm and emotion displayed by foreign tourists towards local churches and ruins (Poulot 2006). At the same time it is swiftly recognized, in line with Urry's (1990) basic concept of the "gaze," that what directs the eye can generate wealth.

Guide books and other media vehicles also act to reinforce what Smith (2006) terms the "authorising discourse of heritage" within the domains of tourism. Heritage, in the form of selected buildings, monuments, landscapes and traditions are highlighted as worthy of tourist visitation. This selectivity and apparent reverence of sites/sights stimulates tourist activity and through a combination of activities and the circulation of records and representations—the sharing of photographs, comments, stories, etc.—reinforces the heritage discourse and locates heritage within routes and itineraries practiced by tourists and commercialized by the tourism sector. Tourists and tourism, although not directly connected to heritage are implicated in its production and development which in many parts of the world acts as a real "machine" to produce wealth (Gravari-Barbas 2009). The enhancement of heritage sites by heritage stakeholders (architects, conservators, protection agencies etc.), even when engaged in 'anti-tourism' discourse, are nevertheless involved in the development of tourism working to standards that are specifically sought after by tourists (Gravari-Barbas and Guichard-Anguis 2003). The example of Mont St Michel in France is paradigmatic in this instance. It was built, having served as a prison, as a "monumental tourism product" by allowing its restoration to be guided by public opinion and the expectations of visitors which sought to preserve its lyrical and romantic aesthetic (Gravari-Barbas 2012). A further example of how tourists are complicit in the production of heritage is provided by Gaudi's Sagrada Familia in Barcelona. Although the reasons for seeking completion of the cathedral are numerous, a persuasive argument relates to the three million tourists that visit the cathedral each year.

Such dialogical relations between heritage and tourism are complex, intimate but now embedded in the discourse of heritage but they take on an additional significance with respect to the category of World Heritage. The global "brand value" that World Heritage status implies, provides enhanced visibility and an "added value" amongst domestic and international tourists and amongst the tourism industry. Actual evaluation of what the touristic implications are from UNESCO inscription are not that common, indicating the practical issues of measurement and the conceptual issues of data interpretation, however, work by DuCros (2006) on the World Heritage Site at Lijiang in China and by Gravari-Barbas and Jacquot (2013) on a number of sites in France would appear to validate the relationship between World Heritage branding and increased tourism summarized in the idea of a "UNESCO effect." However, econometric studies are not clear in this (Prudhomme 2008). Increases in attendance at UNESCO sites sometimes mask the underlying growth of tourism. For example the increase of visitors to Australian natural sites inscribed on the World Heritage List is seen to be bound up with a wider increase in tourist numbers relating to concerted marketing efforts (Buckley 2004). Researchers have also highlighted the differing methodologies used (Van der Aa 2005) and the risk of economic reductionism (Prigent 2011).

From a demand perspective the World Heritage label, like other labels (Reinus and Fredman 2007), can be seen as an additional and attractive feature that taps into wider motivations for visiting heritage sites and also fits with the idea of tourists accumulating symbolic capital (Thurlow and Jaworski 2006) and, in principle, being willing to pay more for a visit to World Heritage properties (Dixon, Pagiloa and Agostini 1998). From the supply side many World Heritage Sites are actively engaging in their own "transformation" into tourist destinations. This involves a web of organizations and local actors involved with tourism development, promotion and marketing (Boyd and Timothy 2006; Shackley 1998), whose interests lie in the wider destination concept and who may not have been involved with the processes of site nomination and designation.

The prospect of World Heritage Sites morphing into World tourism destinations with the promise of attendant economic is clearly attractive to Nation states and specific regions. There is a substantive cost to nominating a heritage site for inscription on the World Heritage list. A report by consultants Price Waterhouse Coopers (2007) on the costs and benefits of World Heritage drew attention not only to a range of benefits that went beyond the economic, but also to the costs of the process of achieving UNESCO designation. Estimates of the costs that included research, the production of technical reports and the management of the process and of the sites, and which excluded direct capital spend upon the Sites themselves varied considerably but were still significant and into hundreds of thousands of pounds sterling. In some cases significant monies have been spent on the inscription process only to have failed. Getting on the World Heritage List therefore has its costs and risks. The Price Waterhouse Coopers (2007) Report did seek to highlight a wider set of benefits that flowed from World Heritage designation—regeneration of places, the building of new partnerships, educational benefits, community cohesion and civic pride. These have been identified in a range of studies (see, for instance, Kim, Wong and Cho 2007; Salazar and Marques 2005), but the implicit, if not explicit benefit sought from designation is some form of economic return most frequently expressed as an increase in tourism activity and related investment.

Tourism: From Threat to Development Tool

Over past decades there has been a marked shift in way that UNESCO has recognized and responded to the international social fact of tourism. The 1972 World Heritage Convention has been characterized as a response to the threats posed by the excesses of urbanization and industrialization evident from the mid 1960s. Francioni (2008) cites the flooding of the Nubian monuments of the Upper Nile and the 1966 floods in Venice and Florence as two events that generated international co-operation directed toward the protection of heritage sites. While the building of the Aswan Dam in the upper Nile Valley was very much a product of wider modernization in Egypt, the flooding of two important "heritage" cities in Italy was, in the main, a natural disaster. Notably, neither of these oft cited stimuli for the 1972 Convention has nothing directly to do with any threat from tourism. By way of context, the perceived threats from industrialization need to be seen as part of longer-term, international governmental recognition of growing environmental concern that was to culminate in the United Nations Conference on the Human Environment in Stockholm and the "Stockholm Declaration" that emerged from that event in the same year of UNESCO Convention. The issue was not that cultural and natural heritage were under immense touristic pressure. Out of the first 12 sites that were accorded World Heritage status in 1978, none could be said to be significantly pressured by large numbers of tourists, although some such as the Galapagos Islands could be said have had an innate sensitivity and capacity issues to tourists. That said, the number of tourists to the Galapagos Islands in 1979 was a mere 12,000 compared to over 180,000 in 2012 (http://www.galapagospark.org/).

In the early days of the operation of the Convention, the protection of cultural and natural sites by putting them on the World Heritage List related more to a general sense of concern for the threat of damage from rapacious industrial growth and attendant rapid urbanization rather than from tourism *per se*, which was still very much in a phase of nascent development. This concern was most prescient with respect to the developing world and less developed countries, which have witnessed rapid phases of economic growth, environmental degradation and social change. It was not so perceptive regarding the long process of de-industrialization that has impacted upon developed nations since the early 1970s. Over the post-1972 period early expressions of concern about industrial development threatening sites have given way to concerns about tourism as economies have sought to diversify and re-build not through primary and secondary development but through the tertiary or service sector. Key to this has been the rapid expansion of global tourism, though with considerable geographical variations. The growth of leisure tourism across the globe over the past 30 years in particular has paralleled increased public and national interest in heritage generating concern that the pace and intensity of the consumption of heritage was becoming a direct threat to some sites.

As is widely accepted tourism rapidly became one the foremost drivers for modernization, particularly in places in the world where heritage, along with associations of the spectacular and the exoticism of otherness, was readily open to appropriation into the wider project of development through tourism. It is thus not surprising to see how the narrative of protection against the excesses of tourism has emerged with regard to World Heritage. Tourists, through their sheer volume, through "inappropriate" behaviors and the commercial tourism sector, through similarly inappropriate development, have largely been portrayed as a threat to World Heritage sites. This essential tension is evidenced by the first ICOMOS Charter on Cultural Tourism (1976) which effectively characterizes tourism as an inevitable, if largely negative force bearing down on cultural heritage. A far more insightful and balanced perspective was echoed in the 1999 version of the ICOMOS Charter (ICOMOS 1999) which recognized the dynamic inter-relationships between tourism and cultural heritage and, importantly, the need to build partnerships to address issues of management in the context of sustainable and responsible development. The ICOMOS Charter, though directed toward a broader conception of cultural heritage and not specifically to "world" heritage and the structures and processes of the 1972 Convention, set out principles aimed at engaging the tourism sector, in both its public and commercial guises, more closely with the heritage conservation sector; predominantly a state/public sector concern.

The ethos of the ICOMOS Charter has been slow to permeate the strategic and operational aspects of UNESCO's World Heritage Centre. The pressures to absorb more explicit actions regarding the interface between World Heritage and tourism have come from various directions. Various meetings and conferences organized through State parties and focusing upon specific regions, types of heritage or approaches to tourism management have been held over the years. Similarly, there have been reports and documents published through UNESCO which have drawn attention to the need to consider tourism as directly relevant to the World Heritage List and that have drawn upon case studies of sites that have been placed under undue pressure from tourist numbers and tourism development. In addition, the negative impacts of tourism have surfaced as part of the normative processes of World Heritage Site reporting, relating to "periodic reporting" and the "state of the conservation reports." Through such reporting, that is a requirement of the 1972 Convention, sites are able to signal issues and problems that are affecting or threatening the "Outstanding Universal Value" (OUV) and impacting upon their authenticity and integrity. This has been very much in line with the idea that tourism is seen as a *threat* to the World Heritage status of sites.

However there has been a gradual re-assessment of the relationship between World Heritage Sites and tourism that can be said to fall into two overlapping phases. The first can be characterized as emphasizing a balanced approach to the management of World Heritage. The Introduction to the ICOMOS (1993) *World Heritage Sites Handbook for Managers* openly called for a balance to be attained between the needs of conservation and access to the public (tourists). However, implicit in this balance was still a hierarchy where conservation concerns preceded those of tourism. Tourism development was seen to logically follow virtuous conservation, and generate revenue that could be ploughed back into conservation. This concept of "balance" is also evident in the manual published by the World Heritage Centre (Pedersen 2002) which states: "visitor management is a balancing act" (p. 12). World Heritage management plans covered the issue of tourism, with the desire to manage its impacts and flows while promoting its benefits. This call for a balanced approach was also informed by developments beyond concern for World Heritage and within a wider context of forms of more sustainable tourism. The heritage–tourism relationship and the need for balance was very much framed in rather narrow economic terms directed to the specificities of the site and the ability of the site to maintain its OUV through the management of tourism and ideally through the income it generated. In a sense, tourism was seen to be an important instrument of the heritage conservation sector. Understanding, rather than measuring, the specific impacts of tourism on World Heritage Sites, was part of a calculus that could open up resources for the management of the site.

A second phase which has emerged more recently relates to a more expansive conception of tourism that is seen to cut across the specifics of World Heritage Sites and into a more integrated and developmental model. Over the past decade or so there has however been a shift in the way that tourism is perceived by UNESCO. In the first instance tourism has been recognized as a phenomenon that cuts across many policy sectors within the remit of UNESCO. The suite of international Cultural Conventions that have emerged post 1972 (the 2001 Convention on the Protection of the Underwater Cultural Heritage, the 2003 Convention on the Safeguarding of Intangible Cultural Heritage and, the 2005 Convention on the Protection and Promotion of the Diversity of Cultural Expressions) while all are still very much dedicated to protection and preservation, are laden with touristic implications both negative and positive. The strand of UNESCO's work that has focused upon the all-embracing concept of sustainable development began to recognize the role that tourism could play in the advancement of the Millennium Development Goals set at the United Nations Summit of 2000. The 2002 Johannesburg Summit on Sustainable Development focused on the mechanisms to achieve the Millennium Development Goals and in line with this tourism began to be recognized not solely as a threat to culture and its expressions through heritage but as a potential agent for sustainable development particularly for developing countries rich in cultural and natural heritage. Robinson and Picard (2006) for instance, examine the ways in which tourism was increasingly central in the relationships across UNESCO's full remit between heritage (tangible and intangible), cultural diversity, biodiversity and the ways it is fundamental to social, cultural and economic development.

Rather than tourism development being seen as polarized against the interests of World Heritage, it is World Heritage that is increasingly being seen as a potential driver for development that includes sustainable tourism. Various recent initiatives point towards this re-orientation. The World Heritage Centre has entered into various partnerships with "non"-heritage organizations in recognition of the potential benefits these relationships can bring and in recognition of the success of, and demand for, the brand value of UNESCO and World Heritage. A partnership with TripAdvisor is indicative of this. In part the partnership was geared to involve tourists in the monitoring of World Heritage Sites but it was also a way of indicating that World Heritage has something to offer TripAdvisor and its millions of users. A partnership with Nokia involved the creation of phone applications relating to World Heritage Sites to provide them with greater visibility and, a partnership with Google Street View aimed to provide virtual tours and new insights into selected World Heritage Sites. These links with commercial operators demonstrate an acceptance on the part of the World Heritage Centre to effectively position World Heritage as a focus for global tourism interest. It is recognized by the World Heritage Centre that local communities and actors now seek to use sites as the focal point for the development of tourism and the economic benefits it can bring. This is recognition of wider UNESCO agendas to address the sustainable development agenda and in particular the alleviation of poverty and the targets of the Millennium Development Goals. In part this can be seen as "top-down" strategy emanating from the World Heritage Centre but it is also recognition of a "bottom-up" strategy which reflects initiatives and demands from the tourist sector.

The institutionalization of this new strand of thinking relating to the World Heritage and tourism relationship came with the signature program on "World Heritage and Sustainable Tourism," passed by the 36th session of the World Heritage Committee in St. Petersburg in 2012. This program seeks to provide answers to the challenges of both World Heritage policy and territorial tourism development. The stated mission of the program states that it will:

Facilitate the management and development of sustainable tourism at World
Heritage properties through fostering increased awareness, capacity and
balanced participation of all stakeholders in order to protect the properties
and their Outstanding Universal Value whilst ensuring that tourism delivers
benefits for conservation of the properties' sustainable development for local
communities as well as a quality experience for visitors. (UNESCO, World
Heritage and Sustainable Tourism, p. 5)

This language, indicative of the program, marks an approach that has come to
embrace tourism not as a threat but as a tool for development. It still has the concept
of OUV and its protection at its heart but recognizes that World Heritage Sites are
indeed attractive and popular tourist destinations. The tourist and importantly the
community, are recognized as co-producers of these World Heritage Sites and need
to participate in their management and in the benefits that can be generated (Casti
2013). This involves effective partnerships and collaboration across a variety of
stakeholders. It is interesting to note that despite the recognition of the tourism
potential of World Heritage as a key driver for national, regional or local policy
makers and indeed, as a driver for inscription, the attendant discourse still appears
to obscure direct references to tourism and surrogate language used that refers to
local development and the upholding of local identity.

The Implications of Inscription

We are witnessing a shift in the meaning of the World Heritage List in social,
political and economic terms. The reasons for what is a re-evaluation of the
World Heritage concept are multiple, complex and require further interrogation
by researchers, however, we can recognize the following. Whatever the
philosophical and ethical challenges the idea of World Heritage still poses and
whatever the inadequacies within the structures that uphold and operate the
concept, it remains highly successful. It exists as a highly visible iconic global
brand and as such has accumulated added value and a commercial potential that
within a world of brands and relational marketing gives it considerable power
and influence. At the same time, within a world still struggling with poverty,
displacement, exclusion and under-development, heritage can be a critical
resource able to lever sustainable forms of development. Furthermore, and
central to this volume, World Heritage is having to be flexible to the very real
pressures but also the opportunities that international tourism presents us with.
The concept of OUV which lies at the heart of the World Heritage idea remains
but other more instrumental values that arise from this are being recognized. We
cannot ignore the reasons why Nation states and communities wish to be part
of the World Heritage List. The desire to be part of the world, to display one's
identity and tell one's story and to reap benefit from tourism and associated
development is real and needs to be managed as well as been acknowledged.

Nor can we dis-invent the List. We can remove Sites against set criteria but we have to deal with not just the properties but also the impacts and implications of these properties for locals, communities, and tourists alike.

The chapters in this book all deal with the implications and impacts of being on the World Heritage List and also of getting onto the List. They each examine different cases and display different methods of approach, but all shed light on the realities of being on the List. Halpenny, Arellano, and Stuart (Chapter 2) examine five Canadian World Heritage Sites and how the label of World Heritage has been used to generate greater consumer awareness of these sites and also has been useful in deterring inappropriate tourism development. Shieldhouse (Chapter 3), using a statistical approach, also looks at the influence of the brand label of World Heritage based on a cases of Mexican historic cities. He demonstrates, as others have, that the label of World Heritage itself may not be sufficient to attract tourists and that investment in supporting infrastructure is also required. The strength of the World Heritage brand can do much to encourage tourists but of course the presence of the latter can change local community life. In Chapter 4, Xiang and Wall examine the implications of designating Mount Taishan as World Heritage on local villagers. Mount Taishan was one of the first sites in China to be inscribed on the World Heritage in 1987 and at the time some locals were relocated. Focusing on a particular village the chapter examines that in the face of loss of land and traditional livelihoods, the locals have become deeply involved with the provision and delivery of tourism services and have adapted their local practices in the face of some over 25 years on the World Heritage List.

In counterpoint to a site listed for a many years, in Chapter 5 Martínez looks at a serial transnational site on the Tentative World Heritage List, the Silk Road. A key issue for making it onto the World Heritage List is the need to deliver a credible and coordinated management plan. Given the diversity of stakeholders involved and their interests this may be problematic and within this there is clear need to understand the possible consequences of being World Heritage. While the tourism potential of the Silk Road is significant Martinez reminds us that that nomination does not necessary guarantee direct and immediate growth in the number of tourists if other conditions regarding protection and management are not previously secured. While inscription on the World Heritage List can generate significant profile for sites and for attendant local communities, Jimura (Chapter 6) suggests that sites may already be well known to national and international tourists and have local and national value. Focusing on Japanese sites and in particular the Hiroshima Peace Memorial, Jimura examines how local identities and wider recognition can pre-date inscription so that the inscription process can act as a form of validation. The impact of listing is picked up by Keshodkar (Chapter 7) who examines the hardships and quality of life experienced by Zanzibar Stone Town residents and questions the "value" of the World Heritage designation imposed on them, implying that inscription fell short of the promises it suggested. Indeed, it is argued that being on the World Heritage List actually prevents positive change for the residents through modernization of the site.

The processes of inscribing World Heritage are complex and remain open to contestation and debate. In Chapter 8 Shortliffe opens up debate around the gendered notion of heritage and asks whether gender should be considered important in terms of (World) Heritage, especially in the fields of site selection, interpretation, marketing and tourism. Shortliffe argues that heritage is not gender neutral and should be taken seriously as an analytical category. This is not only about simply *adding* women to an existing World Heritage framework but is also about recognizing that the heritage of humanity must represent both men and women. The complexities of World Heritage production are also picked up by Salazar (Chapter 9) who in a case study from Indonesia problematizes the management of World Heritage Sites as sustainable tourism destinations. While much of the theorizing on World Heritage management has relied upon inherited or borrowed (Euro-American) conceptions and assumptions about what should be valued and privileged, this chapter illustrates that the significance of heritage—be it natural or cultural, tangible or intangible—is characterized by ever-changing pluri-versality and thus an extended and necessary process of dialogue, negotiation and collaboration.

With the tourist becoming an increasingly important actor in World Heritage Management, understanding the tourist experience has also become important. In Chapter 10 Cutler, Doherty and Carmichael examine the experience of educational tourists at the Historical Sanctuary of Machu Picchu, Perú. Analyzing the immediate reactions of visitors and their use of photography provides an insight into how tourists experience and gain meaning from the World Heritage Site. This in turn can be used to inform planning, policy and interpretation relating to the Site. Reed (Chapter 11) also picks up on the ways in which tourists experience World Heritage in her study of Cape Coast Castle and Elmina Castle, two UNESCO World Heritage sites in Ghana. Reed analyzes the interactions between the Sites and tourists' social lives (including local Ghanians) and identifies different motivations. Central to Reed's discussion are questions of who really owns these sites, who has the right to brand them in a particular light, and what this means for inclusion and exclusion of segments of the public.

The theme of how World Heritage Sites are increasingly managed with the development of tourism in mind is picked up by Khirfan in Chapter 12 where she undertakes a comparative analysis of the Management Plans for two UNESCO World Heritage cities, Aleppo in Syria and Acre in Israel. Blending concepts from urban design and environmental psychology with those from tourism studies, Khirfan focuses on the extent to which these two plans influence the users (both residents and foreign tourists) of these World Heritage cities and how they experience the distinctiveness of place. Hurnath and Sambadoo (Chapter 13) focus upon place and local residents in their examination of the World Heritage Site of Le Morne Cultural Landscape Mauritius. They look at ideas of attachment to the World Heritage Site in terms of "insider"/"outsider" status and problematize these categories as fluid and open to negotiation. This manifests itself in terms of varying senses of attachment and belonging to the heritage site and also in territorial conflicts. Closely related to tourist attachment to a World Heritage Site is the way in which it is interpreted. There is much research to be undertaken on this theme and Crawford (Chapter 14) exemplifies this by focusing upon a geological World Heritage Site, the Giant's Causeway and Causeway Coast in North Ireland, UK. Crawford presents and discusses a case study on tourists' expectations and experiences of the site and reveals a need for interpretation that will generate closer tourist engagement.

Community engagement with World Heritage Sites is picked up in Chapter 15 where Fukushima examines the case of Catholic churches built on the Goto islands in Western Japan. This study examines the changes in value over time, relating not only to the original value of the churches to the community, but also the value in dismantling and relocating the churches. It is argued that the original, intangible values of the churches to the communities need to be taken into account, in addition to the value of the historic buildings. Community is very much at the center of Chapter 16 where McClanahan examines the case of the Neolithic Orkney World Heritage Site in Scotland. She focuses upon how the "values" of a World Heritage Site in Scotland became entangled in competing moral discourses relating to political economy and ideas about cultural and historic "sustainability." The proposal to build a "wind farm" within view of the World Heritage Site, and the subsequent debates that ensued regarding aesthetic "authenticity" of the site and its value as a community "commons" demonstrate how World Heritage values are locked within wider debates of social value. In Chapter 17 da Silva examines different World Heritage Sites of Portuguese origin located outside the boundaries of contemporary Portugal and how these resonate with wider communities and stakeholders. She shows how emotions flow in different directions and are negotiated at different levels in an attempt to understand the attraction of some places while others are forgotten. Finally in Chapter 18 Brantom examines directly the values upon which the World Heritage system is based and those which are embedded in the notion of sustainable tourism. Always open to the process of negotiation, Brantom explores the implications of shared values for World Heritage, associated communities and the process of tourism management.

The diversity of case studies and commentaries presented in this volume deal with the complexities of being inscribed on the World Heritage List, at all stages of the process. In some ways the issues raised are pertinent to *all* heritage sites but are given a heightened profile and intensity by virtue of the "world" status. Collectively, the cases firmly point to the close and inescapable intersections that now exist between World Heritage and tourism to the extent that tourism is no longer a mere "epiphenomenon" of the heritage process (Gravari-Barbas 2012), but rather is both a central factor in its production and a consequence of that production—desired, real and imagined.

References

Anderson, B. (1983). *Imagined Communities: Reflections on the Origins and Spread of Nationalism*. London: Verso.

Arezki, R., Cherif, R. and Piotrowski, J. (2009). *Tourism Specialization and Economic Development: Evidence from the UNESCO World Heritage List*. Washington, DC: IMF (IMF working paper 09/176)

Ashworth, G.J. and van der Aa Bart, J.M. (2006). Strategy and Policy for the World Heritage Convention: Goals, Practices and Future Solutions. In: Leask, A. and Fyall, A. (eds), *Managing World Heritage Sites*. Oxford: Butterworth-Heinemann, pp. 147–58.

Barthes, R. (1972). *Mythologies*, translated by A. Lavers. New York: Noonday (original work published in 1957).

Benhamou, F. (2010). L'inscription au Patrimoine Mondial de l'humanité, la Force d'un Langage à l'appui d'une Promesse de Développement. *Revue Tiers Monde*, April–June, 202: 113–30.

Bourdeau, L., Gravari-Barbas, M. and Robinson, M. (eds) (2012). *Tourisme et Patrimoine Mondial*. Quebec: Presses Universitaires de Laval.

Boyd, S. and Timothy, D. (2006). Marketing Issues and World Heritage Sites. In: Leask, A. and Fyall, A. (eds), *Managing World Heritage Sites*. Oxford: Butterworth-Heinemann, pp. 55–68.

Buckley R. (2004). The Effects of World Heritage Listing on Tourism to Australian National Parks. *Journal of Sustainable Tourism*, 12(1): 70–84.

Cameron, C. (2005). Evolution of the Application of "Outstanding Universal Value" for Cultural and Natural Heritage, Special Expert Meeting of the World Heritage Convention: The Concept of Outstanding Universal Value; Kazan, Republic of Tatarstan, Russian Federation; WHC-05/29.COM/INF.9B. In: Jokilehto, J. (ed.), *The World Heritage List: What is OUV? Defining the Outstanding Universal Value of Cultural World Heritage Properties*. Berlin: Hendrik Bäßler Verlag, pp. 71–4.

Carducci, G. (2008). The 1972 World Heritage Convention in the Framework of Other UNESCO Conventions on Cultural Heritage. In: Francioni, F. and Lenzerini, F. (eds), *The 1972 World Heritage Convention: A Commentary*. Oxford: Oxford University Press, pp. 363–75.

Casti, E. (2013). Modèle de Recherche Participative pour la Valorisation Culturelle et la Promotion Touristique du Patrimoine mondial: les Plans Gravés de la Valcamonica. In: Gravari-Barbas, M. and Jacquot, S. (eds), *Patrimoine Mondial et Développement, au défi du Tourisme Durable*. Quebec: Presses Universitaires de l'Université du Québec à Montréal.

Cavendish, R. (ed.) (2008). *1001 Historic Sites You Must See Before You Die*. London: Barron's Educational Series.

Cellini, R. (2011). Is UNESCO Recognition Effective in Fostering Tourism? A Comment on Yang, Lin and Han. *Tourism Management*, 32(2): 452–4.

Cousin, S. (2008). L'Unesco et la Doctrine du Tourisme Culturel. Généalogie d'un "bon" Tourisme. *Civilisations*, 57, *Tourisme, Mobilités et Altérités Contemporaines*, pp. 41–56.

Di Giovine, M. (2009). *The Heritage-scape, UNESCO, World Heritage and Tourism*. Lanham: Lexington Books.

Dixon, J., Pagiola, S. and Agostini, P. (1998). Valuing the Invaluable: Approaches and Applications. Synopsis of Seminar Proceedings. Available at http://siteresources.worldbank.org/INTEEI/214574–1153316226850/21017832/ValuingtheInvaluableandCaseStudies1998.pdf (accessed January 2013).

Djament-Tran, G., Fagnoni, E. and Jacquot, S. (2012). La Construction de la Valeur Universelle Exceptionnelle dans la Valorisation des Sites du Patrimoine Mondial, entre Local et Mondial. In: Bourdeau, L., Gravari-Barbas, M. and Robinson, M. (eds), *Tourisme et Patrimoine Mondial*. Quebec: Presses Universitaires de Laval, pp. 217–34.

Du-Cros, H. (2006). Managing Visitor Impacts at Lijiang, China. In: Leask, A. and Fyall, A. (eds), *Managing World Heritage Sites*. Oxford: Butterworth-Heinemann, pp. 205–15.

Elliott, M.A. and Schmutz, V. (2012). World Heritage: Constructing a Universal Cultural Order. *Poetics*, 40: 256–77.

Francioni, F. and Lenzerini, F. (eds) (2008). *The 1972 World Heritage Convention: A Commentary*. Oxford: Oxford University Press.

Galapagos Islands. Available at http://www.galapagospark.org/ (accessed December 2012).

Galla, A. (2012). Introduction. In: Galla, A. (ed.), *World Heritage: Benefits Beyond Borders*. Cambridge: Cambridge University Press, pp. 1–3.

Gravari-Barbas, M. (2009). Entre Mise en Tourisme et Affirmation Culturelle. La Mise en Valeur de la Mémoire et des Patrimoines Africains-Américains à Baltimore. In: du Cluzeau, C.O. and Tobelem, J.M. (eds), *Culture, Tourisme et Développement, Les Voies d'un rapprochement*. Paris: L'Harmattan, pp. 75–102.

Gravari-Barbas, M. (2012). Patrimoine et Tourisme, le Temps des Synergies? Le Patrimoine oui, Mais quel Patrimoine? *Internationale de l'imaginaire*, 27: 375–98.

Gravari-Barbas, M. and Guichard-Anguis, S. (2003). *Regards croisés sur le patrimoine à l'aube du XXIe siècle*. Paris: Presses Universitaires de la Sorbonne.

Gravari-Barbas, M. and Jacquot, S. (eds) (2013). *Patrimoine Mondial et Développement, au Défi du Tourisme Durable (à paraître)*. Québec: Presses Universitaires de l'Université du Québec.

Hitchcock, M. (2002). Zanzibar Stone Town Joins the Imagined Community of World Heritage Sites. *International Journal of Heritage Studies*, 8(2): 153–66.

Huang, C.H., Tsaur, J.R. and Yang, C.H. (2012). Does World Heritage Listing Really Induce More Tourists? Evidence from Macau. *Tourism Management*, 33(6): 1450–57.

Hurlingham Travel (2013). *The World's Most Expensive Vacation.* Available at http://hurlinghamtravel.co.uk/ (accessed June 2013).

ICOMOS (1976). *Charter on Cultural Tourism.* Paris: ICOMOS. Available at http://www.icomos.org (accessed December 2012).

ICOMOS (1993). *Tourism at World Heritage Cultural Sites: The Site Manager's Handbook.* Washington: ICOMOS.

ICOMOS (1999). *Cultural Tourism Charter.* Paris: ICOMOS. Available at http://www.icomos.org (accessed December 2012).

Kim, S.S., Wong, K.K.F. and Cho, M. (2007). Assessing the Economic Value of a World Heritage Site and Willingness-to-pay Determinants: A Case of Changdeok Palace. *Tourism Management*, 28(1): 317–22.

Lakoff, G. (1990). *Women, Fire and Dangerous Things: What Categories Reveal about the Mind.* Chicago: Chicago University Press.

Lazzarotti, O. (2003). Tourisme et Patrimoine: Ad Augusta per Angustia. *Annales de Géographie*, 11(629): 91–110.

Leask, A. and Fyall, A. (eds) (2006). *Managing World Heritage Sites.* Oxford: Butterworth-Heinemann.

Marcotte, P. and Bourdeau, L. (2006). Tourists' Knowledge of UNESCO's Inscription of World-Heritage Sites: The Case of Tourists Visiting Québec City. *International Journal of Arts Management*, 8(2): 4–13.

Marcotte, P. and Bourdeau, L. (2012). L'utilisation du Label Patrimoine Mondial Selon son Année d'obtention. In: Bourdeau, L., Gravari-Barbas, M. and Robinson, M. (eds), *Tourisme et Patrimoine Mondial.* Quebec: Presses Universitaires de Laval, pp. 251–63.

New 7 World Wonders Campaign. Available at http://world.new7wonders.com (accessed January 2013).

Parent, M. (1979). Comparative Study of Nominations and Criteria for World Cultural Heritage, CC-79/CONF.003/11. WH Committee. In: Jokilehto, J. (ed.), *The World Heritage List: What is OUV? Defining the Outstanding Universal Value of Cultural World Heritage Properties.* Berlin: Hendrik Bäßler Verlag, pp. 62–6.

Pedersen, A. (2002). *Managing Tourism at World Heritage Sites: A Practical Manual for World Heritage Site Managers.* Paris: UNESCO World Heritage Centre.

Pemberton, J.C. (2001). *Global Metaphors.* Pluto Press: London.

Petzet, M. (2005). Introduction. In: Jokilehto, J. (ed.), *The World Heritage List: What is OUV? Defining the Outstanding Universal Value of Cultural World Heritage Properties.* Berlin: Hendrik Bäßler Verlag, pp. 7–10.

Poria, Y., Reichel, A. and Cohen, R. (2011). World Heritage Site—Is It an Effective Brand Name? A Case Study of a Religious Heritage Site. *Journal of Travel Research*, 50(5): 482–95.

Poulot, D. (2006). *Une Histoire du Patrimoine en Occident, XVIIIe-xxie siècle: du Monument aux Valeurs.* Paris: Presses Universitaires de France.

Price Waterhouse Coopers (2007). *The Costs and Benefits of World Heritage Site Status in the UK: Case Studies.* London: Department for Culture, Media and Sport.

Prigent, L. (2011). Le Patrimoine Mondial est-il un Mirage Économique? Les Enjeux Contrastés du Développement Touristique. *Téoros*, 30(2): 6–16.

Prudhomme, R. (2008). *Les Impacts Socio-économiques de l'inscription d'un Site sur la Liste du Patrimoine Mondial: Trois études.* Paris: UNESCO.

Robinson, M. and Picard, D. (2006). *Tourism, Culture and Sustainable Development.* Paris: UNESCO ((Doc no CLT/CPD/CAD—06/13).

Reinius, S. and Fredman, P. (2007). Protected Areas as Attractions. *Annals of Tourism Research*, 34(4): 839–54.

Russell, J.E. (2011). *Cultural Property and Heritage in Japan.* PhD Thesis, SOAS, University of London. Available at http://eprints.soas.ac.uk/14043 (accessed December 2012).

Salazar, S. and Marques, J. (2005). Valuing Cultural Heritage: The Social Benefits of Restoring an Old Arab Tower. *Journal of Cultural Heritage*, 6(1): 69–77.

Sandholtz, W. (2007). *Prohibiting Plunder: How Norms Change.* Oxford: Oxford University Press.

Shackley, M. (1998). Preface. In: Shackley, M. (ed.), *Visitor Management: Case Studies from World Heritage Sites.* Oxford: Butterworth-Heinemann, pp. xiii–xiv.

Smith, L. (2006). *The Uses of Heritage.* London: Routledge.

Thurlow, C. and Jaworski, A. (2006). The Alchemy of the Upwardly Mobile: Symbolic Capital and the Stylization of Elites in Frequent-flyer Programs. *Discourse & Society*, 17(1): 131–67.

UNESCO (1972). *Convention Concerning the Protection of the World Cultural and Natural Heritage.* Paris: UNESCO Publishing.

UNESCO (2001). *Convention on the Protection of Underwater Cultural Heritage.* Paris: UNESCO Publishing.

UNESCO (2003). *Convention for the Safeguarding of the Intangible Cultural Heritage.* Paris: UNESCO Publishing.

UNESCO (2005). *Operational Guidelines for the Implementation of the World Heritage Convention*, WHC-05/2, 2 February. Paris: World Heritage Centre, UNESCO.

UNESCO (2012). *World Heritage Tourism Programme*, WHC-12/36.COM/5E, Saint Petersburg, Russian Federation 24 June–6 July 2012. Paris: World Heritage Centre.

United Nations (2000). *United Nations Millennium Declaration.* New York and Geneva: UN Publications.

United Nations (2002). *Report of the World Summit on Sustainable Development (Johannesburg, South Africa, 26 August–4 September 2002).* New York and Geneva: UN Publications.

Urry, J. (1990). *The Tourist Gaze.* London: Sage.

Van der Aa, Bart J.M. (2005). *Preserving the Heritage of Humanity? Obtaining World Heritage Status and the Impacts of Listing*. Netherlands Organization for Scientific Research: Doctoral Thesis.

Yang, C.H., Lin, H.L. and Han, C.C. (2010). Analysis of International Tourist Arrivals in China: The Role of World Heritage Sites. *Tourism Management*, 31(6): 827–37.

Chapter 2

The Use and Impact of World Heritage Designation by Canadian Heritage Sites— An Exploratory Media Analysis

Elizabeth A. Halpenny, Alexandra Arellano and Stephen A. Stuart

This chapter presents the results of a research program that looks at the use of World Heritage (WH) designation and tourism-related outcomes at five Canadian natural and cultural WH sites. While some WH sites were well known tourism destinations prior to their WH designation, anecdotal reports suggest that others gained prominence after designation and have received increased, sometimes unwanted, attention as a result. For example, managers of the Joggins Fossil Cliffs located in Nova Scotia reported exponential increases of visitors to the site since its recent designation as Canada's fourteenth WH site in June 2008 (CTV.ca 2008). This parallels observations in other countries that suggest that tourism activity increases at newly designated WH sites; however, rigorously collected data on this phenomenon is lacking. In tandem with this observation is the belief that the United Nation's Educational, Scientific and Cultural Organisation (UNESCO) designation can be used as a marketing tool that can contribute to the branding of a place and increased awareness and attractiveness as a tourism destination. Here we present data that illustrate how five recently designated Canadian WH sites have been (a) portrayed by regional, national, and international media, and (b) speculate on how the WH label is being utilized by site and destination managers to brand/heritagize and promote each site. Data collected on Internet and newspaper coverage is also linked with tourism activity data from the five case study sites to (c) explain the potential implications of WH designation on tourism development.

At a broad level our research seeks to contribute to scholarly dialogue and calls for research related to the use of protected area, public sector and international brands (Fyall and Rakic 2006; Quelch 1999; Wearing, Archer and Beeton 2007), the branding of attractions and destinations (Morgan, Pritchard and Pride 2002; Pike 2007), as well as image-making of tourism destinations and its effects on tourist decision making (Sirakaya and Woodside 2005; Sirgy and Su 2008). We speculate on trends in tourism development and on how the inscription can be used to reposition these heritage places as "top brands" (Buckley 2002).

World Heritage sites represent globally significant examples of natural and cultural heritage. In this chapter we refer to this categorization as representing all forms of heritage that have been designated under the 1972 Convention on World Heritage as being universally important to humanity. These forms of cultural and natural heritage include landscapes, buildings, cities, and unique natural features (UNESCO 1972, 2008).

Tourism as World Heritage Sites

One of the most common challenges for WH sites is the sustainable management of tourism activity (Hawkins 2004; Leask and Fyall 2006). For our purposes the definition of *tourism* includes the activities of recreationists (day visitors) and tourists (overnight visitors), the development and management of tourism at WH sites and nearby regions, and the management strategies and practices employed by tourism businesses. A number of case studies document the positive and negative impacts of tourism at WH sites and their adjacent regions (Harrison and Hitchcock 2005; Shackely 1998) however systematic comparisons of tourism management and impacts at WH sites is nearly non-existent in scholarly literature (Buckely 2002; Leask and Fyall 2006). Systematic and critical assessment of tourism at other types of protected areas has been conducted (Bushell and Eagles 2007; Garrod and Fyall 2000; Hall and McArthur 1998) and some lessons can be taken from these studies. However there are unique elements of WH sites that are not accounted for in these studies. One of these unique elements is the special status that is accrued to a WH site upon its designation. We propose to explore the implications of World Heritage status on tourism development at newly designated WH sites. Based on our own knowledge of tourism and WH sites and published WH case studies (Leask and Fyall 2006; Shackely 1998) some elements at WH sites and their regions that may be affected by WH designation include: a) visitor numbers; b) level and type of tourism development at a WH site/region; c) type of tourism operators and tourists attracted to a WH site/region; and, d) management goals and related outcomes of a WH site (e.g., conservation goals, tourism development goals, and local economic development goals).

A few studies have attempted to probe the effects of WH status on tourism at WH sites and their regions. For example Buckley (2002) compared tourist arrival numbers at six nature-based WH sites in Australia. He compared visitor numbers at WH sites and nearby comparable protected areas over a 20- to 40-year period (i.e., pre- and post-WH designation). A lack of data prohibited firm conclusions about the impact of WH status on visitor numbers. The study raised additional questions such as: Were the WH sites better known? Did they contain more appealing natural or cultural heritage? Did each site's unique image and/or brand demonstrate a stronger attraction effect than the WH designation? Wall Reinius and Fredman (2007) examined visitation to three Swedish protected areas, one of which was a WH site. They compared travel decisions associated with these sites and found that protected area labels acted as "touristic markers" (p. 839) which affected visitors' travel decisions. They also acknowledged the potential impact of other factors such as use history and media coverage in shaping tourists' decisions to travel to these parks. Study limitations included a lack of comparable case study sites (i.e., multiple examples of each protected area type should have been included) and a sole focus of visitors to the case study sites (i.e., visitors to non-study sites and possibly non-visitors would have enhanced understanding). Finally, a survey of tourism operators in New Zealand was used to study operators' attitudes regarding the utility of WH status as a tourism tool (Hall and Piggin 2002). A majority of tourism operators stated they did not use the fact that they operated in or near a WH site to promote their business. Reasons for this included a belief held by operators that it would not influence traveler's decisions (Hall and Piggin 2002: 405). This attitude may be held by operators in other WH site regions; however, no other study has undertaken this approach to examine the impact of WH status.

This tourism operator attitude stands in sharp contrast to the expressed opinions of destination marketing organizations and national tourism offices that are promoting the idea that WH status is a significant tool for fostering tourism development (Boyd and Timothy 2006; Fayall and Rakic 2006; Hawkins 2004; UNESCO World Heritage Committee 2008; Wright 2005). This reification of WH status as a tourism catalyst and, in turn its assumed value as an economic development tool is increasingly expressed through the types of sites that are being nominated by countries for WH site designation (G. Zouais, personal communication, July 2008; Fyall and Rakic 2006). Countries are strategically choosing sites that have tourism potential, perhaps at the expense of equally significant cultural and natural heritage sites in the same countries (Fyall and Rakic 2006). This trend is troubling if indeed the status of WH sites is not the tourism magnet advocates suggest (Shackley 1998). The stakes are especially high for developing countries who lack resources to experiment with economic development, and who are embracing the WH designation without full knowledge of the scope and type of tourism that WH status attracts. We question this trend, particularly based on the slim evidence of WH status' ability to attract greater numbers of tourists, especially over a sustained time period. Practitioners and scholars have called for further investigation of these issues (Boyd and Timothy 2006; Fyall and Rakic 2006; UNESCO World Heritage Committee 2008).

Destination and Attraction Branding and Image Making

WH status can be categorized as a "top brand" that may have strong enough "iconic value" to attract visitors (Buckely 2002: 1). For this chapter, a *brand* is a person's perception of "World Heritage" or WH sites and the experiences they afford. A brand has meaning for individuals beyond its functionality and exists primarily in the audience's mind (Holland 2006; Kapferer 2008; Keller 2008). In the minds of visitors WH status will evoke many kinds of images; some of these will be positive, such as the promise of enriched visitor experiences, others will be negative, including the perspective that WH sites restrict visitor enjoyment with too many rules. WH status is also *iconic* in that for many visitors it is a globally significant cultural phenomenon that humanity shares and recognizes (Holt 2004).

The role of attractions' or destinations' brands and images in affecting tourists' decisions to visit have received increased attention in recent years (Echtner and Ritchie 2003; Morgan, Pritchard and Pride 2002). However some confusion exists in the literature related to the conceptualization and measurement of destination images versus brands and further clarification necessary (Tasci and Kozak 2006). WH status can also be conceptualized as a public sector/non-profit brand; public sector brands, especially those with global associations, have received significantly less attention from researchers than other types of brands (Anholt 2002; Holland 2006).

A brand is communicated via a multitude of media including travel brochures, television programming, news broadcasts, personal blogs, and magazine articles. In this research project, the branding of Canadian heritage sites at WH sites examined thought an analysis of Internet sites and newspaper articles. This is explained next.

Methodology

Data collection focused on three sources of information. The branding of Canadian WH sites was documented through an examination of newspaper articles and Internet sites. The potential impact of the WH branding process was documented through an examination of tourist arrival and park fee figures associated with the five case study WH sites. The five most recently designated WH sites in Canada were selected; they represented both cultural and natural sites, well established (i.e. 10 years post designation) and newly established (i.e., less than two years). The sites included in this study were: Old Town Lunenburg, NS (1995); Waterton-Glacier International Peace Park, AB (1995); Miguasha National Park, QB (1999); The Rideau Canal, ON (2007); Joggins Fossil Cliffs, NS (2008).

Newspapers

For the newspaper analysis, the number and type of local and national newspaper reports related to the WH status of the five case study sites, was examined. The names of each of the five WH sites (e.g., "Rideau Canal") and "World Heritage" were used as key words for the search of the data base. Mentions in the database five years pre-inscription and five years post-inscription were identified and analyzed. This analysis looked at frequency of press coverage, the context in which mention of nomination/inscription appeared, and the potential contribution to the symbolic restructuring of each site. Content analysis of newspapers, limited to the Canadian Newsstand database, was collected and keyword-in-context-analysis was performed. Canadian Newsstand is a full text database providing access to articles, columns, editorials and features from over 170 Canadian newspapers. The database offers an overview of trends on the frequency and amount of media coverage. Furthermore, the analysis of the articles' content indicates how the inscription is portrayed by the media.

Internet Sites

The Internet analysis was conducted in the spring of 2010. Google Search was utilized to search for the same key words that were employed in the newspaper search. The search engine was instructed to list 10 web pages per search page of search results; only the first three pages of search results (i.e., 30 sites) were analyzed for the purposes of this project as the majority of search engine users do not look beyond the first three pages of search results (Henzinger 2007 as cited by Pan et al. 2007). Each page identified by Google Search was analyzed for content; links from the site were followed to determine who the page/site author was, the kinds of interactive tools available and so on. The first web page to appear from each unique web site was analyzed for the following information: page rank (where the site appeared in the first three pages of the search results), agency responsible for its creation (e.g., government, individuals, NGO); use of UNESCO and World Heritage logos; presence of interactive opportunities (e.g., discussion forums or tools for posting comments to WH site managers) including social networking options via a direct link off the web page identified by the search; frequency which the phrase World Heritage appeared on the page; type of medium (e.g., press release, descriptive content, new article (facts), editorial) and type of mention (e.g., personal travel story, description of threat to the site, commercial promotion of site and tourism offerings); existence of tourism content (private or public sector).

Tourism Activity at WH Sites

For the final stage of data collection we undertook a search of available statistics on visitor numbers pre- and post-designation. As some sites did not record visitor numbers prior to, or after WH designation, we relied also on tourist statistics for the regions where each WH site is located. Data sources and methodologies were evaluated and compared from the five sites as to whether or not they provide numbers that indicate significant changes in visitors. Follow up correspondence with site managers helped confirm and explain our observations. In addition to visits and observation of some of the sites, complementary data was gathered through master plans of development and promotional materials from the five WH sites.

Findings

The results of this exploratory research suggest a gap may exist between the intentions of the instigators of the nominations (federal and provincial government, local committees involved in the bidding process, concerned action groups and individuals, etc.), and the actual use of the nomination in the media, as a marketing tool by those responsible for the site and its environs, or as a tourism development agent. While the inscription process is widely seen by those applying for the status as an agent of economic revitalization and/or development, there is an apparent inconsistency regarding promotional activity subsequent to the site being added to the list.

Canadian Press Coverage Observations

The keyword-in-context analysis of the Canadian Press coverage indicated that a site's nomination for WH status was worthy of mention, as a considerably higher word count is attributed directly to the heritagization event after the inscriptions, as opposed to prior coverage (see Table 2.1). It is interesting to see how the Rideau Canal attracted significantly more press coverage than the other four sites. This could perhaps be attributed to the fact that it commences in the Canadian Capital, where more urban Canadians are aware of the meaning of the nomination and the prestige attached to inscription, or maybe its multi-urban location engenders more reactions and adherence sentiment to the concept of heritage. In all five cases, mentions of the heritage sites in the newspapers were much more frequent once they become WH sites.

Table 2.1   Keyword-in-context analysis of Canadian newspapers

WH site	Inscription year	Total articles	Pre-inscription	Post-inscription
Old Town Lunenburg	1995	43	0	47
Waterton-Glacier International Peace Park	1995	87	3	83
Miguasha National Park	1999	25	1	24
The Rideau Canal	2007	198	40	148
Joggins Fossil Cliffs	2008	27	10	17

Most of the press articles which mentioned World Heritage reported on the fact that the nomination process favored conservation practices and improved local awareness for the historic, cultural and natural values of the sites. They also identified the potential the status as a means to draw tourists and help local economic development. In fact, the Canadian Federal Government's tentative list of 11 candidate sites for the UNESCO designation in 2004 reported on how the designation acts as "a magnet for tourism dollars" (Boswell 2004). This ability is clearly reflected by Ballinger (1994) then Director of Operations for the Rideau Canal, who stated that the Canal's Management Plan "regarded … [the canal] … as a valuable tourism and recreational resource contributing substantially to the economy of eastern Ontario." The 2005 version of the Plan contains the same sentence indicating a clear commercial intent over at least a decade (Parks Canada 2005). This plan also identifies tourism development as one of the main incentives behind the activity to get the site inscribed on the WH list.

Interestingly, inscription on the list raises a fundamental contradiction: whilst the development of tourism is often depicted as going hand-in-hand with the conservation and preservation of WH sites, it can also contribute to their contamination and destruction. For example the Niagara Falls were once placed on a Canadian "wish list" for sites to be inscribed, but they were rapidly discarded as tourism was considered to be already too developed and contributed strongly to a spoiling of the integrity and authenticity of the natural wonder (Boswell 2003). Despite the fact that current and future tourism development is now often planned in a "sustainable" manner, a site's inscription on the WH list is still seen as being contested through a series of critiques. While WH status is equated as a "magnet" for tourism, it is also seen as a deteriorating agent where the inscription itself takes a negative connotation, becoming an "academy award like nomination" where inscribing sites as "uninteresting" as the Rideau Canal "cheapens the designation and turns the exercise into nothing more than a money trap for tourists" (Cornish 2004).

Web Page Search Observations

Internet search results produced some observations that ran parallel to the news article analysis. For example, threats to WH site conservation and preservation featured strongly as a theme on many web pages identified by the Google Search engine, largely developed by non-government organizations and private citizens. The value of the WH logo for leveraging protection of heritage resources figured prominently on these pages and their affiliated web sites (e.g., Save the Waterton[1]). Another prominent category of sites were descriptive sites, which listed factual details of each WH site, but no editorial or opinion material (e.g., WH Centre[2]). A third common content theme was tourism promotion, but to a lesser degree than expected; web sites developed and operated by private operators, consortiums of operators or even local destination marketing organization were underrepresented in the search results for each site. However, collaborative marketing efforts did exist (e.g., Rideau Heritage Route[3]). Finally, individual web sites and blogs were

---

1 http://savewatertonglacier.com/ (accessed April 2013).
2 http://whc.unesco.org/en/list (accessed April 2013).
3 http://www.rideauheritageroute.ca/en/ (accessed April 2013).

surprisingly prolific; these featured individual's stories about visiting the WH sites or contained personal photo collections. The WH and UNESCO logos rarely appeared on the identified web pages; this is likely due to the tightened regulations associated with using these logos. However, these increased regulations likely retard the branding process of WH destinations. Exceptions included the US National Park Service's site on Waterton-Glacier and TripAdvisor—the WH logo appeared on these organization's web pages, representing an important co-branding opportunity. Previous Internet studies suggest the rank position of a specific search result has been shown to determine whether it will be reviewed and evaluated by an information searcher (Pan et al. 2007). International (e.g., WH Centre[4]) and national government (e.g., Parks Canada[5]) web pages and the web sites they are affiliated with ranked highest in the Google Search results for all five WH sites. National and international government agencies' web pages were also the most prominent authors of web pages that popped up on the Google Search.

Tourism Activity Observations

Most of the data available on visitor numbers to Canada's WH sites has been gathered using different and varying methodologies and therefore contains deficiencies that invalidate a direct comparison. We have presented these findings below using symbols to indicate generalized trends in visitor numbers and other tourism activity indicators (e.g., park fees collected) for the year directly after designation. Interestingly, whilst Canadian newspapers often depicted such places as high profile sites, no explicit visitor numbers were reported in this media. Despite media claims to the opposite, there appears to have been little positive growth in visitor numbers after the inscription for most of the Canadian sites (see Table 2.2). Indeed, there was a discernable drop-off in visitors to some sites. This study does not address all of the contingent factors affecting individuals' decisions to visit WH sites. However, communication with park managers suggest the decision by the new administration at Miguasha National Park to charge an entrance fee after inscription and the increase of visitor fees at Waterton Lakes National Park after inscription likely had a negative impact on visitor numbers. Lower than expected visitor numbers following the designation of the Rideau Canal could be linked to events that characterized the 2009 tourist season including economic recession, high fuel prices, and poor weather. At all sites it is speculated that a lack of awareness of the meaning of the WH status/brand, lack of appropriate marketing material, and lack of tourism development budget resulted in no or only a small increase in WH site visitation immediately after designation (i.e., within the first year of inscription).

---

4   http://whc.unesco.org/en/list (accessed April 2013).
5   http://www.pc.gc.ca/progs/spm-whs (accessed April 2013).

Table 2.2   General trends in tourism activity after WH site designation

WH site	Visitor #s immediately after designation	Observations from site managers
Old Town Lunenburg	↑[2,3]	
Waterton-Glacier International Peace Park	↓[1]	Park fee increase may have resulted in lower numbers on and after year of inscription
Miguasha National Park	↓[1]	Park fee increase may have resulted in lower numbers on and after year of inscription
The Rideau Canal	=[1,3]	Poor weather, economic recession, high fuel prices affect tourism travel and park fees
Joggins Fossil Cliffs	↑[3]	Little data available prior to designation; a highly remote site

Source: [1]Park or canal use fees collected; [2]Hotel rooms sold; [3]Attraction visitation (e.g., number of museum visitors).

Conclusion

The initial observations from this study suggest that World Heritage sites need to undertake more work in order to understand what specific attributes comprise the World Heritage brand and the individual sites on the List, and how their intrinsic attributes and qualities can be aligned with consumer's existing perceptions, valuations and their tourism requirements in order to optimally leverage the site's resources for today's generation without despoiling them for those yet to come. It also suggests that the authorities controlling such sites could better manage their press and media relations in order to communicate the core values of the overall process of World Heritagization, and the inherent values of the brand and each site to citizens within the local, national and international community, thereby creating a better understanding of the contribution the overall process makes to the impact of tourists, tourism and tourism operators that may support the sustainable management of WH sites and their regions. By viewing the process merely in terms of economic "boosterism" is surely to miss the point of the List, and the values the inscribed sites imbue.

Further research is needed to understand many aspects of this important issue. For instance, little work has been undertaken on Canadian awareness of the inscription process, or the understanding Canadians have of the meaning of the brand and its status. Conducting a survey of WH site visitors that utilizes a stated preference approach would be one valuable method of exploring consumer valuations of the WH brand. Likewise, the difficulties in evaluating the impact of inscription created by inconsistencies in visitor numbers clearly need to be addressed. For example, the reported "exponential increase in visitors" reported at Joggins Fossil Cliffs appears unsupported by any data collected by the authorities. Finally, macro and micro geo-spatial analysis of WH sites would prove of interest in that it would allow researchers to better understand the value created by the proximity of sites to urban areas and their transportation corridors, and the marketing of the WH brand and sites that takes place within them. In other words this could indicate the effectiveness of brand marketing in communicating the core values of the brand and individual sites. This could be further linked to the data gathered in this project to gauge the impact and effectiveness of local press coverage on the branding process.

References

Anholt, S. (2002). National Brands: The Value of "Provenance" in Branding. In: Morgan, N., Pritchard, A. and Pride, R. (eds), *Destination Branding: Creating the Unique Destination Proposition.* Oxford, UK: Butterworth-Heinemann.

Ballinger, D. (1994). Managing the Rideau Canal: Issues of Conservation and Tourism. *ICOMOS Canada Bulletins*, 3(3): 38–40. Available at <http://www.icomos.org/icomosca/bulletin/vol3_no3.html> (accessed June 4, 2009).

Boyd, S.W. and Timothy, D.J. (2006). Marketing Issues and World Heritage Sites. In: Leask, A. and Fyall, A. (eds), *Managing World Heritage Sites.* Oxford UK: Butterworth-Heinemann.

Boswell, A. (2004). Canal Up for World Heritage Designation. *The Ottawa Citizen.* Ottawa, Ontario: May 1, p. A4.

Boswell, R. (2003). Canadian Sites Considered for UNESCO Acclaim. *National Post.* Don Mills, Ontario: August 28, 2003, p. A5.

Buckley, R. (2002). *World Heritage Icon Value: Contribution of World Heritage Branding to Nature Tourism.* Queensland, Australia: Griffith University; Australian Heritage Commission; CRC Sustainable Tourism.

Bushell, R. and Eagles, P.F.J. (eds) (2007). *Tourism and Protected Areas: Benefits beyond Boundaries.* Oxfordshire, UK: CAB International.

Cornish, D. (2004). It's Just a Canal. *National Post.* Don Mills, Ontario: May 3, p. A13.

CTV.ca News Staff (2008). Visitors Taking History from N.S. World Heritage Sites. Friday July 18, 2008. Available at <http://www.ctv.ca/servlet/ArticleNews/story/CTVNews/20080718/joggins_cliffs_080718/20080718?hub=Canada> (accessed October 5, 2008).

Eagles, P.J.F. and Halpenny, E. (2004). *A Sustainable Tourism Plan at Dinosaur Provincial Park—World Heritage Site.* Paul Eagles and Associates: Waterloo, ON. Prepared for Alberta Parks and Protected Areas.

Echtner, C.M. and Ritchie, J.R.B. (2003). The Meaning and Measurement of Destination Image. *The Journal of Tourism Studies*, 14(1): 37–48.

Fyall, A. and Rakic, T. (2006). The Future Market for World Heritage Sites. In: Leask, A. and Fyall, A. (eds), *Managing World Heritage Sites*. Oxford UK: Butterworth-Heinemann, pp. 159–76

Garrod, B. and Fyall, A. (2000). Managing Heritage Tourism. *Annals of Tourism Research*, 27(3): 682–708.

George, E.W. (2004). Commodifying Local Culture for Tourism Development: The Case of One Rural Community in Atlantic Canada, unpublished PhD thesis. Guelph: University of Guelph.

Hall, C.M. and McArthur, S. (1998). *Integrated Heritage Management: Principles and Practice*. London: The Stationary Office.

Hall, C.M. and Piggin, R. (2002). Tourism Business Knowledge of World Heritage Sites: A New Zealand Case Study. *International Journal of Tourism Research*, 4(5): 401–11.

Harrison, D. and Hitchcock, M. (2005). *The Politics of World Heritage: Negotiating Tourism and Conservation*. Toronto: Channel View Publications.

Hawkins, D.E. (2004). Sustainable Tourism Competitiveness Clusters: Application to World Heritage Sites Network Development in Indonesia. *Asia Pacific Journal of Tourism Research*, 9(3): 293–307.

Holland, D. (2006). *Branding for Nonprofits: Developing Identity with Integrity*. New York: Allworth Press.

Holt, D.B. (2004). *How Brands become Icons: The Principles of Cultural Branding*. Boston, MA: Harvard Business School Press.

Kapferner, J.N. (2008). *The New Strategic Brand Management: Creating and Sustaining Brand Equity Long Term*, 4th edn. London: Kogan Page.

Keller, K.L. (2008). *Strategic Brand Management: Building, Measuring, and Managing Brand Equity*, 3rd edn. New Jersey: Prentice Hall.

Leask, A. and Fyall, A. (2006). *Managing World Heritage Sites*. Oxford: Butterworth-Heinemann.

Mazanec, J.A. and Strasser, H. (2008). Perceptions-based Analysis of Tourism Products and Service Providers. *Journal of Travel Research*, 45(4): 387–401.

Morgan, N., Pritchard, A. and Pride, R. (2003). *Destination Branding: Creating the Unique Destination Proposition*. Oxford: Butterworth-Heinemann.

Pan, B. and Fesenmaier, D. (2001). A Typology of Tourism-related Web Sites: Its Theoretical Background and Implications. *Information Technology and Tourism*, 3(3/4): 155–66.

Parks Canada (2005). *Rideau Canal, National Historic Site of Canada, Management Plan*. Ottawa: Government of Canada.

Pike, S. (2007). Consumer-based Brand Equity for Destinations: Practical DMO Performance Measures. *Journal of Travel and Tourism Marketing*, 22(1): 51–61.

Quelch, J. (1999). Global Brands: Taking Stock. *Business Strategy Review*, 10(1): 1–14.

Schiffman, L.G., Kanuk, L.L. and Das, M. (2006). *Consumer Behaviour*, 1st Canadian Edition. Toronto: Pearson Education.

Shackely, M. (1998). *Visitor Management: Case Studies from World Heritage Sites*. Oxford: Butterworth-Heinemann.

Sirakaya, E. and Woodside, A.G. (2005). Building and Testing Theories of Decision Making by Travellers. *Tourism Management*, 26(6): 815–32.

Sirgy, M.J. and Su, C. (2008). Destination Image, Self-congruity, and Travel Behavior: Toward an Integrative Model. *Journal of Travel Research*, 38(4): 340–52.

Tasci, A.D. and Kozak, M. (2006). Destination Brands vs Destination Images: Do We Know What We Mean? *Journal of Vacation Marketing*, 12(4): 288–317.

UNESCO (1972). *Convention Concerning the Protection of the World Cultural and Natural Heritage—Adopted by the General Conference at its Seventeenth Session. Paris, 16 November 1972*. Paris, France: United Nations Education, Scientific and Cultural Organization.

UNESCO (2008). *Operational Guidelines for the Implementation of the World Heritage Convention*. Paris, France: United Nations Educational, Scientific and Cultural Organization—Intergovernmental Committee for the Protection of the World Cultural and Natural Heritage—World Heritage Centre.

UNESCO World Heritage Committee (2008). *Item 5 of the Provisional Agenda: Report of the World Heritage Centre on its Activities and the Implementation of the World Heritage Committee's Decision—Proposal for New Strategic Directions for Partnerships (WHC-08/32.COM/INF.5D)*. Presented at the World Heritage Committee 32nd session, Quebec City, Canada, July 2–10, 2008.

Wall Reinius, S. and Fredman, P. (2007). Protected Areas Attractions. *Annals of Tourism Research*, 34(4): 839–54.

Wearing, S., Archer, D. and Beeton, S. (2007). *Sustainable Marketing of Tourism in Protected Areas: Moving Forward*. Queensland: CRC Sustainable Tourism.

Chapter 3

The Impact of World Heritage on Tourism and the Integrity of Heritage: Some Experience from Mexico

Richard Shieldhouse

Since its inception in 1972, the United Nations Educational, Scientific and Cultural Organisation's (UNESCO) World Heritage List has become a recognized symbol of the world's most important cultural and natural sites. Tourism was not part of UNESCO's original rationale for the list, which now includes 936 properties, but tourism impacts quickly became apparent. The list has evolved to symbolize the best places to visit—an alternative to *Frommer* or *Fodor's*, or even perhaps a kind of alternative to the alternatives, such as *Lonely Planet* and the *Rough Guides*.

There is evidence that World Heritage inscription can trigger an influx of tourists to World Heritage Sites, although demonstrating a relationship between inscription on the list and visitors has proven elusive. This research uses statistical evidence from seven Mexican World Heritage cities to demonstrate that joining the World Heritage List has a significant independent impact on international tourism at World Heritage cities. Although the Mexican World Heritage cities considered here typically experienced increased international visitors after joining the list, the data also revealed wide variation in visitor trends over a longer horizon. Inscription on the World Heritage List may provide an initial bump in visitation, but sustaining these levels may depend on local public policy and planning.

Tourism and World Heritage Cities

UNESCO's Convention concerning the Protection of the World Cultural and Natural Heritage, adopted in 1972, has a number of goals designed principally to encourage the protection of important sites. Increasing tourism is not one of its goals and, indeed, excessive visits indeed threaten some World Heritage Sites to the point where the number of visits are controlled through various means, including advance reservations or ticketing. UNESCO has responded with a World Heritage Tourism Program, designed to encourage benefit for local populations with sustainable management practices.

Mexico has aggressively pursued World Heritage status for its archeological and natural heritage or patrimony, and for numerous historic cities. Including the

Historic Center of Mexico City and Xochimilco, that nation now has 10 cities or towns with major districts designated as World Heritage Sites—which arguably places it in fourth place after Italy (with 27), Spain (with 17), and Germany (with 11). For Mexico, the most recent addition was the Protective Town of San Miguel and the Sanctuary of Jesús Nazareno de Atotonilco (UNESCOb).

There is ample anecdotal evidence of a link between World Heritage Inscription and increased tourism to World Heritage Cities. Ralf Buckley has noted, "Tour companies and tourist accommodation with access to World Heritage areas commonly advertise that fact in their marketing material; and tourism developers and entrepreneurs preferentially pursue opportunities in and around World Heritage areas" (Buckley 2002: 2). There have been some attempts to systematically measure the relationship between inscription and increased tourism, with uncertain results.

The relationship between World Heritage List inscription and tourism has been extensively discussed, but the extent of direct impact of World Heritage inscription on visitor levels has remained elusive. Brijesh Thapa noted that "empirical research is lacking to support the contention" that "designation of a site generally leads to increased tourist visitation" (Thapa 2007: 27).

CCROM's *Management Guidelines for World Cultural Heritage Sites* noted that increased visitors demanding new facilities and services are implied by World Heritage designation (Feilden and Jokilehto 1998). Other observers qualify the relationship between the World Heritage designation and tourism. Francesco Bandarin has noted: "In internationally well-known sites, such as the Tower of London, World Heritage status may have little impact on visitor numbers, but in less established destinations inscription is usually accompanied by an upsurge in tourism" (Harrison and Hitchcock 2005: v).

This was echoed in another analysis (van der Aa 2005: 131), which concludes that non-centrally located cultural World Heritage Sites "see more visitors after their inscription, whereas many centrally nominated sites already receive many visitors before their listing." The same work, however, also suggested that "accessibility and inclusion in tourist routes and tours" drive visitor numbers.

Others claim presence of multiple World Heritage Sites as a predictor of tourism increases. An analysis of 1994–1995 WTO tourist data by country versus the number of World Heritage Sites in each country in 2000 reveals a .75 correlation coefficient, suggesting a strong, positive link between the number of sites and the number of tourists (Lazzarotti 2000).

After a review of 10 case studies, Myra Shackley concluded: "It is frequently assumed that any site awarded World Heritage status will immediately receive a marked increase in visitors. However, this is not necessarily the case and visitor numbers depend on a number of factors including the way in which the site is marketed and issues connected with access" (Shackley 1998: 200).

Looking at quantitative approaches, a study by Ralf Buckley of Griffith University in Queensland, Australia attempted to demonstrate the marginal contribution of World Heritage listing to tourism by examining time-series data for listed sites and comparable unlisted sites during simultaneous periods. Buckley identified numerous analytical problems which are useful for approaching evaluating the impacts of inscription. For example, he noted that World Heritage actually implies a "bundle of attributes which includes heritage value, branding, marketing, and often increased infrastructure funding" (2004: 72). Buckley concluded that "Most of the World Heritage Areas (WHAs) considered here received several times more visitors than the control sites, but it is not clear whether the difference is because WHAs are larger or more accessible, because they are better-known, because they are listed as World Heritage, or because they contain features of natural or cultural heritage which the others do not."

A survey of businesses near two of New Zealand's World Heritage Sites found less than half of the respondents (48.4%) believed the designation plays a role in attracting visitors. Another 31.3% indicated they did not know whether World Heritage inscription has a role in attracting tourists. Only 20.3% indicated it has no role. The authors referenced their work from the previous year which indicated "a causal link between World Heritage listing and increased visitation over and above existing tourism trends is somewhat tenuous" (Hall and Piggin 2002: 402).

International Tourism Trends at Mexican World Heritage Cities

This research employs statistical models for an exploratory analysis of the relationship between World Heritage inscription and foreign tourists to seven World Heritage cities in Mexico. The models isolate the independent effect of inscription, while controlling for other variables: the relative strength of the Mexican peso, the number of available hotel rooms in a given World Heritage City, and the overall trend in international travel.

The goal is to understand the statistical relationship between World Heritage and tourism and—with this information as background—attempt to probe deeper to understand other issues, apart from the three identified exogenous influences, which may have contributed to trends in international visitors.

Tourism can be influenced by the availability of facilities (available hotel rooms), and by price, as defined by the relative strength of currency in the target country. The ability of these two independent variables to explain the dependent variable, international visitors at Mexican World Heritage Cities, is diminished to the extent that global trends in tourism are not held constant. The model accomplished this by including a variable for global international tourist arrivals, as reflected by data from the United Nations World Tourism Organization (WTO).

Data for foreign visitors and hotel rooms for 1986–2008 were provided by Mexico's Secretary of Tourism (*Secretario de Turismo or SECTUR*). The dates of inscription are available from the website of UNESCO's World Heritage Center (UNESCOb). The relative value of the Mexican peso can be defined with historical data for the number of pesos per Special Drawing Right (SDR). SDRs are the unit of account of the International Monetary Fund and other international agencies and represent a basket of securities. Presently it includes the Euro, Japanese Yen, Pound Sterling and US Dollar (International Monetary Fund 2011).

Three Mexican World Heritage Cities were excluded from this analysis. As San Miguel de Allende was inscribed in 2008, few data were available with respect to the post-inscription experience in that city. No data are available for the Historic Monuments Zone of Tlacotalpan, because records have not been kept for that site by Mexico's SECTUR. Mexico City was excluded from the analysis because it is a massive, international city with many commercial, governmental, and cultural draws for foreign visitors, including four different World Heritage Sites. In such an environment, ascribing visitor variation to the 1987 inscription of Historic Center of Mexico City would likely appear to be an intellectual stretch.

The analysis method employed a similar process for each of seven World Heritage cities under consideration. Data for available hotel rooms, number of foreign tourists, and pesos per SDR were combined with a categorical or dummy variable denoting the date of inscription (more precisely, the year in which inscription first had a significant impact on foreign arrivals)—using fixed-effect models where the covariance structure is auto-regressive of lag 1. Six models with significant and directionally logical coefficients were ultimately developed using the Proc Mixed procedure of SAS.

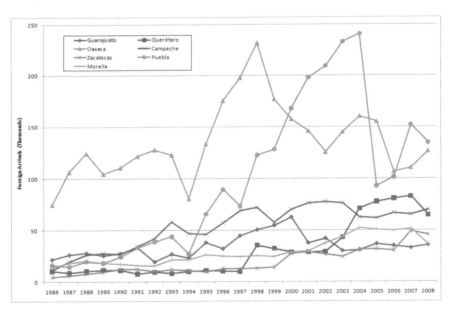

**Figure 3.1   Foreign arrivals to select Mexican World Heritage cities by
            year: 1986–2008**

Source: SECTUR, for dates noted.

Intuitively, one might expect World Heritage inscription to have a delayed effect on tourism. A city should not be inscribed on the list in one year and expect an immediate increase in foreign visitors. It takes time to increase public awareness, to improve access, and to provide facilities. Recognizing this, the analysis sought to explore the period of time required for a significant effect by advancing the year at which the dummy variable was assigned a value of one, beginning with the year of inscription, until meaningful coefficients could be determined for the World Heritage inscription dummy variable. The graph depicted on Figure 3.1 illustrates the trend in foreign tourist arrivals between 1986 and 2008 for the seven subject cities.

In aggregate, it appears the general trend was upward from 1986 to 2000, after which all of the cities had been inscribed. This generally was a period of global economic growth, resulting in a 5.4% compound annual growth rate in global international tourist arrivals, according to WTO data. Additionally, political and economic turmoil in the early 1990s resulted in Mexico's 1994 currency reform which devalued the Mexican peso by 50% (Whitt 1996), and increased the Mexico's appeal as an inexpensive tourist destination.

The statistical analysis indicates that in six of the seven cities examined, inscription on the World Heritage List leads to an eventual statistically significant increase in international visitors, with the mean requiring 5.8 years and the median requiring 6.5 years. The analysis could not discern a statistically significant relationship and international tourism for one of the more recently inscribed Mexican World Heritage Cities, Campeche. Summary results for the seven cities appear in Table 3.1. Coefficients indicate the independent effect of the four exogenous variables on thousands of foreign arrivals per year.

Table 3.1   Summary results for exploratory analysis

City	Year Inscribed	Year at which Dummy = 1*	Coefficients			
			Dummy— World Heritage Designation	Pesos per SDR	Number of Rooms	World Tourism
Campeche	1999	n/a	n/a	n/a	n/a	n/a
Guanajuato	1988	1995	21.7	-0.4	-5.8	-0.1
Morelia	1991	1999	8.8	0.4	14.2	0.5
Oaxaca	1987	1988	41.2	10.7	3.7	-33.1
Puebla	1987	1995	88.7	-5.6	9.1	25.6
Queretaro	1996	2002	18.8	0.2	30.2	-2.8
Zacatecas	1993	1998	8.9	-0.7	3.3	4.6

Source: SECTUR, for dates noted.

Note: *Year at which the dummy variable for World Heritage designation as a value of 1 and generates a coefficient significant at a 95% confidence interval.

At first blush one might assume the inability to obtain a significant result with the Campeche data may be due to nothing more profound than minimal available data points. Campeche, significantly, was one of the last cities in this analysis inscribed in the Word Heritage list—in 1999—and only eight years of historical data were available post-inscription. Digging a bit deeper, it appears the lack of a statistical relationship between inscription and international visitors may equally attribute to an essentially flat trend in visitors between 2000 and 2008. International visitors to that city declined from 70,079 to 69,793 (-0.4%) between 2000 and 2008. With visitor levels flat, one obviously cannot suggest inscription caused them to increase!

SECTUR data indeed indicate that for the period between 2000 and 2008, international visitors to all seven Mexican World Heritage Cities in this analysis were highly variable. Figure 3.2 shows the percentage change in international visitors between 2000 and 2008 for the seven Mexican World Heritage Cities. In addition, to Campeche, which following its inscription in December 1999 experienced eight years with virtually no net change in international visitors (declining 0.4%), half of the remaining six cities demonstrated large increases, with Querétaro, Zacatecas, and Morelia demonstrating increases of 125.4%, 65.4%, and 25.6%, respectively. Simultaneously, international visitor levels *decreased* 43.2%, 19.9%, and 19.7%, respectively, at Guanajuato, Puebla, and Oaxaca, respectively.

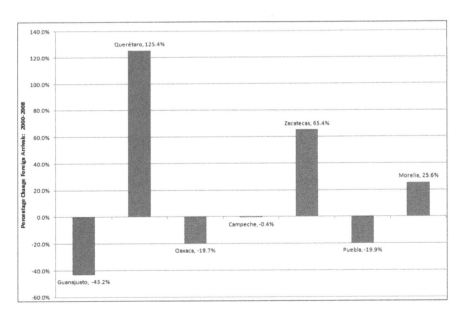

**Figure 3.2   Trends in foreign arrivals—select Mexican World Heritage
                cities: 2000–2008**

Source: SECTUR, for dates noted.

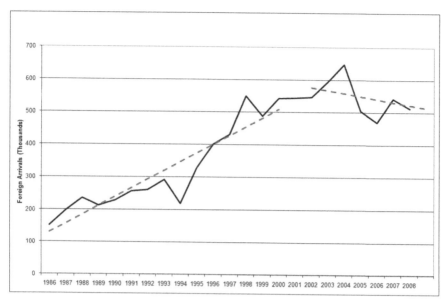

Figure 3.3   Total foreign visitors to select Mexican World Heritage cities: 1986–2008

Source: SECTUR, for dates noted.

Viewed in aggregate, 1986–2008 combined international visitors to these seven Mexican World Heritage Cities can be broken into two distinct trends: 1) a steady progression upward from 1986 to 2000, with a strongly positive (+92.3) correlation coefficient between annual international visitors and the advance of time, and 2) a weaker downward trend between 2001 and 2008, with a -39.9 correlation coefficient between international visitors and time (see Figure 3.3).

This raises two important questions—one statistical and one more practical: 1) Was the previously mentioned statistically significant relationship between inscription on the World Heritage List and international tourism purely an accident related to the fact that six of the seven Mexican cities under scrutiny joined the World Heritage List during the late 1980s and early 1990s, a period of relative prosperity which was generally characterized by large increases in travel? 2) All of these World Heritage Cities operated in a similar environment with respect to the relative value of the Mexican peso, perceived insecurity about flying, and the global economic trends. What was it that caused international visitors to decline in some cities after significant increases in foreign visitors attributable to World Heritage inscription, and increase in others?

Guanajuato, Mexico: A Case Study

To help answer both questions, the analysis focused on one World Heritage City, the Historic Town of Guanajuato and Adjacent Mines, that demonstrated a statistically significant post-inscription increase in international visitors, but subsequently exhibited a precipitous fall in international visitors from after 2000.

From 1986 (two years prior to the city's inscription) to 2000, international visitors to Guanajuato increased at a 7.9% compound average growth rate (CAGR). Going forward from 2000, the trend in international visitors to that city demonstrated a -6.8% CAGR between 2000 and 2008. Extending the window but one year, the 2000–2009 the CAGR becomes -12.4%, reflecting three major influences: the 2009 outbreak of H1N1, which originated in Mexico, the fullest effects of the worldwide recession, which began in 2008, and impact of increasing levels of drug-related violence.

Ignoring 2009's disaster for Mexican tourism, Guanajuato still experienced a 43.2% decline in reported international visitors between 2000 and 2008. Guanajuato remained on the World Heritage List throughout the period, and public and private efforts worked to both improve the appearance of the city and promote it to visitors. What happened?

To find out, semi-structured interviews were conducted with an array of current and former public officials, academics, and preservationists in the city. Interviewees were selected based on reputational and snowball sampling. Interviews were based on a short series of open-ended questions. Their duration ranged from 35 minutes to four hours.

Results revealed a basket of explanations, many of which surfaced repeatedly:

- tourism planning and strategy,
- branding and slogans,
- political issues,
- funding issues,
- the Cervantino Festival, and
- low-quality restaurants, hotels, and shopping (presumably relative to other destinations).

Inconsistent tourism planning and strategies challenge visitor level growth to Guanajuato. The city's heritage comprises much of its allure for visitors, although culture becomes an important attraction during festivals. Guanajuato's weather is typically pleasant—generally warm and arid—but it is located in central Mexico, far from any beach resorts. Built in a narrow ravine, there is little room for parks, and aggressive logging denuded vast areas of nearby mountain forests, rendering them unattractive for hiking and camping. No well-known archeological sites surround the city. Guanajuato, however, figured mightily in Mexico's struggle for independence from Spain 200 years ago, and evidence of a mining history recognized by UNESCO remain abundant, yet the city's principal asset for visitors—heritage—at times becomes ignored or treated casually. A comment from a tourism official epitomizes this:

> We are rich in heritage and culture, but as far as recreation we have nothing to offer. We have no theme parks, no parks. We must remember that, for vacations, it is the children that generate the ideas as to where to go and who decide where the family goes. They come to Guanajuato, they get their fill of history and culture, and then they ask, "Well, what else?" We are missing recreation.[1]

Unique among Mexican World Heritage Cities, Guanajuato's designated area extends beyond a central historic zone and includes surrounding mining communities. The December 1987 UNESCO Designation Report acknowledges that the city's "growth, the layout of its streets, including the picturesque 'subterranean' streets, its plazas, and the construction of hospitals, churches, convents and palaces are all inextricably linked with the industrial history of the region, which with the decline of the Potosi mines in the 18th century, became the world's leading silver extraction center" (UNESCOc).

Unfortunately, efforts to produce recreational offerings and theme parks may conflict with preservation goals of UNESCO and others. With the depressed price of silver soon after 2000, nearby mining assets, which included vast tracts of land and historic communities, were sold by local mining cooperatives (Ferry 2005). Investors subsequently redeveloped the eighteenth-century Guadalupe Mine (also referred to as the "Elephant Mine," because of its multi-story stone exterior buttresses, as a nine-hole golf course and club, with initial plans to build a nine-hole golf course, 100-room hotel, and 21 single family houses (see Figure 3.4). Subsequent visits to this facility suggest it has not been particularly successful. During one glorious weekend in February 2009, a visit revealed the only players were the property's director and a golfing companion. This may reflect a sluggish economy, but it equally may demonstrate public rejection of a facility that appropriates heritage to badly address the desires of the target market, golfers from the United States and Canada, as well as the local market.

Still, development threatens less-populated parts of the UNESCO-designated area near Guanajuato, with or without tourists. An observer noted that the UNESCO World Heritage "declaration is symbolic ... but the city is growing and growing and growing—50 percent of the area of the declaration of World Heritage is empty. We are worried about this area, this ecological area— open space surrounding the historical city."[2]

---

1   Mario Aguado Malacara (Director General of Tourism, City of Guanajuato, Mexico), in discussion with the author, January 2010.

2   Manuel Sánchez Martínez (Professor of Architecture, University of Guanajuato), in conversation with author, January 2010.

Figure 3.4   Guadalupe Mine

One analysis noted that in Mexico, World Heritage Sites "that lie along a tourist route witness the largest increase in international visitors" (van der Aa 2005: 115). This realistic observation has multiple implications for Guanajuato.

A hotelier and former *alcalde* (mayor) commented on how Guanajuato fails to profit from its proximity to other World Heritage Sites. He notes that the State of Guanajuato is the only Mexican state with two World Heritage Cities (Guanajuato and San Miguel de Allende) ... "and they are different." Noting the need to develop links between Guanajuato and the neighboring World Heritage City, which in recent years has attracted more affluent visitors, he continues: "We need to work with the differences between San Miguel and Guanajuato" and encourage tourism to both cities.[3]

Proximity to San Miguel de Allende may be able to provide more visitors, however, but the short duration of visits limits economic impact on the city. "We are so close to the other cities that tourists come just for the day. It happens the same with Toledo and Madrid. People from Madrid go in the morning, visit the city, have

---

3   Arnulfo Vázquez Nieto (former mayor and owner of El Mesón de los Poetas Hotel) in conversation with author, January 2010.

lunch there, and they go back to Madrid."[4] The situation reflects a phenomenon described by Antonio Paolo Russo, who observes that the horde of day-trippers is "less elastic with respect to quality," and much more sensitive to prices. Extreme examples of this produce "a process of 'McDonaldization'" (Russo 2002: 170).

SECTUR data indicate foreign visitors stayed for 2.0 nights on average in four Mexican World Heritage Cities during 2009: Guanajuato, Oaxaca, Puebla, and Querétaro. Two more remote cities, Campeche and Zacatecas are located further from Mexico's center, yet the two cities demonstrate different behavior in this respect, with Campeche's foreign visitors staying only 1.2 nights on average in 2009 and visitors to Zacatecas remaining for 2.3 nights. Morelia, relatively close to Mexico City, Querétaro, San Miguel de Allende and Guanajuato, saw foreign visitors remain for only 1.5 nights on average, while San Miguel de Allende, with its large year-round population of Canadians and Americans saw foreign visitors stay almost twice as long (2.9 nights) in 2009. Based on these data, it appears difficult to attribute these variations entirely to geographic location. Most likely, the number of nights spent in each city is equally a function of a city's proven allure to foreigners (San Miguel), or to well-designed and executed tourism strategies (Zacatecas).

Create a slogan. That summarizes Guanajuato's tourism strategy according to many of those interviewed. "First we select an image—the former one was 'City of Romance,' then from that you develop the strategy; then you put together the blitz," said a city tourism official.[5] Although Guanajuato's basic allure is culture and history, mummies, and monuments, the city's tourism promotion model has led to a proliferation of often disconnected and obscure slogans, including the following:

- City of Lights,
- Cervantino Capital of Mexico,
- City of Romance,
- City of Legends,
- Your Experience Becomes History, and
- Cradle of Independence.

Local observers indicated sloganeering has become a prominent strategy because mayors cannot serve for more than one three-year term. Multiple terms are permitted, but not in succession. Such short terms of office prohibit development and execution of meaningful tourism plans and strategies. Furthermore, tourism promotion staffs tend to turn over with every change of administration. Consequently, in lieu of meaningful long-term planning and strategy, tourism

---

4   Clarisa A. de Abascal (manager of Viajes Georama and former tourism official) in conversation with author, January 2010.

5   Mario Aguado Malacara, (Director General of Tourism, city of Guanajuato, Mexico), in discussion with the author, January 2010.

promotion relies heavily on slogans, with questionable results. Multiple slogans blur the city's brand and confuse potential visitors.

Interviewees identified other policies and issue influencing the apparent 43.2% decline in international visitors to Guanajuato between 2000 and 2008. Guanajuato's principal cultural event is the city's annual Cervantino Festival. The three-week festival of music, dance, and art began in 1972, and has attracted world-famous talent including such artists and performers as Robert Mapplethorpe, Rudolph Nureyev, the Vienna Philharmonic, and Ella Fitzgerald. The international festival attracted increasing numbers of visitors from around the world; however, it also became attractive to a younger Mexican audience craving a party scene. In 2000 this situation reached an unpleasant climax when vast numbers of drunken young revelers motivated some to proclaim Guanajuato had become a large *cantina*. Going forward, Cervantino was modified to provide more regional emphasis and fewer internationally recognized performers and artists. Given the Cervantino Festival's drawing power, some speculate that the festival's reformulation was responsible for the decline in international arrivals to Guanajuato.

This brings us back to the enduring problem faced by others who have attempted to identify and quantify the relationship between World Heritage inscription and tourism, with mixed or little success: the lack of consistent and valid data. In the case of Mexico, SECTUR provides an abundance of data reaching back to 1986. Without considerable investigation, which is beyond the purview of this research, researchers cannot be entirely confident about the veracity of these data. Still, despite some questions from Guanajuatenses about the impact of the impact of hotel and restaurant taxes, the overall impression one can glean from conversations with academics, government officials, and those in the travel industry is that these data are valid, but fail to tell the entire story.

Conclusion

We do know that this investigation's results suggest statistically significant increases in tourism attributable to inscription while controlling for the number of hotel rooms and global trends in international travel. Interviews and simple observation, however, reveal other trends which suggest initial increases visitors may sometimes be a temporary phenomenon, depending on public policy, local management practices, and other causes that may be less controllable. After inscription, World Heritage Cities tend to improve their appearance, infrastructure, and tourism facilities, which may help to increase foreign visitors.

The World Heritage List first appeared in 1978, and some sites have been included for over 30 years. As the World Heritage Movement enters middle age, the research focus must shift its focus away birth and neo-natal periods of sites to a broader view that would begin to understand the life cycle of World Heritage cities. This research suggests that success in retaining and attracting visitors requires solid and consistent planning and management.

A report from the United Kingdom concludes that "World Heritage status is what you make of it" (Price Waterhouse Coopers 2007: 7). The evidence from Mexico appears to support that assertion.

References

Buckley, R. (2002). *World Heritage Icon Value: Contribution of World Heritage Branding to Nature Tourism.* Canberra: Australian Heritage Commission.

Buckley, R. (2004). The Effects of World Heritage Listing on Tourism to Australian National Parks. *Journal of Sustainable Tourism,* 12(1): 82.

Feilden, B.M. and Jokilehto, J. (1998). *Management Guidelines for World Cultural Heritage Sites.* Rome: ICCROM.

Ferry, E. (2005). *Not Ours Alone: Patrimony, Value, and Collectivity in Contemporary Mexico.* New York: Columbia University Press.

Gravari-Barbas, M. and Jacquot, S. (2008). *Les impacts socio-*économiques *de l'inscription d'un site sur la liste du Patrimoine Mondial.* Paris: World Heritage Center.

Hall, C.M. and Piggin, R. (2002). Tourism Business Knowledge of World Heritage Sites: A New Zealand Case Study. *International Journal of Tourism Research,* 4(5): 401–11.

Harrison, D. and Hitchcock, M. (eds) (2005). *The Politics of World Heritage: Negotiating Tourism and Conservation.* Clevedon, UK: Channel View Publications.

INEGI (Instituto Nacional de Estadística y Geografía), Número de habitantes por municipio. Available at <http://cuentame.inegi.org.mx/monografias/informacion/gto/poblacion/default.aspx?tema=me&e=11> (accessed June 30, 2010).

International Monetary Fund (2011). Factsheet: Special Drawing Rights (SDRs). Available at <http://www.imf.org/external/np/exr/facts/sdr.htm> (accessed April 20, 2011).

Lazzarotti, O. (2000). Patrimoine et tourisme: un couple de la mondialisation. *Mappemonde,* 15(1): 15.

OWHC (Organization of World Heritage Cities). World Heritage Cities. Available at <http://www.ovpm.org/index.php?module=ovpm&func=liste&sorte=pays> (accessed July 10, 2010).

PriceWaterhouse Coopers (2007). *The Costs and Benefits of World Heritage Site Status in the UK.* Report prepared for the Department of Culture, Media and Sport, Cadw, and Historic Scotland.

Russo, A.P. (2002). The "Vicious Circle" of Tourism Development in Heritage Cities. *Annals of Tourism Research,* 29(1): 170.

Shackley, M. (1998). *Visitor Management—Case Studies from World Heritage Sites.* Oxford: Butterworth & Heinemann.

Thapa, B. (2007). Issues and Challenges of World Heritage Sites in Nepal. In: White, R. and Carmen, J. (eds), *World Heritage: Global Challenges and Local Solutions*. Oxford, UK: Archaeopress.

UNESCOa. World Heritage Mission Statement. Available at <http://whc.unesco.org/documents/publi_infokit_en.pdf> (accessed July 4, 2010).

UNESCOb. World Heritage List. Available at <http://whc.unesco.org/en/list> (accessed June 28, 2010).

UNESCOc. Advisory Body Evaluation. Available at <http://whc.unesco.org/archive/advisory_body_evaluation/482.pdf> (accessed July 8, 2010).

van der Aa, B.J.M. (2005). Preserving the Heritage of Humanity? Obtaining World Heritage Status and the Impacts of Listing. Unpublished PhD thesis. Groningen: Groningen University.

Weiler, S. and Seidl, A. (2004). What's in a Name? Extracting Econometric Drivers to Assess the Impact of National Park Designation. *Journal of Regional Science*, 44(2): 45–262.

Whitt, J.A. Jr. (1996). The Mexican Peso Crisis. *Federal Reserve Bank of Atlanta Economic Review*, 81(1): 1.

Chapter 4

Implications of World Heritage Designation for Local Residents: A Case Study from Taishan and Taiqian, China

Yixiao Xiang and Geoffrey Wall

Researchers in both the developed and the developing worlds have paid a lot of attention to the resource conservation aspect of heritage, which is realized mainly through heritage tourism (Du Cros 2001; Hall and McArthur 1993; McKercher, Ho and Du Cros 2005; Nuryanti 1996; Stubbs 2004; Timothy and Boyd 2003). Intervention by the United Nations Educational, Scientific and Cultural Organization (UNESCO), in the form of the World Heritage Convention, while enhancing economic significance through international tourism, has exacerbated the intrinsic tension and dissonance in World Heritage designation, especially for local communities.

China places a lot emphasis on application, conservation and development of World Heritage. Research in this area is increasing, but most of it is focused on World Heritage resource conservation including heritage planning and tourism management following the Western tradition or on issues such as management system reforms which are specific to the Chinese context (Su and Deng 2006; Tao 2001; Xie 2003, 2004; Yu and Wan 2007; Zhou 2004). Little in-depth research has been done on the implications of World Heritage designation for local communities and their responses and attempts to cope with the changes. This chapter uses a mixed research method to analyze the implications of designating Mount Taishan a World Heritage Site (WHS) for the villagers living on and around the mountain. Mount Taishan was listed by the World Heritage Convention in 1987 as one of the first four WHSs in China. For conservation purposes, some villagers were relocated and their livelihoods consequently disrupted. This chapter shows how World Heritage designation, while significantly increasing heritage tourism on the mountain, caused a number of changes in local life, as involvement in tourism became a major source of income for the villagers. The village of Taiqian serves as a case study.

World Heritage in China

China ratified the UNESCO Convention Concerning the Protection of the World Cultural and Natural Heritage (WHC), became a contracting party in 1985 and a member state of the World Heritage Committee on October 29, 1999. In 1986, China began to identify and nominate sites in its territory to be considered for inclusion on the World Heritage List. Since its first inscription in 1987, China has been gaining WHSs: in June 2009, it had 38 UNESCO listed WHSs, second only to Italy and Spain, with 25 of them being cultural heritage, seven being natural heritage, and six being mixed cultural and natural heritage, such as Mount Taishan.[1]

Economic Benefits

Aside from conservation, the economic benefits of World Heritage status from tourism are a major incentive for the Chinese government and tourist industry to embrace the idea of World Heritage. Since heritage sites are increasingly favored by visitors, both domestic and international (Dong 2006), they produce substantial increases in local revenues. For instance, the annual tourism revenue of Mount Huangshan reached 200 million CNY (32 million USD) after its inscription on the World Heritage List in 1990, as against 5 million (0.8 million USD) beforehand; the income from the entrance fees of the ancient city of Pingyao reached more than 5 million CNY (0.8 million USD) in 1998 after its World Heritage designation, as against 0.2 million (33,000 USD) in 1997; the tourism revenue from Mount Taishan in 1987 was 182 million CNY (30 million USD), following World Heritage listing, in 1987, it had reached 6.6 billion (1 billion USD) by 2005. Site managers and government at all levels are therefore highly motivated to seek World Heritage designation. The visitor data of several World Heritage mountains presented in Table 4.1 for the Golden Week[2] of May 2006 provide a further illustration. In addition to the existing 35 sites on the World Heritage List, China has had nearly 100 more sites in preparation for WHC nomination (Dong 2006).

---

1   <http://whc.unesco.org/> (accessed March 12, 2015).

2   Golden Weeks are the three week-long holidays at Chinese New Year (January/ February), May 1–7 and October 1–7 approved by the State Council of the People's Republic of China on September 18, 1999 in response to the south-east Asian financial crisis of 1998 to stimulate consumption, spur the domestic economy, and promote internal tourism.

Table 4.1   Golden Week of May 2006, visitor numbers and entrance fee income of six World Heritage Sites in China

Site	Visitors (thousands)								Entrance fee (CNY)	Total income (million CNY)
	May 1	May 2	May 3	May 4	May 5	May 6	May 7	Total		
Mount Taishan	16	32	34	26	24	16	8	156	100	15.6
Mount Wuyi	20	39	29	28	17	9	4	146	110	16.1
Mount Emei	15	23	29	29	17	15	15	143	120	17.2
Lushan National Park	11	22	25	23	16	12	8	117	135	15.8
Mount Huangshan	7	23	20	15	12	5	4	86	200	17.2
Mount Wudang	4	10	12	13	7	5	4	55	110	6.1

Source: Dong 2006.

Local Government

As noted by Dong (2006) and Xie and Zheng (2005), according to the current selection and appointment system of government officials in China, a middle-level (town, district, municipality) official serves on a five-year basis, which means they have to demonstrate satisfactory "political achievements" within these five years to get further promotion. Economic development, especially if it contributes to the GDP, is usually seen as the most important indicator of their achievements. The successful listing of a WHS would be considered a "gold medal" for their leadership, as it would probably lead to a dramatic increase in the local contribution to GDP. Such examples have been taken as role models by many local government officials (Dong 2006). Hence the local governments' desire for World Heritage designation is natural and obvious.

Local Communities

Heritage is multi-functional, subjective and selective (Ashworth and Tunbridge 1996), which can easily lead to conflict and dissonance (Graham, Ashworth and Tumbridge 2000). World Heritage designation adds to the conflict and dissonance already present in national–local relationships within Chinese heritage management. Local residents' lives are often intimately involved in the heritage site: they have usually lived in the area for generations and have strong attachments to it. However, for most large WHSs in China, conservation policy required that local residents be relocated. Research has revealed that this causes economic and mental problems for those relocated: an issue which was overlooked in the past and, in some places in China, has become an threat to social stability (Zhang and Wang 2004). The voices of local communities often seem to be overwhelmed by national and international ones in the heritage chorus. Heritage planners are challenged to determine how to use the multiple functions of heritage to mitigate the dissonance and serve its many stakeholders in a balanced way (Hall 2000). The research conducted for this chapter involved an in-depth study of the implications of World Heritage designation to local life by examining local perspectives on, attitudes to and relationships with the conservation and tourism aspects of Mount Taishan's designation as a WHS. This information could be of use to planners and managers of WHSs for solving problems and maintaining the overall and long-term sustainability of World Heritage in China.

Mount Taishan and Taiqian

Mount Taishan is located in central Shangdong province which is on the lower reaches of the Yellow River and one of the most important coastal provinces of China covering 156,700 square kilometers with a coastal line of 3,100 kilometers and a population of 92.5 million. Shandong is a popular tourist destination with its rich and diverse attractions, including Mount Taishan and the Confucius Complex at Qufu, both WHSs.

Mount Taishan lies across the cities of Tai-an, Jinan and Zibo. Its main peak, Yuhuangding (Jade Emperor Summit), which rises to 1,545 meters above sea level, is located within Tai-an. Tai-an is a popular tourist destination thanks to Mount Taishan, whence it derives its name, which means "the country is prosperous and the people live in peace." Tai-an covers an area of 7,762 square kilometers with a total population of 5.5 million and is less than an hour's drive from Jinan, the capital of the province.

Taishan covers an area of 426 square kilometers. Around 7,000 stone stairs run for 9 kilometers from the foot of the mountain to its peak, symbolizing the route from earthly human life to sacred heaven. Mount Taishan has been held in high esteem by the Chinese people since ancient times. Historical records show that it was a sacred place more than 1,000 years before the Christian era and was visited by emperors to offer sacrifices and to meditate in the Zhou Dynasty (1050–221 BC). In ancient times, the first thing for an emperor to do after ascending the throne was to climb Mount Taishan and pray to heaven and earth or to his ancestors. It has been recorded that 72 emperors of different dynasties made pilgrimages to the mountain, as did many poets and writers. The temples and numerous stone inscriptions and tablets witness to these visits. Mount Taishan also played an important role in the development of Buddhism and Taoism. Local villagers believe in the Goddess of Taishan who is worshiped in the temple on the top of the mountain. People from nearby provinces, such as Henan and Hebei, also make regular pilgrimages to Taishan. In addition the area boasts unique natural scenery: lofty peaks, deep valleys, spectacular waterfalls, enchanting rocks and centuries-old pines and cypresses.

All these attributes make a great tourist attraction. Mount Taishan was recognized by the State Council of China in 1982 as one of the earliest National Scenic Spots and Historical Sites and was opened officially to visitors as a tourism destination. In 1987, Taishan was listed by the UNESCO World Heritage Convention of as a world natural and cultural heritage site, and in 2006 it was designated as a UNESCO World Geological Park.

Technically, the local population is defined as those living inside the Taishan Scenic Beauty and Historic Interest Zone. Statistics showed that, in 2001, this included about 44,300 people, living in over 30 villages within varying distances of the mountain. Only those on or very close to the mountain were relocated. Taiqian was one of them.

Taiqian used to be situated near the bottom of the route up Mount Taishan and some of its inhabitants lived on the mountain. There were about 1,500 villagers and more than half of them were relocated by the Taishan Administrative Committee, although all the villagers experienced disruption to their livelihoods. As compensation, they were granted the rights to provide tourist services and more than half of them have jobs or run small businesses, such as restaurants and souvenir shops, along the route up the mountain.

Methodology

Mixed research methods were employed, as both qualitative and quantitative data can contribute to all aspects of evaluative inquiries (Cook 1995; Sechrest 1992, cited in Patton 2008). Patton pointed out that neither of these two paradigms is intrinsically better than the other, and recent developments in research have led to an increase in the use of multiple methods, including both qualitative and quantitative data (1987). "Triangulation of methods" has found favor with many researchers, because of its emphasis on combining methods and sources of information (Freeman, Rossi and Wright 1979; Patton 1987, 2002; Rossi and Freeman 1993; Shapiro 1973). The four basic types of triangulation are (1) data triangulation, the use of a variety of data sources in a study; (2) investigator triangulation, the use of several different researchers or evaluators; (3) theory triangulation, the use of multiple perspectives to interpret a single set of data; and (4) methodological triangulation, the use of multiple methods to study a single problem (Denzin 1978). Similarly, mixed methods research, as advocated by Creswell and Clark, emphasizes the mixture of qualitative and quantitative approaches in many phases in the research process. It focuses on collecting, analyzing and mixing both quantitative and qualitative data in a single study or series of studies. The central premise of mixed methods research is that "the use of quantitative and qualitative approaches in combination provides a better understanding of research problems than either approach alone" (Creswell and Clark 2007: 5). This does not mean that the more methods used, the better the research.

Rather, decisions about methods should depend on the nature of the research and the context in which it is conducted. According to Shapiro, "research methodology must be suited to the particular characteristics of the situations under study ... . An omnibus strategy will not work" (1973: 543).

Mixed methods or triangulation of methods is appropriate to research into the complicated global–local relationships surrounding a World Heritage Site. Based on a case study and using an ethnographic approach, several methods were employed to collect data. Qualitative data were obtained through interviews of various kinds with two village leaders and three villagers from Taiqian, two of whom received follow-up interviews. Quantitative data were obtained through a seven-point Likert Scale questionnaire, plus information obtained through on-site observation and secondary data collected during field trips. The questionnaire survey for Taiqian villagers was composed of two sections: Section 1 contained 25 attitudinal statements (S1–S25) aiming to uncover the community's perspective on how tourism and World Heritage resources were being used to address their needs; Section 2 contained two open-ended questions together with questions soliciting demographic information. One hundred questionnaires were distributed, of which 83 were returned and 78 were suitable for analysis. The demographic feature of the 78 valid respondents showed that they could reasonably represent the attitudes and perceptions of the village.

Questionnaire Results

The data obtained from the 25 questionnaire statements were analyzed and presented according to three themes: conservation, tourism and local involvement.

Conservation

Table 4.2 reveals the local residents' perceptions of Taishan heritage conservation. The majority of residents felt they were well aware of the importance of protecting the heritage resources of Taishan (S25), and the interviews confirmed this point. When asked if the natural environment was being destroyed by tourism, 56% responded "no" and only 20% said "yes" (S22). This can be interpreted two ways: the villagers are content with the existing status of conservation, or they have positive attitudes to tourism as they hope it will bring them better prospects. Most of them indicated that the previous development of Taishan Scenic Area had not reflected their concerns, nor were they happy about future developments (S20, S21). When asked if they would like to know more about the status of heritage resources and tourism in Taishan and to express their opinions, 39% expressed a reluctance to become involved to varying degrees, 21% did not express an opinion, while 39% indicated that they would like to know more (S19). Qualitative interviews shed some light on why the villagers were not keen to know about conservation and express their opinions: "They would not listen to us," said a retired village leader, "It's merely a waste of time even if we tried to say something."

Table 4.2   **Local responses on resource conservation on and around Taishan (n=78)**

Question	Responses (%)							Mean	SD
	Totally disagree	**Strongly disagree**	**Disagree**	**Hard to say**	**Agree**	**Strongly agree**	**Totally agree**		
	1	2	3	4	5	6	7		
S19: I would like to know about conservation and tourism on Mount Taishan and to express my opinion.	17.8	3.3	18.3	21.2	9.5	7.7	21.2	4.1	2.1
S20: I think the previous development of the Taishan Scenic Area has reflected our concerns.	17.4	21.2	23.7	16.6	11.2	3.3	6.6	3.2	1.7
S21: I am happy about the future development of the Taishan Scenic Area.	24.1	27.8	16.3	13.3	9.5	4.6	4.6	2.9	1.7
S22: I think the natural environment has been destroyed by tourism.	16.6	10.8	27.8	24.5	8.3	5.8	6.2	3.4	1.7
S25: I am keen to protect the cultural and natural heritage of Taishan.	0.4	2.5	18.7	17.0	5.4	10.4	45.6	5.4	1.7

Tourism

The survey results show that local residents were enthusiastic and optimistic about tourism (Table 4.3). Almost all of them (95%, S1) indicated that they were always friendly towards tourists and many of them would offer help to tourists, even for free (61%, S5). The majority (68%) showed a willingness to work in the tourism industry (S2). Only around 20% agreed that the natural environment had been destroyed by tourism development. The majority (76%, S4) did not think tourist activities caused any inconvenience. All this suggests that the local residents have a quite positive attitude to tourism and expect it to improve their lives. Doxey developed an Irritation Index Model (IRRIDEX) for analyzing community attitudes towards tourists (1975). It represents four levels of irritation felt by local residents as the impact of visitors increases: euphoria, apathy, irritation and antagonism. The villagers of Mount Taishan are between euphoria and apathy on this model, although tourism is at a well-developed stage on Mount Taishan and the villagers traditional way of life was actually proscribed because of the World Heritage designation and the consequent conservation measures.

**Table 4.3   Local responses on tourism development on and around
            Taishan (n=78)**

Question	Responses (%)							Mean	SD
	Totally disagree	Strongly disagree	Disagree	Hard to say	Agree	Strongly agree	Totally agree		
	1	2	3	4	5	6	7		
S1: I am always friendly to the tourists at Taishan.	0.0	0.0	2.5	2.9	7.5	32.8	54.4	6.3	0.9
S2: I would like to work in the tourism industry.	0.4	9.1	12.9	9.5	20.3	11.6	36.1	5.2	1.7
S4: Tourist activities do not inconvenience me.	0.4	2.1	5.4	16.2	26.1	19.9	29.9	5.4	1.4
S5: I would help tourists, even for free.	0.8	1.7	15.8	20.3	13.3	20.7	27.4	5.2	1.6
S6: I enjoy interacting with tourists.	1.2	3.3	12.0	26.1	23.7	10.0	23.1	5.0	1.5

Table 4.3 **Local responses on tourism development on and around Taishan (n=78) (*concluded*)**

Question	Responses (%)							Mean	SD
	Totally disagree	Strongly disagree	Disagree	Hard to say	Agree	Strongly agree	Totally agree		
	1	2	3	4	5	6	7		
S7: I feel my activities are an integrated part of the tourist experience.	5.8	8.7	14.5	27.4	19.5	8.7	15.4	4.3	1.7
S13: My quality of life is improved by tourism.	12.0	7.9	22.0	22.8	14.9	7.5	12.9	3.9	1.8
S23: I feel some of my ideas have changed through interaction with tourists.	1.7	13.3	24.5	26.6	21.2	5.8	7.1	4.0	1.4
S24: Interacting with tourists is an important source of information.	4.1	17.4	32	20.7	16.6	1.7	7.5	3.6	1.5

However, many of them either disagreed (44%, S13) or felt it hard to say (23%) when asked if they felt their quality of life was improved by tourism. A majority (57%, S6) said that they enjoyed interacting with tourists. However, more than half (cumulatively 57%, S7) disagreed or felt it hard to say if their activities were a part of the tourists' experience. When asked about the consequences of tourist–local interactions, such as whether some of their ideas were changed through interaction with tourists and whether interacting with tourists was an important source of information, the positive response was low (34.1%, S23; 25.8%, S24).

Local Involvement

The data also provide useful information for examining local benefits and local involvement (Table 4.4). Many respondents (58%, S3) held jobs related to tourism, but only a small proportion (29%, S8) were satisfied with their income from tourism. It appears that, according to the villagers, the Taishan Administrative

Committee (TMC) did not pay satisfactory wages or provide community facilities (S9, S10, S11), although, in the interviews, the management personnel claimed that they had provided sources of income. Locals did get reduced or free entry to the WHS (S12). There was a very negative response to inquiries about training in conservation or tourism (S14, S15, S16). This may be one reason for the low level of local involvement.

Many respondents felt that their voices were not heard (75%, S18; 70%, S17), so only a small number (39%, S19) were concerned about acquiring more information. The majority were not happy with the previous development of Taishan Scenic Area or its future development (62%, S20, 68%, S21). This may be the reason why 39% expressed their concern, 21% found it hard to say and another 39% were uninterested in learning about the status of the heritage resources and tourism of Taishan and expressing their opinions about them (S19).

Given these findings, it is not surprising that only a few respondents answered the open-ended question, No. 26: "Presently the most serious problem with tourism development on Taishan that I am concerned about is _____ ." Some of the few answers were related to lack of employment opportunities, lack of financial support and being ignored. As for No. 27: "The best way I hope to solve the problem is _____ ," even fewer responded, with one suggestion being: "Think about us, and listen to us" and another being "More financial and policy support."

Table 4.4   Local responses on benefits and involvement (n=78)

Question	Responses (%)							Mean	SD
	Totally disagree	Strongly disagree	Disagree	Hard to say	Agree	Strongly agree	Totally agree		
	1	2	3	4	5	6	7		
S3: My daily work is highly relevant to Taishan tourism.	2.9	3.4	7.5	20.1	20.7	17.0	20.3	4.9	1.6
S8: I am satisfied with my income from tourism.	19.9	15.8	13.7	22.0	13.7	10.0	5.0	3.4	1.8
S9: A good part of my income is from the TMC.	63.1	10.0	5.8	6.6	6.2	3.7	4.6	2.1	1.8
S10: The TMC often provides us with welfare.	66.0	7.9	6.6	5.9	10.4	3.3	0.8	2.0	1.6

Table 4.4   Local responses on benefits and involvement (n=78) (*continued*)

Question	Responses (%)							Mean	SD
	Totally disagree	Strongly disagree	Disagree	Hard to say	Agree	Strongly agree	Totally agree		
	1	2	3	4	5	6	7		
S11: Quite a few of our community facilities were built by the TMC.	34.9	19.9	12.9	14.5	3.3	11.2	3.3	2.8	1.8
S12: I enjoy reduced or free entry to Taishan.	0.4	0.0	1.2	3.7	12.0	39.8	42.7	6.2	0.9
S14: I can get training on how to interact with tourists.	19.9	23.7	28.6	11.2	5.0	4.1	7.5	3.0	1.7
S15: I can get training on heritage conservation.	21.6	29.5	24.5	9.5	5.8	5.0	4.1	2.8	1.6
S16: I can get training on occupational options.	24.1	37.8	17.4	7.9	7.5	2.5	2.9	2.6	1.5
S17 The TMC listens to our opinions about conservation and tourism.	38.2	9.5	22	9.5	2.4	4.1	4.1	2.8	1.8
S18: We have effective ways to express our opinions to the TMC.	34.9	18.7	21.2	10.8	7.1	5.0	2.5	2.6	1.6
S19: I hope to learn about the conservation and tourism of Taishan and to express my opinion.	17.8	3.3	18.3	21.2	9.5	8.7	21.2	4.1	2.1

Table 4.4   Local responses on benefits and involvement (n=78)
(*concluded*)

Question	Responses (%)							Mean	SD
	Totally disagree	**Strongly disagree**	**Disagree**	**Hard to say**	**Agree**	**Strongly agree**	**Totally agree**		
	1	2	3	4	5	6	7		
S20: I think the previous development of the Taishan Scenic Area has reflected our concerns.	17.4	21.2	23.7	16.6	11.2	3.3	6.6	3.2	1.7
S21: I am happy about the future development of the Taishan Scenic Area.	24.1	27.8	16.3	13.3	9.5	4.6	4.6	2.9	1.7

Interviews

The villagers showed a deep attachment to Mount Taishan and positive attitudes to conservation, agreeing with the result of the questionnaires. To the villagers, Taishan is their root, their life sustainer and their asylum god: one villager referred to it as the "mother mountain" (Villager 1, interview). Most of the villagers and their families had been living in and around Taishan for generations, had an instinctive love for the mountain, and had rich experience of living in harmony with it. One villager claimed to know what kind of trees grew best on the mountain. Their ancestors had a tradition of building their houses and walls of scree or cobblestones from the dry riverbed rather than quarry the mountain itself. They worshiped Taishan and believed that even the smallest cobblestone in the dry riverbed was blessed and would bring good luck to the house built with it (Villager 2, interview). A village leader said that the villagers had the greatest enthusiasm for conserving Taishan. They reported fires to the TMC and would be the first to arrive at the spot and start extinguishing it. As he put it, "since what we eat and drink are from Taishan, we should take good care of it and protect it. All the villagers understand this better than anyone else" (Village Leader 1, interview).

Conservation

On one hand, the villagers had no strong objections to the World Heritage status of Mount Taishan; on the other, constant complaints could be heard about the impact of the conservation project on their lives. Relocation was the foremost problem, which led to several others, including loss of land and livelihoods.

Relocation is a big issue at many of China's World Heritage Sites. It started at Taishan soon after UNESCO designated it a WHS in 1987 and still not been completed, according to the Taishan Conservation Master Plan (2000–2020). In their interviews, the leader of Taishan Administrative Committee and the village leaders were positive about how the relocations had been conducted, claiming that a lot of effort had been put in to it. A new community of standard residences had been built near Taishan, and the villagers were compensated if their new houses were smaller than their old ones and only had to pay cost price for any extra space if they were bigger. According to the committee, most of the villagers were supportive of heritage conservation and were happy to move to the new community, although a few had some problems. These problems were being dealt with through communication, persuasion, negotiation and regulation, especially by the village leaders, who acted as brokers between the TMC and the villagers.

Nevertheless, a different story was heard in the interviews with the villagers. One street-corner fruit-vender stated that the relocation policy was little more than a license to take from the villagers. The villagers said they were well aware of the value of Mount Taishan and supported its conservation, even though they were reluctant to move from the houses their families had lived in for generations. This was especially true for older people. Meetings were organized by the village committee to keep the villagers informed, and the village leaders also went to see families who found it difficult to accept the policy. The interviews with the villagers revealed five problems with relocation: (1) it meant changes of tradition and lifestyle; (2) some families already had tourist businesses, which many of them lost; (3) many were not satisfied with the compensation, either because it was les than they expected or had been promised; (4) it was felt to be inequitable—some had to move, but others could stay, some got jobs from the village committee, but others did not—(5) some villagers believed they had a better feeling for the area and more local knowledge than the conservation professionals and could not be convinced that they should not live on the mountain as its custodians.

Positive messages were also received from the Taishan Administrative Committee and the village leaders regarding loss of land and livelihoods. It was reported that "Taishan District Government was exploring a long-term mechanism to guarantee the farmers who lost their land due to heritage resource conservation as well as urbanization to live in peace and enjoy their lives."[3] The

---

3   <http://www.dzwww.com/xinwen/xinwenzhuanti/ffcl/qlfj/t20051028_1239245. htm> (accessed March 12, 2015).

report cited several measures adopted by the government for dealing with the challenge, including: providing policy support and training for young and middle-aged villagers to set up their own businesses catering to tourists and residents of Tai-an; providing technological support and training in growing high-economic-return plants such as fruits and herbs; and establishing a social security system for aged villagers to provide pensions and medical treatment.

Taiqian is one of the three villages which suffered most from land loss due to heritage conservation and urban sprawl. The village became a victim of urban sprawl after relocation, with almost all the land being purchased by the government and traditional livelihoods being completely disrupted. Observation revealed that Taiqian was no longer a village but more like a town neighborhood with cement or asphalt streets and neat standardized houses. Traditional rural attitudes could still be seen in the dried products such as mushrooms, chili peppers and garlic hung on the front walls of the building and the yards full of chickens. There was a "local food street" lined with about 30 family-run restaurants serving local, homemade meals for visitors and residents of Tai-an. Most were owned by local villagers.

Over half of the Taiqian villagers between the ages of 18 and 55 work in tourism-related businesses run by the village, all of which were under the umbrella of a tourism company owned and managed by the village committee. The others were "nong-min-hongs," regular or irregular non-agricultural workers in Tai-an or other cities. People reaching retirement age did not work but enjoyed pension and medical benefits arranged by the village committee whose major financial source was tourism.

The Interviews with the villagers confirmed that the various levels of government provided policy support and financial assistance. As noted by a village leader, policy support from the government meant a lot to the villagers, considering the long-standing, centralized, top-down institutional system in China. Only with government assistance could they do what they had to do to adapt and make the best of their situation. Also, it was confirmed that the pension and medical insurance system was implemented in Taiqian. It was a compulsory policy enforced and supervised by the government although all the costs were borne by the village committee. However, finance had always been a big problem. Some villagers felt the compensation they were supposed to receive could not always be obtained in a satisfactory way; others were not happy with the amount of compensation for relocation and land requisition and felt it was far from enough to cope with their life afterwards. Complaints arose most from those villagers who did not have the guarantee of a long-term means to sustained future life, such as a job in the village-run tourism business.

Qualitative data also showed that there were some villagers, especially the older ones who were nostalgic about life on the mountain. They were not used to the new accommodation and lifestyles, which caused physical and psychological discomfort. However, many of the young villagers interviewed, especially those who were financially well off, preferred the change of livelihood and living an urban lifestyle. They liked interacting with tourists, knowing more about the world and making more money than they did farming. Equity issues were raised again, mostly that relocation was not arranged fairly, compensation rules were not applied evenly, and job opportunities were not equally distributed.

Tourism

All the interviewees showed a very positive and enthusiastic attitude towards tourism. The village had been actively seeking opportunities to develop and benefit from tourism. Observations also showed that local residents who worked in souvenir shops, restaurants and hotels at the foot of or on the route up the mountain were polite and friendly towards tourists. Asked if they felt any inconvenience caused by tourism or any offensiveness by tourists, almost no one in the villages said they did. On Doxey's Irritation Index, their attitude was still between euphoria and apathy, which is remarkable, as tourism development in Taishan started in the mid 1980s and had reached a stage between "consolidation" and "stagnation" (Butler 1980). The villagers hoped to receive more tourists, even though the mountain was flooded with them during the high seasons.

Local Involvement

Taiqian was one of the first two villages involved in tourism at Taishan because of its location. Many of the villagers who lived on the mountain undertook tourism-related work, either running their own small business or selling local products as souvenirs even before the village committee took over in 1983. At the time of this research, there were five hotels, one coach service with a capacity of 624 seats, 35 souvenir shops, tourist convenience stores, family-based restaurants, and a number of seasonal kiosks providing food and beverages or photography services on the route up the mountain. They were operated by Taiqian Tourism Service Company set up by the village committee. There were about 1,000 employees, more than half of the village's total labor force and involving three-quarters of the 400 families. According to the village leader in charge of tourist affairs, tourist income made up to almost 70% of the total revenue of the village and the average annual income of an employee was 5,000–6,000 CNY (900–950 USD).

The management and employees of the Taishan Tourist Service Company were all from Taiqian. The village leaders automatically became the management team. They decided what hotels restaurants and souvenir shops were needed and sought contractors to bid for them at village meetings. Villagers could bid singly or as a group. Usually the contractor would be paid a basic salary by the company and was required to provide a certain return. If the actual revenue was higher than the promised return, the surplus would belong to the contractor; if lower, then the contractor had to make good the deficit. The contractors also had to accommodate a certain number of employees depending on the business. Those were also employees of the company rather than the contractors, and they earned basic salaries from the company and received a bonus from the contractor if business was good, but were not held responsible if business was bad. All the employees of the company have pensions (men at 60; women at 55) and medical insurance. Most of the company's income went on salaries, pensions and medical insurance, part went on governmental fees and tax and part went on the free education provided to all school-age children.

Interviews and observations in the village revealed some positive aspects of tourism in Taishan. However, problems were also exposed. There were still villagers hoping to benefit from tourism, although tourist capacity is limited and the tourism labor market had reached saturation point. According to the village leader, many "outsider non-registered tour guides" also wanted a share of Taishan tourism; however, their non-professional behavior damaged the image and reputation of the locals, and they did not follow the regulations or pay tax or management fees. They misled tourists with low-quality interpretations and by directing them to overpriced restaurants and souvenir shops, which often led to tourists claiming they had been cheated by the locals. Almost all the village leaders hoped for more financial support from the Taishan Administrative Committee and the government. They complained that they had good projects which they were confident would attract investors, but the TMC did not consider them appropriate for the scenic zone of Taishan.

There was also fierce competition between villages and between villagers. Tourism was regarded as an important means of making a living and the most effective and acceptable way to practice the old tradition that "those who live near the mountain, live off the mountain."

Discussion

As was pointed by Ross and Wall (1999), the well-being of the local community is central to the sustainability of tourism. The damage or weakening of community relations effects the overall stability of heritage and local residents should not be disadvantaged by conservation or tourism development. In the case of Taishan, World Heritage designation and consequent tourism should have contributed to local well-being; however, it seems it did not quite do this. Some major problems with the heritage–local relationship resulted from World Heritage designation.

The villagers felt strongly about Mount Taishan and took pride in its World Heritage designation. They were also content with the existing state of the heritage conservation under the Taishan Administrative Committee. However, their sense of belonging to the mountain was affected by relocation, unsatisfactory compensation and loss of the right to use the mountain in the traditional way. Relocation and loss of land were a major threat to the livelihoods of the villagers. In response they were keen to become involvement in tourism. However, there wee problems due to limited resources and opportunities, lack of training, inequity and fierce competition. All these issues should be considered in developing and implementing a World Heritage conservation and development plan.

Nonetheless, the strategy developed by Taiqian village committee to get the villagers actively involved in the tourism is worth of note and can provide practical experience to draw on. It brought the majority of the villagers under its umbrella by setting up a tourism company, contracting out services to the villagers and taking responsibility for social welfare. To a great extent, this alleviated the tension and stress caused by World Heritage designation. However, it should be noted that local life can not depend solely on tourism, since it is seasonal, sensitive to natural disasters, and dependent on political, social, and economic factors beyond the village's control. More tourists also means more pressure on the conservation aspect of the WHS. Local issues and objectives need to be addressed in both resource conservation and tourism planning.

References

Ashworth, G.J. and Tunbridge, J.E. (1999). Old Cities, New Past: Heritage Planning in Selected Cities of Central Europe. *GeoJournal*, 49(1): 105–16.

Butler, R.W. (1980). The Concept of a Tourist Area Cycle of Evolution: Implications for Management of Resources. *Canadian Geographer*, 24(1): 5–12.

Cook, W.D., Kress, M. and Seinford, L. (1994). A Multi-criteria Composite Index Model for Quantitative and Qualitative Data. *European Journal of Operational Research*, 78(3): 367–79.

Creswell, J.W. and Clark, V.P. (2007). *Designing and Conducting Mixed Methods Research*. Thousand Oaks, CA: Sage.

Denzin, N.K. (1978). *The Research Act: A Theoretical Introduction to Social Methods*, 2nd edn. New York: McGraw Hill.

Dong, Y. (2006). Protection and Development of the World Heritage in China Available at <http://www.shanshuang.gov.cn/bsshanzhuang/download/pdf/0040.pdf> (accessed December 23, 2011).

Doxey G. (1975). A Causation Theory of Visitor-Resident Irritants: Methodology and Research Inference. In: *Travel and Research Association, Sixth Annual Conference Proceedings*. San Diego, CA.

Du Cros, H. (2001). A New Model to Assist in Planning for Sustainable Cultural Heritage Tourism. *International Journal of Tourism Research*, 3(2): 165–70.

Freeman, H.E., Rossi, P.H. and Wright, S.R. (1979). *Evaluating Social Projects in Developing Countries*. Paris: OECD.

Graham, B., Ashworth, G.J. and Tunbridge, J.E. (2000). *A Geography of Heritage: Power, Culture and Economy*. London: Arnold.

Hall, C.M. (2000). *Tourism Planning: Policies, Processes and Relationships*. Harlow: Prentice Hall.

Hall, C.M. and McArthur, S. (1993). *Heritage Management in New Zealand and Australia*. Auckland: Oxford University Press.

McKercher, B., Ho, S.Y. and Du Cros, H. (2005). Relationships between Tourism and Cultural Heritage Management. *Tourism Management*, 26(4): 539–48.

Nuryanti, W. (1996). Heritage and Postmodern Tourism. *Annals of Tourism Research*, 23(2): 249–60.

Patton, M.Q. (1987). *How to Use Qualitative Methods in Evaluation*. Thousand Oaks, CA: Sage.

Patton, M.Q. (2002). *Qualitative Research and Evaluation Methods*, 3rd edn. Thousand Oaks, CA: Sage.

Patton, M.Q. (2008). *Utilization-Focused Evaluation*, 4th edn. Thousand Oaks, CA: Sage.

Ross, S. and Wall, G. (1999). Evaluating Ecotourism: The Case of North Sulawesi, Indonesia. *Tourism Management*, 20(6): 673–82.

Rossi, P.H. and Freeman, H.E. (1993). *Evaluation: A Systematic Approach*, 5th edn. Thousand Oaks, CA: Sage.

Sechrest, L. (1992). Roots: Back to Our First Generations. *Evaluation Practice*, 13(1): 1–7.

Shapiro, E. (1973). Educational Evaluation: Rethinking the Criteria of Competence. *School Review* (November): 523–49.

Stubbs, M. (2004). Heritage-sustainability: Developing a Methodology for the Sustainable Appraisal of the Historic Environment. *Planning, Practice and Research*, 19(3): 285–305.

Su, Y. and Deng, H. (2006). Current Status, Issues, and Countermeasures of World Heritage Conservation and Management in China. *Research on Development Study*, 5: 76–80.

Tao, W. (2001). *Study on the Sustainable Tourism Development on the World Heritage Sites in China*. Beijing: China Tourism Press.

Timothy, D.J. and Boyd, S.W. (2003). *Heritage Tourism*. Harlow: Pearson Education Limited.

Xie, N. (2003). Discussion on Some Problems with National Key Tourist Attractions. *Planners*, 19(7): 23–6.

Xie, N. (2004). An Urgent Need for Reforming World Heritage Management System in China. Interview, February 2. Available at <www.news.sohu.com> (accessed December 23, 2012).

Xie, Z. and Zheng, X. (2005). Some Theoretical Thoughts about Study of Cultural Heritage Tourism. *Journal of Guilin Advanced Tourism College*, 14(2): 21–5.

Yu, X. and Wan, J. (2007). Study on the Limitation of the Definition of World Cultural Heritage. *Journal of Yunnan Normal University*, 39(4): 79–82.

Zhang, M. and Wang, L. (2004). Co-management: Transformation of Community Affair Model in Chinese Nature Reserves. *Journal of Forestry Research*, 15(4): 21–5.

Zhou, W. (2004). The Motive behind the World Heritage Application. *Economic Reference* (July 5).

Chapter 5

Cultural Routes as World Heritage Sites: Challenges of the Nomination of the Ancient Silk Roads

Isabel Maria Torres Martínez

Tourism is claimed to be one of the world's largest industries, bringing economic benefits and contributing to the development of countries, especially those in the less-developed world (Roe and Urquhart 2001). It is also considered to be beneficial for the preservation and revival of local cultures, which might otherwise decline (Werner 2003). Moreover, the increasing interest in "cultural routes" is creating new opportunities for tourism (Zhou 2005), and, since the independence of the former Soviet states (1991), there has been a revival of the Silk Road for tourism and cultural purposes.

The Silk Road was an important trade route for many centuries (139 BC – AD 1400), connecting, through its many branches, eastern, southern and western Asia with the Mediterranean world including North Africa and Europe. It was not just silk that was traded but also other goods such as spices, Chinese porcelain, jewelry, silverware, livestock and slaves. This extensive network served as a bridge for political, economic and cultural exchanges, including religions, technology and science, between Asia and Europe and helped in the development of the great civilizations of China India, Egypt and Persia, laying the foundations for the modern world (UNWTO, UNDP and UNCTAD 2005).

The Great Silk Road

The length of the Silk Road, its development over centuries and the multiple intercultural exchanges that it facilitated have all contributed to the heritage of the Silk Road, which consists of more than the built heritage such as mosques, pagodas and mausoleums. Seeing the possibilities, the United Nations Educational, Scientific and Cultural Organization (UNESCO) started the "Integral Study of the Silk Roads: Roads of Dialogue" in 1988 in order to promote tourism in central Asia. Since then, many workshops, forums and agreements have been made to increase awareness of the immense potential of the Silk Road to the international community. The World Tourism Organization

(UNWTO) started the Silk Road Project in 1994 and has been offering its support in organizing meetings and developing marketing strategies for the region. The Fifth International Meeting on the Silk Road took place in Uzbekistan, where key issues relating to tourism development along the Silk Road were debated, and the Silk Road Action Plan 2010/11 was approved (UNWTO 2010). The plan focuses on the three priority areas: (1) marketing and promotion, (2) capacity building and destination management and (3) travel facilitation (UNWTO 2011).

In addition, UNESCO is assisting central Asian countries in the preparation of a proposal to include a Serial Nomination of the Silk Road in the Tentative List for World Heritage status. Indeed, China has already submitted the Chinese section of the Silk Road in their Tentative, and the Chinese Government has approved a five-year plan for the conservation of the Xinjiang section of the Silk Road (Zhou 2005). However, being nominated as a World Heritage Site (WHS) does not necessary guarantee an immediate growth in the number of tourists. In fact, if sites are not carefully managed, negative first-time experiences would have a stronger effect on tourists and on the overall reputation of the site.

Methodology

This chapter is part of a larger research study whose purpose was to investigate the development of the Silk Road as a tourist destination. Data collection methods included questionnaires to gather primary data from tour-operators along the Silk Road and secondary data analysis from official reports and statistics sources. Questionnaires were emailed to 159 tour-operators based mainly in China and central Asia: 34 were collected. In the broader study, the questionnaire covered other questions related to the Silk Road, its development, attractions and concerns of tour-operators. However, in this chapter just those questions related to the nomination of the Silk Road as a WHS will be discussed; specifically, the question: How do you think nomination as a World Heritage Site will influence the region?

A five-point Likert Scale ranging from "Strongly disagree" to "Strongly agree" was used, with the following statements: World Heritage status will increase tourist numbers; more help will be received from international organizations such as UNESCO and the WTO; more training will be available; the region will be better known; nothing will change.

Results show that most tour-operators (79%) thought the nomination would increase tourist numbers, with 32% strongly agreeing and 47% agreeing, and that the region would become better known, with 35% strongly agreeing and 44% agreeing. Designation as a WHS would definitely have an impact at the international level, although it is not be completely clear which region or countries of "The Great Silk Road" would receive the attention, as this would depend on where marketing campaigns focused and where investment was made.

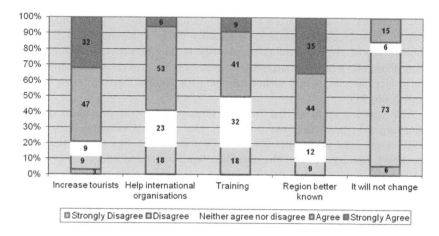

Figure 5.1   Effects of nomination as a World Heritage Site

Opinions regarding help from international organizations and training were more varied: 23% neither agreed nor disagreed and 18% disagreed that World Heritage status would lead to more help from international organizations; 32% neither agreed nor disagreed and 18% disagree that it would lead to more training becoming available. It is possible that the help received from UNESCO and UNWTO up to now has not been extended to all stakeholders in the region and their opinions are influenced by these experiences. The last statement "nothing will change" confirmed the responses regarding tourist numbers and awareness of the region, with 73% disagreeing and 6% strongly disagreeing. All the percentages are shown in Figure 5.1.

Considering these results, it seems that the nomination of the Silk Road as a WHS would increase tourism in the region. The issue that would arise is how to manage that tourism or, better, how to manage the heritage.

Managing Heritage

UNESCO has listed 1,007 properties in 161 countries on its World Heritage List since the adoption of the Convention Concerning the Protection of the World Cultural and Natural Heritage in 1972 (World Heritage Centre 2014). Although the aim of the convention is to ensure the "identification, protection, conservation, presentation and transmission to future generations of the cultural and natural heritage" (UNESCO 1972: 3), World Heritage status has been increasingly used as a marketing tool: it is seen as the "coveted prize" that will increase tourism (Li, Wu and Cai 2008: 308). However, World Heritage status does not automatically result in financial support from UNESCO, unless the site is at risk and funding is often for less-developed countries (Shackley 1998). Furthermore, Hall questions whether World Heritage status necessarily leads to increased visitor numbers, citing Rodwell, who pointed out that there was no proven relationship between World Heritage status and visitor numbers for cultural heritage sites in the UK (Hall 2006: 31).

The rapid growth of the World Heritage List has provoked discussion regarding the threat that mass tourism can cause to heritage sites (Garfield 1993), especially in countries with high populations like China (Li, Wu and Cai 2008). McKercher and Ho state that "both over- and under-use pose threats to the sustainability of cultural tourism products" (2006: 473). Over-use can cause damage to the site and consequent loss of value, whilst under-use may result in neglect and lack of conservation, which would also lead to loss of value (McKercher 2001).

Therefore, the challenge is to find a balance between tourist activity and conservation: a complicated task when a large number of stakeholders are involved (Leask 2006). Thompson remarks that maintenance of heritage sites is not the highest priority for central Asia governments and this has hindered preservation (2004). Nonetheless, conservation and tourism must go together. The integration of tourism and land management at all levels is essential for the management of a WHS (ibid), and a holistic approach should be sought when planning the development of any site. This is particularly important in the case of a Serial WHS where several stakeholders are involved. The new concept of cultural routes, compared to other forms of cultural heritage, requires a multidimensional and integrated perspective to better understand and identify the cultural heritage and provide for the conservation of the entire route (Eman 2005; Suarez-Inclan 2005).

Cultural Routes as World Heritage Sites

Cultural routes were included as a new category of WHS by UNESCO in 2005. The International Committee on Cultural Routes of the International Council on Monuments and Sites (ICOMOS) prepared the Charter on Cultural Routes that was ratified in 2008. In it, the concept of cultural route entails "a value as a whole which is greater than the sum of its parts and gives the Route its meaning" (ICOMOS 2008: 1).

Cultural routes are the result of dynamic and interactive processes of movements of people (Eman 2005), and they illustrate the interaction of geographical, economical, political, social and cultural aspects (Rosas Moscoso 2005). They are also believed to be more deeply connected to intangible heritage than other forms of cultural heritage (Ono 2005). Mason calls cultural routes "testimonies of epic journeys" (2005), and, even though they sometimes initiated conflicts, today they can be used to promote a culture of peace (Suarez-Inclan 2005).

The Silk Road is an outstanding example of a cultural route:

> A cultural route is a land, water, mixed or other type of route, which is physically determined and characterized by having its own specific and historic dynamics and functionality; showing interactive movements of people as well as multi-dimensional, continuous and reciprocal exchanges of goods, ideas, knowledge and values within or between countries and regions over significant periods of time; and thereby generating a cross-fertilization of the cultures in space and time, which is reflected both in its tangible and intangible heritage. (ICOMOS 2003)

Even though the significance of the Silk Road seems obvious and there is an indisputable argument for its inscription as a WHS, the process of nomination is hindered by the number of countries and heritage sites involved. However, even if the nomination proceeded by stages, every additional extension would enhance the whole Outstanding Universal Value (OUV) of the site. Zhou states that, although the concept of cultural routes does not address all the difficulties that heritage conservation faces, by adopting the wider approach a new side of the history and culture can be explored and better understood (2005).

Serial World Heritage Site Nomination

According to the World Heritage *Operational Guidelines*, serial properties include component parts that are related because they belong to either

> the same historico-cultural group; the same type of property which is characteristic of the geographical zone; the same geological, geomorphological formation, the same biogeographic province, or the same ecosystem type; and provided it is the series as a whole—and not necessarily the individual parts of it—which are of outstanding universal value. (UNESCO 2008a: 35)

Since the introduction of serial and transnational nominations, there has been a significant increase in interest in its use by State Parties. The Silk Road is considered for serial nomination as well as being a transnational site that will be nominated in stages. The Chinese section has already been inscribed on the Tentative List, and the other sections will be included progressively. However, difficulties may be encountered by State Parties when submitting the Silk Road on their Tentative Lists, especially in central Asian countries that have fewer resources. For this reason, UNESCO has organized several meetings to provide capacity building to State Parties and to guide them through the process of preparing the nomination files. Likewise, UNESCO is helping similar sites, such as Le Qhapaq Ñan and the Incas Trail in Latin America to prepare for nomination as cultural routes (Herdoíza and Fustillos 2005).

There are various issues that require attention: the large demands on resources occasioned by complex serial nominations for both State Parties and the World Heritage Committee and the criteria used to evaluate serial nominations that are submitted in stages (UNESCO 2008b). The committee recommends that State Parties express on the first nomination the wish to extend the property on subsequent nominations. However, this has not always been done, since some of the current serial properties were first listed before the introduction of the serial nominations. Hence, some controversies arise as to whether it is acceptable that in these cases, just the first property but not subsequent additions demonstrate OUV. Feng points out the need to structure the nomination process so that places to be included in the Serial WHS are not selected randomly and a wide perspective is taken (2005).

Another issue is whether just Samarkand or Khiva, which in fact are already WHSs, need to have OUV and the additional sites along the Silk Road are not that relevant or all parts need to have OUV. The *Operational Guidelines* mentions the relevance of the series "as a whole," without emphasizing the importance of the sites individually (UNESCO 2008a: 35). Feng distinguishes between "anchor sites" and "support sites or structures" (2005). While the anchor site should have OUV, the support sites do not necessarily need it but "complement the picture." However, this raises the question of whether, in a nomination by stages, support sites could be included as extensions to a serial site or if they needed to have an anchor site as well. Coherence must be sought for extensions to WHS, particularly when dealing with serial and transnational nominations.

Limiting numbers is also a contentious issue. For instance, the WHS, Belfries of Belgium and France, was firstly listed in 1999 as Belfries of Flanders and Wallonia in Belgium comprising 32 belfries. It has now been extended with the addition of 23 belfries in northern France and the belfry of Gembloux in Belgium as a group. Although in this case the extension shows a good example of shared architecture in north-western Europe, it would not make sense to add more individual sites in the future that exhibit the same characteristics. The site is already representative of the heritage and further sites would not enhance the actual value.

With regards to the Silk Road, the choice of the number of sites will be a complex matter. The Chinese section alone already has 46 sites on the Tentative List. According to Zhan, "selected sites shall be directly related to the attributes, functions and effects of the Silk Road(s), rather than merely located along the Silk Road" (2010: 62). Management of Serial WHSs is a key issue for IUCN (International Union for Conservation of Nature). They noted the need for "clearer direction and guidelines to ensure strong nomination and effective management post-inscription" (cited in Leask 2006: 14). Support and resources are needed not only during the nomination process, but also for post-inscription and actual management of the site, especially considering the increase in the number of visitors that is likely to happen when the site is inscribed as a WHS.

The *Operational Guidelines* require that together with the nomination file, "a management system or mechanisms for ensuring the co-ordinated management of the separate components" is included (UNESCO 2008b). Joint-management can suffer from difficulties when State Parties have different political, economic, legal and social characteristics; stakeholders' interests and approaches differ; characteristics of local communities are not shared; or in general when communication is not fluent and appropriate (ibid).

To create and run an efficient management system for the Silk Road represents a challenge. UNESCO recommends following best-practices achieved by already inscribed serial sites, but these are not as complex as the Silk Road. Moreover, the cultural routes that are being considered for nomination as WHSs, like the Inca Trail in Latin America, are approximately at the same stage of development and cannot be used as examples. The management system for the Silk Road Serial WHS entails very ambitious relationships and organizational structures.

UNESCO has provided some guidelines for the establishment of a management system for serial transnational properties and it includes acknowledgment of the common thematic framework and understanding of the OUV, agreement of joint management and arrangements for collaboration for the protection, management and conservation of the property through all the institutions (2008b). Whereas sharing a common vision and objectives can be achievable, arranging protection and management measures might be more difficult and conflicts of interest may occur, especially when the economic benefits of tourism are involved.

In addition, it is important to highlight that serial nominations are assessed with "the same criteria, requirements for integrity, authenticity and management as are all other nominations" (UNESCO 2008b). This means that if a component of the serial site is not well managed and its value is under threat due to inappropriate heritage conservation, the whole serial site is likely to be inscribed on the World Heritage in Danger List. This needs to be perfectly understood by State Parties wishing to jointly work on the preparation and management of serial sites. Sugio proposes that a heritage assessment should be made prior to the nomination of the site, which should include potential impacts on the cultural route, their likeliness and dimension. Preventive and corrective measures should also be indicated (Sugio 2005).

The Silk Road is a very complex cultural route and inappropriate management of a single place would affect the whole site and put it at risk. UNESCO recommends that China establish a National Management Unit supported by clusters that represent various themes, for instance, art, architecture, archeology, religion, military engineering, agriculture, trade and manufacture, travel and transportation and so on (UNESCO 2004: 22). It is essential for China to have a well-structured organization, since the area and number of sites are greater than in the central Asian countries.

This same structure with clusters could be adapted by the other countries at the national level, but also at the regional level. If Kazakhstan, Kyrgyzstan, Tajikistan, Turkmenistan and Uzbekistan together present the nomination of the "Central Asian Section of the Silk Road," then a "Central Asian Management Unit" should be created. These countries are already benefiting from the development of a multiscale Cultural Heritage Information System that, with funds from UNESCO and BELSPO (Belgian Science Policy), will support the nomination of the Central Asian Silk Roads Cultural Heritage Sites (BELSPO 2009). It is recommended that the central Asian countries work together on the management of their section for a short period of time, before they merge with China, so that the preservation of all the sites is not compromised.

UNESCO maintains that it is essential to bear in mind constraints due to cultural, social and political differences in countries and to avoid complex nominations that have little chance of being manageable (2008b). Even though it is a very complex cultural route, the complexity is what makes the Silk Road rich in history and culture and why it needs to be recognized as a WHS. Small, steady and consistent steps should guide the process of nomination and post-management of the sites along the route. For both the nomination of the Silk Road as a WHS and the promotion of the site as a tourist destination, a holistic approach is needed to show the whole OUV and the unique destination. It "should never lose sight of the meaning and historic significance of the Route as a whole" (Suarez-Inclan 2005: 6).

According to UNESCO, the starting point should be "the identification and justification of those aspects and elements that will 'tell the story' of the Chinese Silk Road in a comprehensive manner" (2004: 7). If this approach is taken, it can be seen that the support sites play a significant role in the storytelling, and it is not just the most beautiful mosques, temples or pagodas that are the attractions, but also the small villages, caravanserais and the landscapes, as well as the intangible heritage that complement the destination. This approach is consistent with Thorne's notion of a "place-based" approach to cultural tourism, which must:

> possess a holistic understanding of culture,
> understand the city or region's cultural character, and
> understand the travel motivations and behaviours of cultural tourists.
> (Thorne 2008: 1)

A place-based tourist destination should be a "tapestry of place" composed by "the destination's people, its history, its folklore, its cuisine, its natural and built heritage, its art and music, its language and traditions—along with its museums, galleries, festivals, heritage sites, and the other 'usual' cultural experiences that a visitor might expect" (Thorne 2008: 4). This tapestry of place corresponds with the concept of "crossroads of cultures," as the Silk Road has been widely described. It is therefore essential that a place-based approach is taken to both the promotion and understanding of its OUV when identifying a site to be included on the Tentative List. By these means, the Silk Road can be promoted as an integrated and unique destination with a wide array of natural, cultural and intangible heritage, which will hopefully be preserved for future generations through its nomination as a WHS.

Conclusion

The ancient Silk Road has significant tourism potential as an outstanding example of a cultural route, created and shaped by the movements of peoples over centuries. As a result, there has been an increasing interest by international organizations, such as UNWTO and UNESCO to promote cultural tourism in the region, including nominating the site for World Heritage status. Nomination as a Serial Transnational WHS could be hampered by the numerous sites, differences of cultures, level of development of the countries and the stakeholders involved. The identification of the OUV of the sites also presents some controversies. For this, it has been recommended that a staged nomination process that adapts best-practices gained on similar sites or more advanced sections be followed. By adopting the holistic approach of cultural routes, the OUV is better identified and the conservation of the cultural heritage is enhanced. This improves joint-management of the WHS, as well as increasing inter-cultural understanding and co-operation. In short, an integrated and multi-dimensional approach should be taken to the storytelling and heritage conservation of the ancient Silk Road.

References

BELSPO [Belgian Science Policy] (2009). Motivated Expression of Interest for the Silk Road (Central Asia) Project Related to the Development of an Information System in View of the Nomination of the Serial WH-Site. Available at <http://www.belspo.be/belspo/home/calls/forms/SILKROAD_Proj2009_en.pdf> (accessed August 17, 2009).

Eman, A. (2005). The Dynamic of Linear Settings: Hijaz Railroad. *Monuments and Sites in Their Setting: Proceedings of ICOMOS 15th General Assembly and Scientific Symposium, Xi'an, China.* Available at <http://www.international.icomos.org/xian2005/papers.htm> (accessed March 5, 2015).

Feng, J. (2005). UNESCO's Efforts in Identifying the World Heritage Significance of the Silk Road. *Monuments and Sites in Their Setting: Proceedings of ICOMOS 15th General Assembly and Scientific Symposium, Xi'an, China.* Available at <http://www.international.icomos.org/xian2005/papers.htm> (accessed March 5, 2015).

Garfield, D. (1993). *Tourism at World Heritage Cultural Sites: The Site Manager's Handbook.* Washington, DC: ICOMOS.

Hall, M. (2006). Implementing the World Heritage Convention: What Happens after Listing? In: Leask, A. and Fyall, A. (eds), *Managing World Heritage Sites.* Oxford: Butterworth-Heinemann, pp. 18–32.

Herdoíza, W. and Fustillos, A. (2005). Le Qhapaq Ñan ou la Route des Incas. *Monuments and Sites in their Setting: Proceedings of ICOMOS 15th General Assembly and Scientific Symposium, Xi'an, China.* Available at <http://www.international.icomos.org/xian2005/papers.htm> (accessed March 5, 2015).

ICOMOS [International Council on Monuments and Sites] (2003). Preliminary Ideas for the Drafting of an International Charter on Cultural Routes. Available at <http://www.icomos-ciic.org/CIIC/reportZimPrelimiIdeas.htm> (accessed April 18, 2011).

ICOMOS (2008). Charter on Cultural Routes. Available at <http://www.international. icomos.org/charters/culturalroutes_e.pdf> (accessed December 16, 2011).

Leask, A. (2006). World Heritage Site Designation. In: Leask, A. and Fyall, A. (eds), *Managing World Heritage Sites*. Oxford: Butterworth-Heinemann, pp. 5–19.

Li, M., Wu, B. and Cai, L. (2008). Tourism Development of World Heritage Sites in China: A geographic perspective. *Tourism Management*, 29(2): 308–19.

Masson, G. (2005). Cultural Route and the Heritage Management Challenge: The Klondike Gold Rush: A Case Study'. *Monuments and Sites in their Setting: Proceedings of ICOMOS 15th General Assembly and Scientific Symposium, Xi'an, China*. Available at <http://www.international.icomos.org/xian2005/ papers.htm> (accessed March 5, 2015).

McKercher, B. (2001). Attitudes to a Non-viable Community-owned Heritage Tourist Attraction. *Journal of Sustainable Tourism*, 9(1): 29–43.

McKercher, B. and Ho, P. (2006). Assessing the Tourism Potential of Smaller Cultural and Heritage Attractions. *Journal of Sustainable Tourism*, 14(5): 473–88.

Ono, W. (2005). A Case Study of a Practical Method of Defining the Setting for a Cultural Route. *Monuments and Sites in their Setting: Proceedings of ICOMOS 15th General Assembly and Scientific Symposium, Xi'an, China*. Available at <http://www.international.icomos.org/xian2005/papers.htm> (accessed March 5, 2015).

Roe, D. and Urquhart, P. (2001). Pro-Poor Tourism: Harnessing the World's Largest Industry for the World's Poor. Available at <http://www.propoortourism.info/ documents/Roe2002PPT.pdf> (accessed September 3, 2009).

Rosas Moscoso, F. (2005). Lima–Cordoba del Tucuman: Camino Imperial Incaico y Camino Real Español. *Monuments and Sites in their Setting: Proceedings of ICOMOS 15th General Assembly and Scientific Symposium, Xi'an, China*. Available at <http://www.international.icomos.org/xian2005/papers.htm> (accessed March 5, 2015).

Shackley, M. (ed.) (1998). *Visitor Management: Case Studies from World Heritage Sites*. Oxford: Butterworth-Heinemann.

Suarez-Inclan, M.R. (2005). A New Category of Heritage for Understanding, Cooperation and Sustainable Development; Their Significance within the Macrostructure of Cultural Heritage; the Role of the CIIC of ICOMOS: Principles and Methodology. *Monuments and Sites in their Setting: Proceedings of ICOMOS 15th General Assembly and Scientific Symposium, Xi'an, China*. Available at <http://www.international.icomos.org/xian2005/papers.htm> (accessed March 5, 2015).

Sugio, K. (2005). A Consideration on the Definition of the Setting and Management/ Protection Measures for Cultural Routes. *Monuments and Sites in their Setting: Proceedings of ICOMOS 15th General Assembly and Scientific Symposium, Xi'an, China.* Available at <http://www.international.icomos.org/xian2005/ papers.htm> (accessed March 5, 2015).

Thompson, K. (2004). Post-colonial Politics and Resurgent Heritage: The Development of Kyrgyzstan's Heritage Tourism Product' *Current Issues in Tourism*, 7(4): 370–82.

Thorne, S. (2008). Place and Product. A Place-Based Approach to Cultural Tourism. Available at <http://www.torc.on.ca/documents/REVISEDPlaceasProduct_000. pdf> (accessed August 7, 2009).

UNESCO [United Nations Educational, Scientific and Cultural Organization] (1972). Convention Concerning the Protection of the World Cultural and Natural Heritage. Available at <http://whc.unesco.org/archive/convention-en. pdf> (accessed July 28, 2009).

UNESCO (2004). *UNESCO Mission to the Chinese Silk Road as World Cultural Heritage Route: A Systematic Approach towards Identification and Nomination: 21–31 August 2003.* Paris: World Heritage Centre.

UNESCO (2008a). *Operational Guidelines for the Implementation of the World Heritage Convention.* Paris: UNESCO.

UNESCO (2008b). *Point of Information on the Preparation of Serial Transnational Nominations.* Paris: World Heritage Centre.

UNWTO [World Tourism Organization] (2010). Silk Road Action Plan. Available at http://www.unwto.org/silkroad/events/en/pdf/Silk_Road_Action_Plan_2010. pdf (accessed July 7, 2011).

UNWTO (2011). Silk Road Programme. Available at <http://www.unwto.org/ silkroad/> (accessed April 7, 2011).

UNWTO, UNDP [UN Development Programme] and UNCTAD [UN Conference on Trade and Development] (2005). Tourism Pearls of the Silk Road. Available at <http://www.unwto.org/silk_road/pub/en/pdf/silk_road. pdf> (accessed June 14, 2009).

Werner, C. (2003). The New Silk Road: Mediators and Tourism Development in Central Asia. *Ethnology*, 42(2): 141–59.

World Heritage Centre (2014). World Heritage List. Available at <http://whc. unesco.org/en/list> (accessed November 12, 2014).

Zhou, L. (2005). Cultural Routes and the Network Construction of the World Cultural Heritage Conservation. *Monuments and Sites in their Setting: Proceedings of ICOMOS 15th General Assembly and Scientific Symposium, Xi'an, China.* Available at <http://www.international.icomos.org/xian2005/ papers.htm> (accessed March 5, 2015).

Chapter 6

The Relationship between World Heritage Designation and Local Identity

Takamitsu Jimura

As of 2011, many countries are competing for the acquisition of World Heritage status for their historical sites. Such fierce competition is not limited to between countries. It can also be observed within countries such as the UK or Japan, countries with long Tentative Lists of candidate sites. Hence, it could be said that the interests of States Parties in obtaining World Heritage status are still very high and their aspiration to use that status for various positive purposes is still very strong. Interest in World Heritage status is not limited to the real world. World Heritage Sites (WHSs) have been one of the main research areas in heritage and tourism studies since the late 1990s. For instance, various cases studies focus on issues in the visitor management at WHSs (Shackley 1998a); others look at different issues in managing WHSs, from conceptual framework to site management (Leask and Fyall 2006). Moreover, Jimura examines the impact of World Heritage designation on local communities (2007a; 2011) and the concept of "historic urban landscape" (2009). On the other hand, the establishment of identities at the national, regional and local levels through heritage creation and representation have also been a key area of research (e.g. Hewison 1987; Lowenthal 1998; Waterton and Watson 2010). However, none of these focuses specifically on WHSs and their implications for the creation of identity, especially at the local level. This chapter, therefore, aims to build a bridge between studies about WHSs and those on local identity. Thus, the chapter examines what kind of requirements WHS designation must meet to make a vital contribution to shaping or enhancing a local identity. First, earlier studies of WHSs and local identity are reviewed, and three requirements are identified and discussed.

Theoretical Framework:
World Heritage Convention and the Mission of World Heritage Sites

The United Nations Educational, Scientific and Cultural Organization (UNESCO) is trying to promote the identification, protection and preservation of cultural and natural heritage in the world (UNESCO 2011a). This is embodied in an international agreement known as the World Heritage Convention (WHC).

Article 27.1 of the WHC requires State Parties to enhance appreciation and respect by local and global communities through all suitable means, and in particular by educational and information programs (UNESCO 2011b); Article 5.1 also requires that State Parties not only to protect and rehabilitate WHSs but also to give the sites a function in the life of the communities they belong to (ibid.).

According to the UNESCO, the mission of World Heritage is to:

- encourage countries to sign the WHC and to ensure the protection of their natural and cultural heritage;
- encourage State Parties to the WHC to nominate sites within their national territory for inclusion on the World Heritage List;
- encourage State Parties to establish management plans and set up reporting systems on the state of conservation of their WHSs;
- help State Parties safeguard World Heritage properties by providing technical assistance and professional training;
- provide emergency assistance for WHSs in immediate danger;
- support State Parties' public awareness-building activities for World Heritage conservation;
- encourage participation of the local population in the preservation of their cultural and natural heritage;
- encourage international co-operation in the conservation of our world's cultural and natural heritage. (UNESCO 2011a)

No contribution to national, regional and local identity is included in the mission of World Heritage. However, it could be assumed that an identity at national, regional and local levels could be established or increased through the mission mentioned above as Shackley implies works at the national level (1998a).

The Impact of World Heritage Site Designation

Previous studies have examined the changes caused by WHS listing. Not all, but many WHSs see an increase in the visitor numbers after WHS designation (Asakura 2008; Hall and Piggin 2003; Jimura 2007a, 2011), and this could lead to overcrowding of local communities (Bianchi and Boniface 2002; Smith 2002) and disruption of local people's lives (ICOMOS 1999). Simultaneously, however, this also means the site is newly "discovered" and "acknowledged" as a WHS by outsiders. Shackley (1998b) and Smith (2002) assert that WHS designation can make a site highly visible and known to the public. World Heritage status also has a symbolic value: it brings huge prestige at international and national levels, and it eventually influences the decisions of local planning (Shackley 1998b; Smith 2002). WHS designation can also enhance the site's image and is likely to work as a marker of authenticity and quality for international tourists (Bianchi 2002; Smith 2002). These processes could enable local people to think that their site has something special and unique which will attract numerous tourists (Jimura 2007a), and this could lead to the shaping or enhancing of a local identity. In other words, local people can rediscover themselves and their heritage through the discovery of the site by outsiders. The most basic standard which can measure how the site is acknowledged and celebrated by the public should be a comparison of the visitor numbers before and after WHS designation. In short, to examine this difference would be useful to establish a requirement WHS listing must meet to make a vital contribution to shaping or enhancing a local identity.

The Role and Position of World Heritage Sites

The process of WHS designation is complicated; however, its main part is the submission of a dossier about a particular site by a national government (Shackley 1998b). The dossier on cultural heritage is examined by ICOMOS (International Council on Monuments and Sites) and that on natural heritage is reviewed by IUCN (International Union for Conservation of Nature). WHS designation can be withdrawn if the site loses its criteria for designation through inadequate conservation measures, over restoration or natural disasters (Shackley 1998b). However, such a withdrawal is rare; therefore, the number of WHSs has been increasing (Evans 2002). Consequently, the total number of WHSs as of March 2011 is 911: 704 cultural, 180 natural and 27 mixed properties in 151 countries (UNESCO 2011c). Evans states that WHS listing means that the site is awarded the same status as other existing WHSs and this means that the newly inscribed WHS becomes a competitor for tourists with other WHSs (2002). Bazin argues that nomination for World Heritage status is conducted by a nation without the agreement of local people (1995), but this view seems to be somewhat extreme. However, it is true that in many cases there are different aspirations for WHS designation between national government, local government and local people. This implies that it could sometimes happen that, even if the national government regarded a site as representative of a national, regional or local identity which deserves World Heritage status, local communities might not agree. In other words, a WHS could be seen by local people as just part of their ordinary life and need did not think that it has universal value or plays a vital role in their daily life.

Tasks for World Heritage Sites

Graham, Ashworth and Tunbridge stress that the concept of World Heritage encapsulates themes which are significant to humanity as a whole, but they also warn that it often creates ideological discord as well (2000). For example, the problem of imbalances in WHSs was raised in 1994, and the issue has been addressed through various measures. However, it is still not resolved, and the geographical and numeric imbalance in the World Heritage List remains.

As Smith suggests, in the future, questions might be raised about the indefinite expansion of the World Heritage List and the depreciation of meaning and significance of WHSs (2002). As tourism occupies a central position at most WHSs, questions about the appropriate balance between visitation and conservation frequently emerge (Bianchi and Boniface 2002), and finding the proper balance between these two demands will always be a contentious task for WHS managers (Shackley 2006). However, this is quite difficult, because conserving heritage for future generations and displaying heritage to the public for their education and enjoyment have basically opposite aims (ICOMOS 1999). If the WHS has not been managed properly due to an inappropriate balance between conservation and tourism development, the quality of the WHS will be compromised and the national, regional and local identity created or enhanced through World Heritage designation will also be weakened. In the light of this point, the contribution that World Heritage designation can make in shaping or enhancing local identity will be larger when the WHS is a place to live rather than a monument or archeological site. This is because local people feel a much stronger sense of unity in the former case than in the latter.

World Heritage Sites in Japan and Investigation of Requirements

Three requirements that a site must satisfy for World Heritage designation make a significant contribution to shaping or enhancing a local identity are how well known the site is to tourists, the value ascribed to the site by the local population and that it be where the local population live.

How Well Known is the Site to Tourists before World Heritage Designation

Japan has 14 WHSs as of March 2011: 11 cultural and 3 natural (UNESCO 2011c) (see Table 6.1). Of these, several were already well known to domestic and international tourists and attracted numerous visitors even before their WHS listing. In Japan, several cultural WHSs which were already famous amongst tourists as visitor attractions or tourist destinations did not show a noticeable increase in the visitor number, though some of them saw a temporary increase immediately after designation (Naikakufu Seisaku-tokatsukan-shitsu 2005). In these WHSs, there were various factors which made them visible and attractive for visitors, including long histories as tourist destinations: attractive or significant histories, culture or natural features; physical and emotional accessibility; and the impact of the media. For instance, Historic Monuments of Ancient Kyoto (Kyoto, Uji and Otsu Cities) (Table 6.1, No. 5) encompasses 17 properties and all of these, especially Kiyomizu-dera, Rokuon-ji, Nijo-jo, Kyo-o-gokoku-ji and Jisho-ji, had attracted visitors from all over the world for a long time before their WHS designation. This point also applies to other "established" sites such as Historic Monuments of Ancient Nara (No. 9). This WHS includes eight properties and all of these, particularly Todai-ji, Kofuku-ji and Yakushi-ji, have been very popular amongst domestic and international tourists. The only cultural WHS near the Greater Tokyo area, Shrines and Temples of Nikko (No. 10) has also been visited by a large number of tourists even before its WHS designation.

Table 6.1   World Heritage Sites in Japan

Number	Name	Type	Year of Inscription
1	Buddhist Monuments in the Horyu-ji Area	Cultural	1993
2	Himeji-jo	Cultural	1993
3	Shirakami-Sanchi	Natural	1993
4	Yakushima	Natural	1993
5	Historic Monuments of Ancient Kyoto (Kyoto, Uji and Otsu Cities)	Cultural	1994
6	Historic Villages of Shirakawa-go and Gokayama	Cultural	1995
7	Hiroshima Peace Memorial (Genbaku Dome)	Cultural	1996
8	Itsukushima Shinto Shrine	Cultural	1996
9	Historic Monuments of Ancient Nara	Cultural	1998
10	Shrines and Temples of Nikko	Cultural	1999
11	Gusuku Sites and Related Properties of the Kingdom of Ryukyu	Cultural	2000
12	Sacred Sites and Pilgrimage Routes in the Kii Mountain Range	Cultural	2004
13	Shiretoko	Natural	2005
14	Iwami Ginzan Silver Mine and its Cultural Landscape	Cultural	2007

Source: UNESCO World Heritage Centre 2011c.

According to Jimura, the number of visitors to Buddhist Monuments in the Horyu-ji Area (No. 1) before and after WHS designation are also similar to those of the three WHSs mentioned above. It saw a slight increase and accepted more overseas tourists, especially from the UK, France, Germany and Italy, only immediately after its WHS inscription (Jimura 2007b). Asakura, however, argues that the average annual visitor numbers for the five years after its WHS listing decreased 33% compared with those before WHS designation (2008). The results from two different studies do not match very well; however, at least it could be said that Buddhist Monuments in the Horyu-ji Area have not experienced a undeniable growth in visitor numbers. Shiretoko (No. 13) can be seen as the only Japanese WHS whose visitor numbers have gradually decreased since its WHS listing, though the latest year will see some increase (Shari-cho 2011).

Asakura and Naikakufu Seisaku-tokatsukan-shitsu note that several Japanese WHSs have seen an extensive increase in the number of visitors and tourists after WHS designation: Shirakami-Sanchi (No. 3), Yakushima (No. 4), Historic

Villages of Shirakawa-go and Gokayama (No. 6) (Asakura 2008; Naikakufu Seisaku-tokatsukan-shitsu 2005) and Gusuku Sites and Related Properties of the Kingdom of Ryukyu (No. 11) (Naikakufu Seisaku-tokatsukan-shitsu 2005). For example, Shirakawa-go was designated a WHS together with Gokayama in December 1995. Before WHS designation, the numbers of visitors to the village were around 671,000 in 1994 and 771,000 in 1995 (Shirakawa-mura 2010). In 1996, the numbers of visitors and tourists showed a marked increase (1,019,000) and have kept increasing until 2008 (1,861,000) (ibid.). The common features of these four WHSs are that tourism has not developed much there and they did not have many tourists before their WHS listing. In other words, they have relatively short history as established tourist destinations, and it would have been difficult for local people to recognize that their community has something with the potential to attract a large number of tourists. It could be said that if a WHS sees a huge increase in the number of tourists, WHS listing can make a vital contribution to shaping or enhancing the local identity.

The Value Ascribed to a Site by Local Communities before
World Heritage Designation

The value of the site for local people and its role before WHS listing are closely related to the difference in local people's recognition of the site before and after WHS inscription. For example, the Hiroshima Peace Memorial (Genbaku Dome) (No. 7) has been an important icon for all Japanese people, especially for elderly local people, because of its witness to the devastation of the atomic bomb. Needless to say, it is meaningful for everyone on earth that the site is now a cultural WHS. However, a local identity as "Hiroshima people" seems to have been created not by a World Heritage status but by the dropping of the atomic bomb and the existence of the memorial itself. In this case, the spirit of place of the Hiroshima Peace Memorial will not be affected by whether the site is a WHS or not or whether the site is a dark tourism destination or not.

Sacred Sites and Pilgrimage Routes in the Kii Mountain Range (No. 12) and Iwami Ginzan Silver Mine and its Cultural Landscape (No. 14) are two WHSs described as "cultural landscapes." This is different from the Hiroshima Peace Memorial, which is also a cultural WHS but is designated as a "monument." World Heritage status has improved the value of these two sites for Japanese people, especially local people. However, like the Hiroshima Peace Memorial, these two sites also had important values for Japanese people before WHS listing. Sacred Sites and Pilgrimage Routes in the Kii Mountain Range have a historic and religious link with both Shintoism and Buddhism. Japanese people recognize that the site is very important for them and a sacred area whose cultural and natural features are deserving of respect even without its World Heritage status. In contrast, Iwami Ginzan Silver Mine and its Cultural Landscape is the Japan's first industrial heritage listed as a cultural WHS. However, even without World Heritage status, most Japanese people recognize its historic and industrial significance: it had a large impact on commercial activities and international trades in the Sengoku, Azuchi-Momoyama and Edo periods (Iwami Ginzan World Heritage Centre n.d.).

In the cases of three WHSs, World Heritage designation could only make a limited contribution (Sacred Sites and Pilgrimage Routes in the Kii Mountain Range, Iwami Ginzan Silver Mine and its Cultural Landscape) or almost no contribution (Hiroshima Peace Memorial) to shaping or enhancing a local identity. This is because both local and Japanese people already understand the value of the sites, and the sites themselves have already played an essential role as part of a local community and established a strong presence in society at local and national levels. It could be argued that if the site itself did not play an important role in a local community and local people did not attach especially significant value to it before WHS inscription, and World Heritage listing had a positive influence on these attitudes, World Heritage designation made a significant contribution to shaping or enhancing a local identity.

The World Heritage Site as a Place to Live

Of the three natural WHSs, Yakushima and Shiretoko are National Parks (Ministry of the Environment 2010a, 2010b) and Shirakami-Sanchi is a mountainous land covered by virgin forest with a large variety of flora and fauna (Ministry of the Environment 2010c). There are, therefore, no people who use these natural WHSs as places of residence, though many people work there for conservation and other purposes. Hence, these natural WHSs cannot be seen as part of a local community.

In contrast, most of the 11 cultural WHSs are monuments or cultural landscapes, and all of these seem to have a closer link with local people's daily life than the three natural WHSs. This is because the whole of, or at least a part of, each cultural WHS is physically (location and area) and mentally (local people's recognition of the site) encompassed in local communities and their daily life. However, it is doubtful that WHS designation of all of these cultural WHSs has actually made a vital contribution to shaping or enhancing a local identity. For example, Himeji-jo (No. 2) is a castle and can be seen as a monument. The castle has existed in its current location since its main structures were constructed in 1580 (City of Himeji 2011). Before the Meiji period, the castle was a place of residence for feudal lords. In the past 140 years, however, it has not been used as a place of residence. Moreover, it has been open to the public for a long time, with admission fees. In other words, Himeji-jo has a long history as a historic visitor attraction and an icon of the City of Himeji. For the reasons above, it would be difficult to claim that there is a strong link between the World Heritage listing of Himeji-jo and any change in the level of local identity. The level of contribution that the WHS designation of Itsukushima Shinto Shrine (No. 8) could make should be similar to the case of Himeji-jo. Itsukushima Shinto Shrine is also a monument; however, unlike Himeji-jo, the

Figure 6.1   Gassho-style houses in Ogimachi
Source: © 2011 Takamitsu Jimura.

site includes its water gate, pavilions and extensive precinct. As of 2000, around 2,200 people live on Miyajima Island where Itsukushima Shinto Shrine is located (Hiroshima Prefecture n.d.); however, the shrine is no-one's residence and only the chief priest and some workers live there. Therefore, it would be possible to conclude that, like the Himeji-jo, there is no significant relationship between the WHS status of Itsukushima Shinto Shrine and any change in the level of local identity. Cultural landscapes such as Sacred Sites and Pilgrimage Routes in the Kii Mountain Range and Iwami Ginzan Silver Mine and its Cultural Landscape are also difficult to see as people's places of residence.

Of the 11 cultural WHSs in Japan, the only exception in terms of people's place of residence is Historic Villages of Shirakawa-go and Gokayama, which can be categorized as a group of buildings. The important point is that definite areas with clear boundaries where local people actually live there (Ogimachi in Shirakawa-go, Gifu Prefecture, and Suganuma and Ainokura in Gokayama, Toyama prefecture) are inscribed as a cultural WHS. All three of these areas have conserved their historic houses (Figure 6.1) and many people still live in them. Now local people can feel that they live in a WHS, although some of them find it inconvenient to live in such houses (Jimura 2007a). Of 14 WHSs in Japan, therefore, Historic Villages of Shirakawa-go and Gokayama is the only WHS which can be regarded as a place people live. Orbasli notes that WHS listing can increase the level of local people's interest in their town (2000), and Ogimachi, Suganuma and Ainokura would be cases in point. In the case of Ogimachi, several intangible changes in local people's minds were confirmed after its WHS designation: these changes included an increase in interest in heritage conservation and attachment to and pride in their place of residence (Jimura 2007a, 2011). All of these changes are positively related to local identity. It could be concluded that if a WHS includes definite areas where people live and local people feel that the WHS is their place of residence, World Heritage listing can make a critical contribution to shaping or enhancing a local identity.

Conclusion

In conclusion, there are three requirements WHS designation must have to make a significant contribution to shaping or enhancing local identity. First, the site must not be well known to tourists before WHS listing, but become well known and see a large increase in the number of tourists afterwards. This also means that after World Heritage listing, local communities can rediscover themselves and their heritage through the discovery of the site by outsiders. Second, the sites must not play an important role in the local community before World Heritage designation, and World Heritage status must have a positive impact on this, and the local community's awareness of the value of the site must been enhanced. Third, the site must be somewhere where people live. These requirements have been identified through the investigation of WHSs in Japan. Needless to say, the examination of diverse WHSs in various countries in different regions would be essential to suggest more comprehensive and rigorous requirements WHS designation needs to satisfy in order to make a significant contribution to shaping or enhancing a local identity.

References

Asakura, S. (2008). Impacts of Registration for World Heritage in Japan. In: Japan Institute of Tourism Research [JITR] (ed.), *Proceedings of the 23rd JITR Annual Conference*. Ueda: JITR, pp. 329–32.

Bazin, C.-M. (1995). Industrial Heritage in the Tourism Process in France. In: Lanfant, M.-F., Allcock, J.B. and Bruner, E.M. (eds), *International Tourism: Identity and Change*. London: Sage, pp. 113–26.

Bianchi, R. (2002). The Contested Landscape of World Heritage on a Tourist Island: The Case of Garajonay National Park, La Gomera. *International Journal of Heritage Studies*, 8(2): 81–97.

Bianchi, R. and Boniface, P. (2002). Editorial: The Politics of World Heritage. *International Journal of Heritage Studies*, 8(2): 79–80.

City of Himeji (2011). Himeji-jo no Rekishi. Available at <http://www.city.himeji. lg.jp/guide/castle/history.html> (accessed March 4, 2011).

Evans, G. (2002). Living in a World Heritage City: Stakeholders in the Dialectic of the Universal and Particular. *International Journal of Heritage Studies*, 8(2): 117–35.

Graham, B., Ashworth, G. and Tunbridge, J. (2000). *A Geography of Heritage: Power, Culture and Economy.* London: Hodder Arnold.

Hall, M. and Piggin, R. (2003). World Heritage Sites: Managing the Brand. In: Fyall, A., Garrod, B. and Leask, A. (eds), *Managing Visitor Attractions: New Direction.* Oxford: Butterworth-Heinemann, pp. 203–19.

Hewison, R. (1987). *The Heritage Industry: Britain in a Climate of Decline.* London: Methuen.

Hiroshima Prefecture (n.d.). Miyajima-cho. Available at <http://db1.pref. hiroshima.jp/data/FigureOfTown/toshi/html/toshi27-a/toshi27-a.html> (accessed July 6, 2010).

ICOMOS [International Council on Monuments and Sites] (1999). *Tourism at World Heritage Sites: The Site Manager's Handbook*, 2nd edn. Madrid: WTO.

Iwami Ginzan World Heritage Centre (n.d.). Iwami Ginzan Iseki to sono Bunka-teki Keikan. Available at <http://ginzan.city.ohda.lg.jp/wh/jp/culture/index. html> (accessed July 4, 2010).

Jimura, T. (2007a). The Impact of World Heritage Site Designation on Local Communities: A Comparative Study of Ogimachi (Japan) and Saltaire (UK). Nottingham Trent University: unpublished PhD thesis.

Jimura, T. (2007b). How Cultural Heritage is Consumed by Tourists: A Case Study of Horyu-ji Temple. Paper presented at the 2007 International Tourism Biennial: Tourism, Lessons from the Past, Directions for the Future, Canakkale, April–May 2007.

Jimura, T. (2009). Examination of the Concept of Historic Urban Landscape (HUL) in the Japanese Context through a Case Study of the City of Kyoto, Japan. World Heritage, Tourism and Identity, 12th International Seminar Forum UNESCO: University and Heritage: Historic Urban Landscapes: A New Concept? A New Category of World Heritage Sites?, Hanoi, April 2009.

Jimura, T. (2011). The Impact of World Heritage Designation on Local Communities: A Case Study of Ogimachi, Shirakawa-mura, Japan. *Tourism Management*, 32(2): 288–96.

Leask, A. and Fyall, A. (eds) (2006). *Managing World Heritage Sites.* Oxford: Butterworth-Heinemann.

Lowenthal, D. (1998). *The Heritage Crusade and the Spoils of History.* Cambridge: Cambridge University Press.

Ministry of the Environment (2010a). Kirishima-Yaku Kokuritsu Koen. Available at <http://www.env.go.jp/park/shiretoko/> (accessed July 6, 2010).

Ministry of the Environment (2010b). Shiretoko Kokuritsu Koen. Available at <http://www.env.go.jp/park/kirishima/index.html> (accessed July 6, 2010).

Ministry of the Environment (2010c). Mori no Hakubutsukan. Available at <http:// www.env.go.jp/nature/isan/worldheritage/japanese/shirakami/about.html> (accessed July 6, 2010).

Naikakufu Seisaku-tokatsukan-shitsu (2005). Sekaiisan no Kankokyakusu. Available at <http://www5.cao.go.jp/j-j/cr/cr05/chr05_1-01.html> (accessed March 4, 2011).

Orbasli, A. (2000). *Tourists in Historic Towns*. London: E. & F.N. Spon.

Shackley, M. (ed.) (1998a). *Visitor Management: Case Studies from World Heritage Sites*. Oxford: Butterworth-Heinemann.

Shackley, M. (1998b). Conclusions: Visitor Management at Cultural World Heritage Sites. In: Shackley, M. (ed.), *Visitor Management: Case Studies from World Heritage Sites*. Oxford: Butterworth-Heinemann, pp. 194–205.

Shackley, M. (2006). Visitor Management at World Heritage Sites. In: Leask, A. and Fyall, A. (eds), *Managing World Heritage Sites*. Oxford: Butterworth-Heinemann, pp. 83–93.

Shari-cho (2011). Kanko-tokei-shiryo. Available at <http://www.town.shari.hokkaido.jp/shiretoko/data/index.htm> (accessed March 4, 2011).

Shirakawa-mura (2010). Shirakawa-mura kanko tokei. Available at <http://www.shirakawa-go.org/lifeinfo/info/kankou/kankouka.htm> (accessed March 4, 2011).

Smith, M. (2002). A Critical Evaluation of the Global Accolade: The Significance of World Heritage Site Status for Maritime Greenwich. *International Journal of Heritage Studies*, 8(2): 137–51.

UNESCO [United Nations Educational, Scientific and Cultural Organization] (2011a). World Heritage. Available at <http://whc.unesco.org/pg.cfm?cid=160> (accessed March 4, 2011).

UNESCO (2011b). World Heritage Convention. Available at <http://whc.unesco.org/en/conventiontext> (accessed March 4, 2011).

UNESCO (2011c). World Heritage List. Available at <http://whc.unesco.org/en/list> (accessed March 4, 2011).

Waterton, E. and Watson, S. (eds) (2010). *Culture, Heritage and Representation: Perspectives on Visuality and the Past*. Farnham: Ashgate.

Chapter 7

Local Consequences of Global Recognition: The "Value" of World Heritage Status for Zanzibar Stone Town

Akbar Keshodkar

In 2000, Zanzibar Stone Town (ZST) was designated a World Heritage Site (WHS). The United Nations Educational, Scientific and Cultural Organization (UNESCO) and the World Heritage Committee indicated that ZST earned this designation because it represented, "an outstanding material manifestation of cultural fusion and harmonization" and served as "a fine example of the Swahili coastal trading towns of East Africa ... retain[ing] its urban fabric and townscape virtually intact and containing many fine buildings that reflect its particular culture," bringing together and homogenizing disparate elements of cultures from around the Indian Ocean.[1] This description of Zanzibari heritage fails to recognize the history of struggle and hardships that continue to epitomize Zanzibar as a socially and ethnically diverse and politically contested country (Keshodkar 2005). However, as others have already rejected notions of Zanzibar as a harmonized culture (Bissell 1999; Syversen 2007), this chapter will examine other dimension of the heritage discourse. The hardships and quality of life experienced by ZST residents question the "value" of the global designation imposed on them. This chapter argues that given the present physical state of ZST, it is the continuing dilapidation and the rising poverty and hardships of its residents that is celebrated by the World Heritage designation, as the quality of life and access to resources and services for these residents could substantially improve if many areas of ZST were torn down and replaced with more modern facilities and infrastructure.

The Path to World Heritage Designation

The buildings that define UNESCO's idea of "heritage" for ZST were built in the nineteenth century. The majority of these structures emerged after 1828, when the Omani Sultanate established their rule in Zanzibar. Prior to that, mud brick huts dominated the landscape (Syversen 2007: 103). As Zanzibar evolved into

---

1   <www. whc.unesco.org/en/list/173> (accessed March 12, 2015).

a commercial entrèpot under Omani rule, most of the mud huts were torn down and replaced with more modern structures, inhabited primarily by merchants involved in the slave trade and clove plantations. It was during this period that the general layout and architecture of ZST acquired the characteristics of an Arab town, with main streets and residential quarters crisscrossed by narrow lanes (Bissell 1999: 443; Walls 1995: 121).

Today, however, less than 25% of total building stock in ZST can be characterized as being of Arab origin (Siravo 1995: 136) and the "traditional" Swahili structures which UNESCO claims to be "virtually intact" are almost non-existent.[2] The structures depicted as representing the "heritage" of Zanzibar were built by social, political and economic elite of the time, primarily Arabs and Indians, to reflect their wealth (Keshodkar 2010: 227). These merchants possessed the wealth to decorate the buildings with expensive imported materials, often containing intricate wood designs. Moreover, these structures were designed for a drier climate, thus requiring constant maintenance as the foreign materials deteriorated in the humid local climate (Syversen 2007: 109). Much of the African population of Zanzibar lived in Ng'ambo, "on the other side," of the creek that divided ZST from the rest of Zanzibar town (Myers 1993).

Only after the 1964 Revolution, when an African insurgency overthrew Arab rule and forced many Indians and Arabs to flee Zanzibar, did the orientation and composition of ZST change. Perceived as a center of the inequalities that defined Zanzibar before the Revolution, the revolutionary government developed a new city center outside ZST (Hitchcock 2002: 160) and forcefully marginalized ZST. With the expulsion of Arabs and Indians, most structures in ZST were confiscated and converted into multi-family houses for low-income residents from rural areas of Zanzibar (Syversen 2007: 107). Given that these new residents of ZST did not have an urban tradition nor any interest in or means of maintaining the elaborate and ageing structures (Hoyle 2002: 151), the post-revolutionary period marked the beginning of a sharp decline in the physical conditions of buildings and in economic life of ZST (LaNier et al. 1983, in Bissell 2007: 186–7).

In 1979, UNESCO identified 17 structures in ZST which it felt needed to be saved and preserved (Bissell 1999: 449). Subsequently, in 1982, Zanzibar applied for World Heritage status for these 17 buildings, but their application was rejected on the grounds that the character of the city was no longer of sufficient integrity or authenticity (Syversen 2007: 127). Subsequently numerous conservation consultants, including those from UNESCO, Habitat and the Aga Khan Trust for Culture (AKTC) among others, came to help Zanzibar identify ways to "preserve" its history and become a WHS.

---

2   Over 30% of total building stock in Stone Town today, constituting the majority as representative of any particular cultural heritage, is characterized as being of Indian origin, built in the late nineteenth and early twentieth centuries (Siravo 1995: 136).

Though existing research at the time highlighted that tourism offered no solutions to Third World countries struggling for economic growth (Turner 1976) and led to unequal and uneven development (Britton 1982) and greater dependency on the West (Mowforth and Munt 2009: 52), conservation and urban development consultants recommended that Zanzibar invest in tourism to save its heritage and reverse the decay of the buildings in ZST and create new economic opportunities for local residents (Balcioglu 1995: 131; Bissell 1999: 479). Consequently, Zanzibar started promoting tourism in the 1980s and applied for the World Heritage designation four more times over the next 16 years. Finally, in 2000, ZST joined the World Heritage List. However, the designation was not centered around the 17 buildings that UNESCO initially identified in 1979, but included the entirety of Stone Town. Now, all of ZST needed to be preserved. It is noteworthy that when Zanzibar initially applied in 1982, the application was rejected because the site was considered to lack sufficient integrity or authenticity to authorize its inscription. Yet, with the development of tourism and the involvement of outside agencies in renovating and "preserving" some buildings, it somehow acquired integrity and authenticity. Furthermore, in 1982, Zanzibar lacked a tourism infrastructure. However, by 2000, when a manageable tourism infrastructure was developed to support all those tourists interested in celebrating its heritage,[3] ZST became a WHS, and Zanzibar now acquired its new global identity.

Between 1985 and 2000, tourism to Zanzibar increased dramatically, and more tourists continue to visit Zanzibar since WHS designation (Table 7.1). An official at the Stone Town Conservation and Development Authority (STCDA), which monitors and enforces UNESCO policies, suggested that "WHS designation provides a 'Brand' for Zanzibar to the world. ... It makes a huge difference in marketing and promoting tourism" (interview, January 13, 2010), and it supports the government's goals of bringing approximately 500,000 tourists to Zanzibar annually by 2015 (ZATI 2008: 11). There was also a concerted effort by the government to primarily promote upper-class tourism, with the idea that wealthy tourists were more interested in learning about Zanzibar culture (Hitchcock 2002: 163): ironically, backpackers were primarily responsible for putting Zanzibar on the tourist map. But, as the "value" of visiting the WHS increases for tourists, as determined by the increase in visitor numbers, it is the local residents who have to cope with these new intrusions.

---

3   Approximately 73% of tourists that visit Zanzibar come from western European countries (ZATI 2008: 9).

Table 7.1   Visitors to Zanzibar, 1985–2009

Year	Total Number of Tourists	Year	Total Number of Tourists
1985	19,368	1998	86,455
1986	22,846	1999	86,918
1987	20,011	2000*	97,156
1988	32,119	2001	76,329
1989	37,850	2002	87,511
1990	42,141	2003	68,365
1991	50,827	2004	92,161
1992	59,747	2005	125,443
1993	68,597	2006	137,111
1994	41,433	2007	143,283
1995	56,415	2008	128,440
1996	69,159	2009**	97,711
1997	86,495	2010	Figure not available

Source: Zanzibar Commission for Tourism *Zanzibar Stone Town declared a World Heritage Site **January–September.

The Physical Challenges of Living in Zanzibar Stone Town

As tourists venture through ZST, immersed in its "heritage," they often remain unaware of the non-tourists around them. The residents of ZST now represent part of the exhibit on display. Rarely do tourists realize, as it was succinctly expressed by one resident, that "Stone Town is a living city, not a monument" (interview, January 10, 2010). With urban tourism becoming a major global industry in the twenty-first century (Ashworth and Tundbridge 1990, in Hoyle 2002: 154), areas such as ZST are being turned into museums for the enjoyment of tourists who are eager to experience the other side of cities (cf. Mowforth and Munt 2009: 280) with complete disregard for the object of their gaze. However, residents living in these urban sites are forced to cope with the consequences of accommodating this tourist gaze.

In 1995, approximately 75% of the 1,713 buildings in ZST were categorized as deteriorating (Siravo 1995: 137), and less than 14% of all structures were in good shape (Bissell 1999: 476). Many of these structures collapse each year (Hitchcock 2002: 160). However, the rubble from them remains behind (Figure 7.1).

Initiatives to clean up these areas or build other structures now require approval from STCDA and for new structures to have features correlating with the "heritage" theme, which is extremely expensive. For the over 18,000 residents who live in the 1,400 remaining structures in ZST, many barely earning enough to survive, embarking on such projects remain an impossible endeavor (Siravo 1995: 102). Consequently, many of the collapsed structures become rubbish dumps (Figure 7.2).

Figure 7.1   Collapsed and dilapidated structures in Zanzibar Stone Town and rubble around them

Source: Author, January 2010.

Figure 7.2   Open areas in Zanzibar Stone Town used as dumping grounds

Source: Author, January 2010.

Figure 7.3   Water tanks and pipes on the outside of buildings in Zanzibar Stone Town
Source: Author, January 2010.

When many of the structures were built, they required extensive upkeep. However, after their original owners left, the poor inhabitants that moved in lacked the resources to maintain them. Often, they modified the buildings to their own liking, usually to multi-family homes (Syversen 2007: 108–10). Over time, the need for "modern" facilities led the occupants to place water-tanks and sewage pipes on the exterior of the buildings (Figure 7.3), resulting in soiled water leaking through pipes, spreading bacteria and fungi on the walls and polluting the groundwater (Walls 1995: 123–5). Accessing electricity became possible only through connecting into existing services, leading to wires crossing between houses (Figure 7.4).

While living under these conditions is difficult, the World Heritage status of the entire ZST has prevented many residents from improving their living conditions. STCDA policies require all renovations to follow UNESCO guidelines for the preservation of heritage buildings. Given the exorbitant costs of such repairs, most residents are unable to afford them. Furthermore, after the Revolution, the government expropriated over 90% of buildings in ZST (Syversen 2007: 175) and still maintains control of about 60% of them (Boswell 2008: 308). Many structures are also *waqf*, "religious endowments" controlled by authorities, further limiting prospects of private ownership (see Hitchcock 2002: 164). Since the government owns the majority of the buildings, residents lack any incentive to embark upon renovations.

**Figure 7.4   Electric wires crossing the narrow streets of Zanzibar
Stone Town**

Source: Author, January 2010.

Those that dare, have to engage in longwinded bureaucratic procedures to acquire permission, first, from the government and, then, from the STCDA. In addition to acquiring permits from STCDA, residents have to contract STCDA consultants to monitor the restorations and often have to pay fines if any renovation is found to be in violation of ambiguous UNESCO policies (see Bissell 1999: 522).[4]

---

4   Pendlebury, Short and While discuss the lack of a clear, internationally agreed-upon set of conservation principles and policies for conservation of structures in urban areas by UNESCO (2009).

Figure 7.5   Residents of Stone Town waiting in line for water
Source: Author, January 2010.

Government regulations have also further intruded upon the lives of the residents of ZST. As the value of many ZST properties have substantially increased in recent years, the government has, often arbitrarily ,declared properties in desired locations unsafe and inhabitable. However, after forcing residents to evacuate, these properties are sold to investors (Bissell 1999: 503). The government has also raised rents substantially, forcing many residents to move (Bissell 2007: 188). A number of respondents claimed that their rents increased 10-fold over the past few years, with one claiming that their monthly rent increased from 20,000 shillings to 200,000 shillings (interview, January 19, 2010). As the value of properties in ZST appreciates, these developments highlight how the government, which once actively marginalized ZST and encouraged the rural poor to occupy it, now facilitates gentrification to benefit from recent developments in tourism.

Though property values have increased recently, there continues to remain larger infrastructure problems in ZST, with the inability of the government to provide adequate water supply, drainage, sewage and rubbish collection and disposal (Siravo 1995: 138). While hotels in ZST seem to have easier access to these services, many residents continue to experience daily hardships accessing water and electricity. Residents often wait in line for hours to fill buckets with water (Figure 7.5). It has been suggested that these problems were related to recent political developments on the islands. The rising corruption and continuing ineffectiveness of the government led many residents to support the opposition party. Consequently, some respondents claimed that the government punished them by restricting their access to services. They indicated that in areas outside ZST, where there was greater support for the government, there was greater access to basic services. Yet, despite increasing revenues acquired from tourism, the basic quality of life of many ZST residents continues to deteriorate.

Additionally, tourism has failed to bring the economic prosperity that many consultants claimed would follow World Heritage status. Employment figures over the past decade suggest that rather the opposite is taking place. Between 2001 and 2009, urban unemployment in Zanzibar increased from 25% (United Nations 2001: 24) to 34% (ILO 2009: 27). Many tourism jobs in Zanzibar are taken by migrants from mainland Tanzania and other parts of East Africa. With no access to adequate secondary and tertiary education, many Zanzibaris do not possess the linguistic and work skills required in the tourist industry and are thus only qualified for unskilled work (see Keshodkar 2005). Consequently, many residents operate small curio shops, selling goods that primarily originate from outside Zanzibar. However, to operate these shops in ZST, they have to follow STCDA and UNESCO policies. These policies, many shopkeepers claim, restrict them from displaying their products outside their shops, consequently limiting their ability to attract tourists and recently forced them to purchase "authentic" board signs for their businesses (Boswell 2008: 308). In instances that these policies were not followed, shopkeepers were fined.

While the situation of many residents is dire, there are efforts by various individuals and groups to restore parts of ZST. A major issue for restoring any building in ZST is the cost. An official at AKTC in Zanzibar emphasized how, when they restored and converted the Ex-Tel Com building into Serena Hotel,[5] it cost 10 times more than just demolishing the existing structure and building another one would have (interview, January 18, 2010). Those with political connections have also managed to acquire exclusive rights to various buildings and have used them as leverage in the market, selling them to private investors looking to make them into hotels (Bissell 2007: 188). The government has also condemned buildings as unsafe, evicted their residents and then sold them to investors (Bissell 1999: 500). Consequently, only few people are in a position to revive any of these structures—namely international organizations, affluent residents and businessmen who restore the structures to increase their social prestige and standing; government officials, whose source of wealth is questionable; Zanzibari families returning from the Gulf and Europe; and expatriate private investors (Yahya 1995: 117). Without wealth or connections, the majority of ZST residents remain excluded from this process.

---

5   The Ex-Tel Com building, overlooking the sea, served as a library for local residents before it was "restored" as the Serena Hotel (see Bissell 1999).

The "Value" of World Heritage Status

These prevailing circumstances question the value of World Heritage status for ZST residents, who receive no or minimal benefit from developments associated with the status of the site. Conservationists argue that ZST needs to be saved, but in the process, the social lives and urban concerns of its residents continue to be blighted (Bissell 2007: 195). Conservationists further argued that restoration of ZST would accelerate the economic revitalization of its people (Balcoiglu 1994: 130–31), but, for many residents, restoring these structures remains more a financial burden than cultural obligation (Meffert 1995: 110). Furthermore, conservationists see local residents as an obstacle to restoration, claiming that they do not see the value of the local heritage (Bissell 1999: 503–4), a sentiment also iterated by a STCDA official, who claimed that "locals need to be educated ... as they do not see value of living in a heritage site" (interview, January 13, 2010). In all of these instances, calls for preserving the heritage of Zanzibar is made primarily by outsiders and those in positions of power, who do not live in ZST, not ZST residents, who continue to be excluded from the process (Bissell 1999: 518).

The rationale for ZST being designated a WHS is itself quite revealing. When Zanzibar first applied, in 1983, with the 17 structures which UNESCO considered worthy to be preserved and representative of Zanzibari culture, its application was denied. Only after all structures of ZST, even those that were dilapidated and in the process of collapsing, were included in the application was it designated a WHS. Consequently, structures which locals saw of no value were forced to remain standing, irrespective of how dangerous and unsafe they were. With the growing prominence of urban tourism, UNESCO's decision of to designate the entirety of ZST as a WHS can be perceived as an effort to create a new, non-Western urban product for Westerners to consume. Urban WHSs in other industrializing nations encounter similar realities. Old Havana, Islamic Cairo, Luang Prabang, Cartagena, among others are the few urban destinations whose heritage UNESCO wants to celebrate. However, the fate of these cities is similar to that of Zanzibar—many areas within them are dangerously dilapidated, massively overcrowded and with many residents living in poverty (Mowforth and Munt 2009: 279).

In Zanzibar, tourism has accelerated urbanization. Presently, over 40% of Zanzibar's population live in and around Zanzibar Town (ILO 2009: 3). As the poor are forced out of ZST in favor of investors and local elites interested in restoring buildings (Bissell 2007: 187), they have fewer options available to them, not only in ZST, but also in the surroundings slums and shanty towns. Again, this situation is not unique to Zanzibar, but is prevalent in many urban WHSs in non-Western nations, where gentrification is increasingly an unavoidable product of urban conservation and tourism development (Mowforth and Munt 2009: 280). Conservationists in Zanzibar have suggested that to conserve ZST, overcrowding must be controlled, and, to that effect, the government should move people out of the historic area and offer them alternative housing (Walls 1995: 122).

However, this solution would displace residents from the only home that many of them have ever known.

ZST is a "living city, and not a monument," and it is this living city that Western tourists come to consume. If it was uninhabited, tourists would then come and take pictures of the ruins, but people do live there. In its present form, Western tourists consume the omnipresence of poverty, the filth of Third World urban areas, romanticizing and experiencing it by walking through the middle of it, which they would never dare back in their own societies (see Mowforth and Munt 2009: 285). Furthermore, as patterns of tourism development in Zanzibar illustrate, this experience is increasingly reserved for affluent Westerners, who apparently exhibit the disposition to appreciate Zanzibar's culture (Hitchcock 2002: 163).

UNESCO, by virtue of designating ZST a WHS and forcing Zanzibar to follow specific models of heritage and preservation, is complicit in constructing and advocating this new gaze onto Third World cities. There is no recognition of the fact that urban settlements cannot be frozen at a particular point in time and are subject to continuous development (Pendlebury, Short and While 2009: 351). ZST residents require modern structures to live in, with indoor plumbing, electricity and other basic services. However, the only modern structures in ZST today are the ones that were either built before the World Heritage designation or are restored homes and hotels. Many of these newer buildings are often in violation of UNESCO conventions, but as an STCDA official indicated, "there is pressure [to look the other way] because officials are often bribed" (interview, January 13, 2010), and as one resident asserted, "if one pays, they can get their way around UNESCO regulations" (interview, January 13, 2010).

There is a desperate need to modernize ZST, but World Heritage designation and convention prohibits that modernization from taking place. Modernization would lead to removal from the World Heritage List, resulting in dramatic consequences for the island's economy, given its increasing reliance on tourism. The dependency that Zanzibar now has on UNESCO and the World Heritage brand was recently tested when Zanzibar embarked upon renovating the port at the northern edge of ZST. With more people and goods coming to Zanzibar, the decaying old port required urgent renovation and expansion. However, the expansion resulted in the demolition of several warehouses built in 1927 adjacent to the port. The port, now refurbished, handles more passengers and cargo. Nevertheless, UNESCO rebuked the Zanzibar authorities and warned that any further unauthorized renovations could warrant the site be placed on the list of World Heritage in Danger (UNESCO 2008: 8). Since this reprimand, STCDA has become more obedient towards UNESCO policies, as they do not want Zanzibar to suffer the same fate as Dresden, which was delisted in 2009 for building a bridge, seen as essential to ease local traffic congestion, across the cultural landscape designated a WHS. Being in Germany, Dresden can turn to its national government for financial assistance with development; Zanzibar is in no such position. With the government bankrupt and unable to provide many services, Zanzibaris increasingly rely upon tourism for foreign exchange. World Heritage status promotes tourism, and, consequently, Zanzibar does not have the luxury of going against the wishes of UNESCO. It now remains hostage to UNESCO's "heritage" policies. In the process of rebuilding the port, Zanzibar found out the limits of the value World Heritage status offers local residents under the current heritage discourse.

Conclusion

The history of Zanzibar has been one of hardship. Since the 1980s, the promotion of tourism tied to the restoration of ZST was marketed as bringing a brighter future for Zanzibaris, epitomized by the designation of ZST as a WHS. However, many ZST residents not only continue to experience great hardship but also live in dangerous and unsafe structures. Present UNESCO policies and Zanzibar's rising dependence on tourism contribute to this situation. Nevertheless, UNESCO, proclaiming high, moral and enlightened goals, has the power to change the premises on which it facilitates the development of the societies that depend upon it. There is no doubt that existing UNESCO policies regarding WHS management require modifications, if not in re-defining "heritage," then certainly in determining the value of that heritage for people on whom the designation is imposed. Zanzibaris have risen up in the past against those that exacerbated their hardship. As these hardships increase, the degree to which UNESCO re-evaluates existing World Heritage policies will determine the value of World Heritage status for ZST and how and to what extent Zanzibaris actually benefit from the inscription of ZST as a WHS.

References

Ashworth, G.J. and Tundbridge, J.E. (1990). *The Tourist-Historic City.* London: Belhaven.

Balcioglu, E.M. (1994). *The Historic Cities Support Programme of the Agan Khan Trust for Culture and its Activities in the Stone Town of Zanzibar.* Geneva: Aga Khan Trust Switzerland.

Bissell, W. (2007). Casting a Long Shadow: Colonial Categories, Cultural Identities, and Cosmopolitan Spaces in Globalizing Africa. *African Identities,* 5(2): 181–97.

Bissell, W. (1999). City of Stone, Space of Contestation: Urban Conservation and the Colonial Past in Zanzibar. University of Chicago: unpublished PhD thesis.

Boswell, R. (2008). Scents of Identity: Fragrance as Heritage in Zanzibar. *Journal of Contemporary African Studies,* 26(3): 295–311.

Britton, S. (1982). The Political Economy of Tourism in the Third World. *Annals of Tourism Research,* 9(3): 331–58.

Hitchcock, M. (2002). Zanzibar Stone Town Joins the Imaged Community of World Heritage Sites. *International Journal of Heritage Studies*, 8(2): 153–66.

Hoyle, B. (2002). Urban Waterfront Revitalization in Developing Countries: The Example of Zanzibar Stone Town. *Geographical Journal*, 168(2): 141–62.

ILO [International Labor Organization] (2009). *Zanzibar: Social Protection Expenditure and Performance Review and Social Budget*. Geneva: ILO.

Keshodkar, A. (2005). Movement of Asian and Swahili Identities: Impact of Tourism on Constructions of Community, Ethnicity, and Gender Relations in Zanzibar Town. Oxford University: unpublished PhD thesis.

Keshodkar, A. (2010). Marriage as the Means to Preserve "Asian-ness": The Post Revolutionary Experience of the Asians of Zanzibar. *Journal of Asian and African Studies*, 45(2): 226–40.

LaNier, R., McQuillan, D.A., Flemming, A., McAuslan, P. and McPhelim, P. (1983). *The Stone Town of Zanzibar: A Strategy for Integrated Development*. Report commissioned by UN Center for Human Settlement (Habitat) for Ministry of Lands, Housing and Construction, Zanzibar.

Meffert, E. (1995). Will Zanzibar Stone Town Survive? In: Sheriff, A. (ed.), *The History and Conservation of Zanzibar Stone Town*. Athens: Ohio University Press, pp. 109–15.

Mowforth, M. and Munt, I. (2009). *Tourism and Sustainability: Development, Globalization and New Tourism in the Third World*, 3rd edn. London: Routledge.

Myers, G. (1993). Reconstructing Ng'ambo: Town Planning and Development on the Other Side of Zanzibar. Los Angeles: University of California: unpublished PhD thesis.

Pendlebury, J., Short, M. and While, A. (2009). Urban World Heritage Sites and the Problem of Authenticity. *Cities*, 26(6): 349–58.

Sheriff, A. (ed.) (1995). *The History and Conservation of Zanzibar Stone Town*. Athens: Ohio University Press.

Siravo, F. (1995). The Zanzibar Stone Town Planning Project. In: Sheriff, A. (ed.), *The History and Conservation of Zanzibar Stone Town*. Athens: Ohio University Press.

Syversen, I.L. (2007). Intentions and Reality in Architectural Heritage Management: In Search of the Influence of International Policy Documents on Contemporary Sustainable Local Heritage Management. Case Zanzibar Stone Town, Tanzania. Gothenburg: Chalmers University of Technology: unpublished PhD thesis.

Turner, L. (1976). The International Division of Leisure: Tourism and the Third World. *World Development*, 4(3): 253–60.

United Nations (2001). Common Country Assessment for Zanzibar, July, 2001. Available at <http://www.tzonline.org/pdf/thecommoncountryassistancefor zanzibar2001.pdf> (accessed April 10, 2011).

UNESCO [United Nations Educational, Scientific and Cultural Organization] (2008). Report on the Mission to Stone Town of Zanzibar, United Republic of Tanzania, from 5 to 10 May 2008 presented at the 32nd session of World Heritage Committee, Quebec City, Canada, July 2–10. Available at <http://whc.unesco.org/en/documents/100794> (accessed March 12, 2014).

Walls, A. (1995). The Revitalization of Zanzibar Stone Town. In: Sheriff, A. (ed.), *The History and Conservation of Zanzibar Stone Town*. Athens: Ohio University Press, pp. 118–29.

Yahya, S.S. (1995). Zanzibar Stone Town: Fossil or Foetus? In: Sheriff, A. (ed.), *The History and Conservation of Zanzibar Stone Town*. Athens: Ohio University Press, pp. 102–17.

ZATI [Zanzibar Association of Tourism Investors] (2009). Tourism: More Value for Zanzibar, Value Chain Analysis prepared for ZATI, October 22.

ZATI (2008). Zanzibar Tourism Sector: Current Issues and Potential Constraints to Growth, A Study on Tourism Development in Zanzibar for ZATI by Acorn Consulting Partnership Ltd, Zanzibar, May.

Chapter 8

Gender and (World) Heritage:
The Myth of a Gender Neutral Heritage

Sarah Ellen Shortliffe

From the earliest conservation attempts to the modern day heritage movement the scope and understanding of heritage has increased and evolved to include ever more aspects of history and culture. The cultural rights of religious and ethnic minorities and Indigenous peoples all around the globe are beginning to receive due attention as are alternate ways of defining heritage. The creation of the *Burra Charter* (ICOMOS 2007) expanded the Eurocentric and tangible heritage focused concept of "authenticity" to include ideas and issues stemming from Asian perspectives. The Global Strategy launched by the United Nations Educational, Scientific and Cultural Organization (UNESCO) built upon previous definitions of heritage to include a variety of new themes in areas which were not traditionally thought of as heritage, such as industrial sites. Yet despite this trend towards a democratization of heritage, one major factor has been continuously overlooked: gender.

The role of gender in heritage has largely been considered irrelevant, something which the lack of literature concerned with this area, supports. Even a long time professional in the field of heritage, familiar with issues of minority and marginalized heritage, did not see the need for such research, stating: "… perhaps women's issues already get a fair go" (Logan 2007). If a "fair go" means more than mere tokenism then it can be argued that "women's issues" more often than not, do not "get a fair go." Gender plays an important role in different areas related to heritage such as policy development, site selection, interpretation and tourism. In order to make gender visible, so that change can occur, a holistic approach to mainstreaming gender within the heritage field and within the UNESCO World Heritage program is required. From the major heritage documents to scientific research, interpretation and tourism there exists a serious lacuna in terms of understanding the role that gender relations play in the heritage field. Heritage is not gender neutral and therefore gender as an analytical category must be taken seriously and effective gender mainstreaming initiatives must become the norm instead of the exception.[1]

---

1   Throughout this chapter the term "women" is often used instead of the term "gender." This is not because the terms are considered interchangeable but because the negative impacts of gender roles and gender relations are often best illustrated using women as examples, this however, should not be understood to imply that women are the only

Methodologies and Methods

While there are scant resources dealing directly with gender and heritage some efforts have been made to broach the subject, especially in disciplines related to heritage. Cultural, tourism and environmental and development studies have many interesting contributions concerning gender. Much work has also been done within the United Nations Educational, Scientific and Cultural Organisation (UNESCO) and the United Nations (UN) in terms of publications regarding women and gender though tellingly no publications were found discussing gender and heritage, aside from one document dealing with gender and intangible heritage. The research used for this chapter is predominately based on literature from a variety of disciplines and from a variety of print media; journals, books, UN and UNESCO documents. The theoretical backbone of this work is based on feminist epistemologies but does not rely on one specific school of thought as it is informed by post-modern feminist as well as liberal, cultural and radical feminist thought.[2] Analytically, one specific method was not employed but the work was informed by various content analysis frameworks including, but not limited to: critical discourse analysis, gender analysis frameworks as created for the international development field and gender and development theories.

---

gender negatively affected or limited by existing gender roles. The cultural ideals of what it means to "be a man," something often represented in museum and heritage interpretation, can also limit and have a negative impact upon men. The term "women" is also used because women are more often the victims of marginalization and stand to benefit the most from efforts to increase their visibility in the heritage sector.

2   I, like many other feminists do not subscribe to one school of feminist theory but rather am influenced by various aspects of different schools. The second-wave feminist schools such as liberal, cultural and radical feminism are the foundations upon which my understanding and appreciation of third wave feminism, namely postmodern feminism is built. A short description should highlight when which modes of thought from the different schools are employed: *Liberal Feminism* takes its influence from Enlightenment thought and focuses on the use of rational, critical and objective thinking. An important belief is that women deserve equality because they have the same capabilities as men. Oppression is seen to stem from rigid gender roles and the erroneous belief that women are less capable than men. *Cultural Feminism* focuses on the special abilities and qualities of women and aims to reinstate the value of women's nurturing roles and use these roles to solve problems. It challenges the belief that women must think like men in order to succeed and places value on female ways of knowing. *Radical Feminism* emphasizes social transformation (ex. of the heritage field) and aims to transform cultural values. It also underlines the oppression of women as a potent form of oppression and suggests that patriarchy controls women's bodies, which influences all aspects of social interaction. Much attention is also given to the way in which research is affected by this patriarchal rule. *Postmodern Feminism* looks at language as a source of oppression and aims to deconstruct gender and gender relations in order to discover the sources of oppression. It also is somewhat more open to relativism though this is a slippery slope, especially when dealing with culture. For more information regarding feminist schools of thought see Zerbe Enns and Sincore (2001).

UNESCO and Gender

UNESCO's mandate of promoting education, science and culture ensures that there are high expectations for the support and advancement of women's rights. Due to its work in the fields of education, science and culture, UNESCO is seen, by the world and within the UN system, to be in a position to address gender and women's rights in a broad way (UNESCO 2000: 10). In some ways UNESCO does live up to these expectations. There is a clear interest in advocating and affirming women's rights. Various publications exist covering topics such as gender neutral language, gender trainings and a *Passport to Equality* which contains information regarding the *Convention for the Elimination of All Forms of Discrimination against Women* (CEDAW). UNESCO offices also have individuals who are assigned to act as *Gender Focal Points* within their unit. The *Focal Point's* job is to encourage and assist gender awareness, to organize gender trainings and to answer questions related to women and gender in terms of projects and the Organization (Ruprecht 2005: 22). UNESCO also provides access to these and additional materials online.[3] However, despite these commitments to women's rights and advancements in mainstreaming gender there remain areas, most notably in the World Heritage Section, which have not kept up.

Gender and World Heritage

Despite the laudable steps taken by UNESCO to incorporate gender sensitive approaches into its strategies—gender has been selected as one of the global priorities for the Medium-Term Strategy 2008—2013 (UNESCO 2008a: 10)—and the goal to integrate issues of gender equality into the policies and practices related to cultural heritage conservation (UNESCO 2008b: 7) there still remain gender mainstreaming issues within the Organization and with the implementation of these gender streaming tools. The *Gender Mainstreaming Implementation Framework for 2002–2007* (GMIF) makes it clear that "a profound transformation of the structures and systems, which lie at the root of subordination and gender inequality, is required" (Ruprecht 2005: 6). In order to incite change the 'hidden biases' which impede women and men from achieving equality must be uncovered and brought to light (Ruprecht 2005: 6). One of the most important aspects of the GMIF is that one of its guiding principles is Recognition. Before change can occur and gender sensitive approaches and projects can be carried out it must be recognized that "Gender issues permeate all aspects of international co-operation ..." and that "Acknowledging this fact is necessary to tackle the systematic barriers to gender equality" (Ruprecht 2005: 9). The idea that it is essential to recognize that gender plays a role in all areas of UNESCO's competencies is essential.

---

3   www.womenwatch.org and www.unesco.org/women (accessed July 10, 2013).

In a study conducted by Dr. Sophia Labadi which analyzed nomination dossiers submitted for inclusion on the *World Heritage List* it was discovered that women were being marginalized. As Labadi points out, this could suggest that women were not historically important figures in terms of the nominated sites, however, Labadi also revealed that contemporary women were being marginalized as well. In the nomination dossiers included in the study only two female academics were quoted in comparison to 15 male academics. In situations where female researchers or academics were involved with a particular site, contemporary male specialists were still given more credibility (Labadi 2007: 163). Another issue revealed through the study was the fact that the sites being nominated were most often associated with historical men or successful male entrepreneurs, especially in the case of industrial heritage. When women were mentioned, they were solely from privileged economic backgrounds and were "… with few exceptions, described in a neutral way …" while "… famous men tend to be described in a more positive and praiseworthy manner." The way in which men are presented provides a stereotypical definition of masculinity which is marked by power, success and admiration. In addition to this, it is primarily men from the middle and upper economic classes who are included in the nomination dossiers. This version of history, which focuses on "… heroism, power and grandeur … exclude other dimensions and histories" (Labadi 2007: 162). This one-sided presentation of the past is not only harmful to women, who do not see themselves reflected in history, but also to men who are presented with specific ideas of what it means to be a man. The fact that gender is so clearly present in the nomination dossiers, whether it be through the omission of women or women's stories and achievements or through the support and propagation of the myth of the "real male" (Labadi 2007: 162), it becomes difficult to accept that World Heritage is gender-neutral.

In order to lift the veil of gender neutrality, analysis is required in all heritage related areas with the goal of balancing the "voices" of heritage. Language is a key factor in "balancing" these voices. Analysis has shown that gender neutral language has often been used in an attempt to avoid discrimination, unfortunately this can actually conceal the fact that not all members of a group are represented thus privileging the opinions and interests of the dominant group. Gender neutral language can also act as camouflage for gender blindness. In research the use of gender neutral terminology often hides the fact that no analysis of gender and social relations has been undertaken, not only because of scarce resources but also because researchers are often not aware and do not take into consideration that differences in responsibilities, preferences and perceptions exist because of gender. Due to gender blindness within institutions, organizations, communities and among individuals, gender "… is either ignored or overlooked" (Vernooy 2006: 232). This lack of acknowledgement of the role that gender plays in research was noticed early on in the development sector which is far ahead of the heritage sector in terms of gender awareness. Development projects were thought to affect women and men in the same way which often led to negative outcomes for either one or both sexes. It is only within the last decade that more attention has been paid to the role that gender plays in development and which has led to the increased visibility of women within this sector (Wilkinson and Pratiwi 1995: 288). Unfortunately, it seems that the heritage sector has been slow to realize the value and necessity of taking gender into consideration. Labadi's analysis revealed additional values which have suffered marginalization in the nomination documents, among them are the lower-socio economic classes, local populations and women (Labadi 2007: 159–60). This discovery echoes the observation made by Jane Austen that history is "the quarrels of popes and kings ... and [there are] hardly any women at all ..." (Austen 1993: 113).

Gender Analysis and Power

The explicit inclusion of women and the recognition of gender as inseparable from culture would be a major step towards having a truly diverse representation of cultural heritage. Reports and documents such as *Our Cultural Diversity* which do recognize the importance of gender provide hope that changes will occur in terms of World Heritage and in the heritage sector in general. However, gender is an extremely sensitive topic. Documents such as the *Universal Declaration on Cultural Diversity* often mention the rights and value of minority and indigenous cultures yet fail to mention women or gender. Those in favor of gender neutral documents may argue that women are implicitly included. Yet the evidence presented does not support this argument and it leads to the suspicion that gender or women may not be mentioned because of conscious or unconscious resistance to changes in the status quo and for fear that female empowerment threatens male privilege. Bureaucratic resistance to women's programmes or special initiatives to empower women often meet more opposition then new mandates or changes in other areas for just those reasons (Moser 1993: 109–10) and UNESCO is almost certainly no exception. It should be noted that UNESCO as well as its advisory bodies, ICOMOS, IUCN and ICCROM all have their headquarters in Europe: UNESCO and ICOMOS in Paris, IUCN in Gland, Switzerland and ICCROM in Rome. So while they represent international organizations they cannot avoid being influenced by their cultural surroundings. The explicit inclusion of indigenous and minority rights is something which is perhaps more comfortable for these 'European' institutions than gender. A certain distance can be placed between "them" and "us" meaning the minority or indigenous groups and those belonging to the majority. In no way does this suggest that non-Europeans are not involved in the drafting of these documents and in decision-making but it does suggest that despite a variety of influences, being located in Europe and having a history of employing European modes of thinking create a situation which lends itself to Eurocentrism.[4] Any discussion of gender

----

4   The best example of that is the need for the Global Strategy due to the use of criteria which favored the listing of European and Christian sites on the World Heritage List.

and any transformation in this area "… inevitably disrupts the patterns of identity of both genders and touches upon issues of dominance (and hence power)" (Moser 1993: 130). With changes to gender relations and the empowerment of women there can be no distance placed between "them" and "us" because the relationships are symbiotic. There can be no "man" without "woman" and vice versa because the roles and values ascribed to each gender are dependent on those ascribed to the other. It is therefore much easier to discuss minority and indigenous rights because it does not automatically imply change or shifts in power for the dominant group.

Gender Blind Research and Site Interpretation

It is not as easy as only recognizing gender bias and then adding women. The areas in which gender bias is manifested, whether through gender blindness or through blatant discrimination, must first be identified and action must be taken at those levels. Language is one area in which bias is manifested but is not the only one. Scientific research which leads to the identification of new sites and new information is just as interesting and important in terms of gender. Research informs not only which sites are selected and listed but also the information which is presented and then interpreted. So just as gender neutral or gender bias language plays a role in the heritage sector so does gender blind research, especially in the area of interpretation.

Site interpretation is dependent on research to provide the information upon which it is based and bias in this research and in the subsequent interpretation of the research is another factor contributing to the marginalization of women's history. The belief that the use of scientific methods can "… eliminate biases and yield the 'truth' about the past" (Read 1996: 123) is highly questionable as it has been noted by researchers using a gender perspective that traditional approaches are in fact "… not scientifically 'objective'" and that "… they generally ignore women's knowledge by showing bias towards the male perspective" (Beetham and Demetriades 2007: 199). The issue of bias in research has received far more attention in the fields of development and environmental conservation then in heritage because issues of access to information based on gender play a very important role. Male researchers may not have access to women informants because of cultural restrictions or it may be taken for granted that the males represent the family. In addition, women's own lack of experience working with researchers, and/or limited mobility can also lead to biased research results (Howard 2003: 21). While the previous issues relate more generally to field research, historical research provides a plethora of areas in which gender bias can be manifest. History, as written, is rife with gender bias because "… ideas about gender are woven into the very fabric of history, running beyond the mere presence or absence of women" (Read 1996: 122). That is why the accurate interpretation of historical sites is of vital importance in achieving a more balanced and equitable heritage.

The dominant discourse regarding history and heritage plays a key role in terms of research and interpretation. The ideas, beliefs and concepts which come to be taken for granted regarding gender and are accepted as knowledge or fact, necessarily influence all aspects of research and interpretation. Underlying this dominant discourse are issues of power which may inhibit equal participation within the heritage field. Those whose understanding of heritage runs contrary or which deviates from the dominant discourse will be excluded (Waterton, Smith and Campbell 2006: 340). One might consider if this is the case with women's heritage; the dominant discourse provides an understanding of heritage which is predominantly male and which relies on the creation of history through great feats and which marginalizes the more intangible aspects of heritage and the more everyday acts of living. It is this discourse which then acts as a normative force granting authority to certain voices and to certain "truths." Discourse, of course, is not something static and it does not only sustain and legitimize the status quo but it can also change it (Read 1996: 343). The introduction of women's studies and gender studies have worked to change the status quo, if only ever so slightly, creating the possibility for women's history to emerge from the sidelines through the development and acceptance of a more gender sensitive heritage discourse. These changes to the dominant discourse have also allowed for changes in research practices, with a move away from the assumption that "traditional" research methods "… are essentially benign and gender neutral" (Beetham and Demetriades 2007: 200).

Changes to traditional research methods would provide more opportunity for women's histories to be discovered and their voices to be heard. There must be a move away from accepting research as something which is apolitical and gender neutral. Every decision that the researcher makes informs the version of facts and the stories which will be presented and told (Beetham and Demetirades 2007: 206). New research methods can provide new insight into histories in which women were absent or misrepresented. In Australia new research has revealed that Aboriginal women play major roles in spiritual life both in ceremonial functions and in land management. This revelation is contrary to previous research during which only Aboriginal men were interviewed creating the assumption that women did not play an active part in these areas. In another example, it was discovered that female convicts shipped to Australia made vital contributions to the work force and were also independent and active in the areas of farming, industry and within their communities. This presents a very different picture of female convicts who were all previously assumed to be sex workers (Cowley 2001: 57). Gender is not only important for the way in which research is carried out and interpreted but also for the way in which women and men are represented within heritage sites. This is an issue which gains additional importance when tourism to is taken into consideration.

Tourism, Representation and Heritage

Increasing tourism is not a goal set out by the World Heritage Convention yet it is something which may accompany the listing of a site and therefore the changes it can bring merit consideration in terms of gender issues. Tourism is based on social relations and complex interactions informed by different realities and experiences and gender is one aspect of these social relations and interactions which are "… are often hierarchical and unequal." Because they are hierarchical and unequal women and men "… are involved differently in the construction and consumption of tourism." The same can be said of the different roles which the visitor plays in comparison to that of the host. The dominant gender discourse informs the way tourism is marketed, the motivations that visitors bring with them, and the behavior of the hosts (Swain 1995: 249).

The way in which tourism is marketed and presented to tourists is very much related to the way sites are selected, the way they are interpreted and the representations which are provided. Despite these connections, the role of gender in "… both the representation and consumption of heritage places and products has not been widely acknowledged" (Aitchison 2001: 59). Gender is manifested in several important areas of tourism: in employment and in the marketing of sites to visitors as well in issues of preservation of cultural practices. In terms of tourism employment, gender plays a very important role. Cara Aitchison categorizes tourism as the "… most sex-segregated industry or the world's most sex role stereotyped industry" (Aitchison 2001: 61). Within the tourism industry often the only jobs available to women are those which do not challenge the roles considered appropriate for women, such as housekeeping, food and sexual services, something Maria Mies has termed the "housewifization of labor" (McKenzie Gentry 2007: 478). Tourism has been associated with globalization and the homogenization of culture. This could have created space for a break down and challenging of traditional gender roles and constraints but instead, contemporary tourism development has "… served to strengthen, rather than destabilize, gendered representations of space and place alongside notions of nationalism and bounded cultural identity" (Aitchison 2001: 61). This gendered employment is significant in terms of heritage in that it necessarily affects the way in which a heritage site is experienced and consumed by visitors as well as reinforcing the local and international notions of gender appropriate work and the intensification or re-creation of cultural identities. Aitchison stresses that "… tourism needs to be considered … as a powerful cultural form and process which both shapes and is shaped by gendered constructions of space, place, nation and culture" (Aitchison 2001: 61).

These gendered constructions inform the way in which sites are marketed and the way in which the culture is represented. Tourism Studies has raised the issue of the "… masculinity of the abstract 'tourist' subject" (Swain 1995: 252). In the same way that women are the "… unintended *readers* of history …" they are also the unintended tourists. Men are assumed to be both the "… 'readers' as well as the 'actors' of history ..." (Read 1996: 118) in the same way that the tourist subject is assumed to be male. The masculinity of the abstract tourist becomes visible through the analysis of the way in which heritage sites are marketed. Sites, especially natural sites, are marketed as "feminine"; something wild to be conquered. This is also true for sites in host societies which differ from the visitors in terms of colonial history, race/ethnicity or economic and social status (Read 1996: 249). In the same way that representations of women and men in museum exhibits or at heritage sites uphold and reinforce dominant historical and contemporary views of gender roles, marketing and tourist information brochures are often full of very gendered representations. The "... representations of men [are often] associated with action, power and ownership, while women are associated with passivity, availability and being owned." Women also represent the exotic "Other" and in this way the tourism industry reinforces gender stereotypes (Read 1996: 249). Tourism not only reinforces gender stereotypes, but also the dominant history discourse that men are the "actors" of history while women are either ignored or are presented as objects whose bodies and images serve as representations of male ideals. According to Linda K. Richter "... the impact of tourism continues to socialize generations to the importance of what men have done while women are ignored or immortalized on postcards, nutcrackers and T-shirts" (Richter 1998: 400).

It is this *impact* which must be taken into consideration in the heritage field. Tourists come to expect certain behaviors from the host community based on various factors; cultural stereotypes, the historical relationship of the guest's nation/ethnicity with the host community, economic status and the marketing of the site and space. Many of these expectations are based on hierarchical and gendered notions of the "Other." This search for the "Other" is often a major motivating factor for travel (Aitchison 2001: 64). Women, who are often seen as the "bearers of culture," frequently become "... caught in the paradox of authenticity ..." that results from heritage and cultural tourism. They are expected to maintain tradition without modification and yet are also supposed to be attractive to tourists (Abbott Cone 1995: 322). Individuals who choose to challenge these stereotypes are often met with strong resistance, with arguments based on appropriate gender behavior or the sanctity of culture. An example of this can be found in the heart of the World Heritage city Venice in Italy. In 2007, despite having not passed the exam, a woman of German and Algerian decent won limited rights in court to steer a gondola in the canals of Venice, a position which had been exclusively male since its inception, in fact fathers often pass the trade down to their sons. While many applauded the move, the other gondolier operators were opposed to opening the trade to women because they fear it will destroy their cultural tradition. One gondolier was quoted as stating that "... it is a question of skill and not gender" and he also states that "Being a gondolier is a tradition and it is very difficult work." The assumption that women are not fit for such "difficult work" is as clear as the fact that gender does in fact matter to the gondoliers because allowing a female gondolier flies in the face of tradition. Though there is room for hope. In 2010, a Venetian woman, whose father broke with tradition and passed the trade down to her, became the first woman to pass the exams and receive a gondolier license. The Mayor of Venice is quoted as saying that this "… is another step towards parity between sexes and I'm sure her male colleagues will share her delight. In the past there has been a tendency of excessive machismo" (Pisa 2010). Whether the new *gondoliera* will be accepted by her peers is still unknown as even her father who passed the tradition down to her is quoted as saying that he still thinks "… being a gondolier is a man's job …" (Kington 2009). There are many arguments against women breaking into "men's jobs"; that they lack the strength or skill, that it is a question of aesthetics or tradition. Though when one considers the real issue at stake, it becomes clear that it is not whether a woman has the strength or the skill, for surely there are women who do, or that it has to do with aesthetics, for women are often employed *for* aesthetic reasons, but rather that it has to with what may be perceived as an attack on appropriate gender roles as well as an attack on tradition, a tradition which is very important for the "authenticity" of culture for tourists. Tourists have expectations conditioned by marketing campaigns which often do not present the culture "authentically" and local peoples' behavior becomes conditioned by the expectations of the tourists (Alsayyad 2001: 4, 17) often leading to the "carnivalization" of their culture.

Final Analysis

World Heritage represents the legacy of humanity's and natures greatest achievements. It is presented as an exclusive club on the one hand but it is also presented as something inclusive, something which breaks down boundaries; regional, national and even religious, on the other. World Heritage is the inheritance of all humanity but "if we entertain the ideas of heritage and inheritance then we must also acknowledge the possibility of disinheritance …" (Saltmarsh 2006: 537). Disinheritance occurs when members of society are marginalized and their contributions to history ignored. Women should not be disinherited of their heritage. In light of the burgeoning awareness of the importance of indigenous and minority heritage the dominant heritage discourse may have expanded the definition of "history makers" from "white male" to "male," but the "other" sex still finds no space within this definition. It has been written in reference to culture that "culture has terrific power. We stand in awe of what our fellow men have done and can do" (Boniface 1995: 5). This statement could not be more true; at heritage sites around the world tourists and locals alike, stand in awe of what *men* have done and yet as has been pointed out, women have always been at least half of history, so why does the opportunity to stand in awe of what they have done rarely exist?

The answer to this question should at this point be clear. The effects of gender blindness are far reaching, not only for women but also for men. This is not a problem which only affects the heritage sector. The lack of gender awareness in heritage, and more specifically World Heritage, is merely a product of the society in which it was produced. The dominant discourse which posits man as the neutral subject rejects the possibility that women be included, *unless* specific steps are taken, for neutrality in language and actions often hide a male perspective. The blinders must be removed and gender acknowledged in the field of heritage. It has been shown that "neutral" is not really neutral and that gender relations are the foundations upon which all other relations are built. The consequences of this are that history and heritage are products of these gender relations and are products of the dominant discourses of their time. Gender blindness and male bias permeate all aspects of (world) heritage from the selection of sites to the language and the images presented in the interpretation and representations of the site and in tourism.

While the situation may seem bleak, positive steps have already been taken. The mainstreaming of gender within organizations is a small but powerful step in this direction, the fact that gender has been a topic in the fields of education, development and environment for decades suggest that the heritage field may also open to change. In fact the first signs of change can be observed at the local level. In Australia, Canada[5] and the United States (Cowley 2001: 37) women's heritage is beginning to be included on traditional heritage lists and new research by women's history academics is beginning to correct the under-representation and misrepresentation of women in history (Cowley 2001: 57). In terms of World Heritage, some steps have also been taken to address gender and women at sites around the world.[6] A diverse and equitable heritage can only be achieved by expanding the definition and understanding of heritage to include this wide array of realities and experiences. The "historical truth" must be replaced by "historical truths."

The need for change within the World Heritage system is clear. As a leader in heritage issues change within its operations may act as a catalyst for change within the entire heritage field. The inclusion of women's experiences, stories and contributions to the importance of a site should be valued and explicitly encouraged in the nomination dossiers. In addition, the use of gender neutral language in partnership with gender disaggregated statistics and gender specific language, when appropriate, should be encouraged. Further research might also reveal ways in which to construct a type of gender analysis framework suitable for heritage sites which would ease the mainstreaming of gender into heritage and tourism management, and the interpretation and representation of sites, for heritage professionals and site managers. It would also provide a tool to better understand the site specific effects of gender and gender relations and therefore

---

5   Parks Canada has a section of their internet site devoted to women's history for more information see: www.pc.gc.ca/progs/lhn-nhs/femmes-women/index_E.asp (accessed June 9, 2012).

6   One example is from the Genderinstitut Gotland in Sweden which undertook a twinning partnership with the World Heritage Site, Old Stone Town in Zanzibar, Tanzania and Visby, Sweden. The project entitled "(Re)claim women's space in World Heritage" was financed by the Swedish International Development Agency (SIDA) for a three-year period from 2004–2007.

allow for more appropriate decision making, especially in dealing with living heritage sites. It is important to note however, that it is not just about simply *adding* women to an existing framework, but about changing the framework to recognize that the heritage of humanity must represent both men and women. It is about writing women back into history as opposed to merely adding them on as a footnote. The analysis and suggestions which have been discussed and presented aim not to position men against women, but rather aim to look at the way in which gender and the dominant gender discourse inform the field of heritage. Looking at heritage through a "gender" lens is not about asking different questions, but about asking the same questions differently (Kabeer 1999: 4).

References

Abbott Cone, C. (1995). Crafting Selves: The Lives of Two Mayan Women. *Annals of Tourism Research*, 2(22): 314–27.

Aitchison, C. (2001). Heritage and Nationalism: Gender and the Performance of Power. In: Crouch, D. (ed.), *Leisure/Tourism Geographies: Practices and Geographical Knowledge*. London: Routledge, pp. 59–73.

Alsayyad, N. (ed.) (2001). *Consuming Tradition, Manufacturing Heritage: Global Norms and Urban Forms in the Age of Tourism*. London: Routledge.

Austen, J. (1993). *Northanger Abbey*. Ware, England: Wordsworth Editions.

Beetham, G. and Demetriades, J. (2007). Feminist Research Methodologies and Development: Overview and Practical Application. *Gender and Development*, 2(15): 99–216.

Boniface, P. (1995). *Managing Quality Cultural Tourism*. London: Routledge.

Crouch, D. (2001). *Leisure/Tourism Geographies: Practices and Geographical Knowledge*. London: Routledge.

Cowley, J. (2001). Place and Gender: Applying Gender Theory to the Documentation and Management of Cultural Landscapes. *CRM Cultural Resources*, 7: 37–40.

Howard, P.L. (ed.) (2003). *Women and Plants: Gender Relations in Biodiversity Management and Conservation*. New York: Zed Books.

ICOMOS Australia. (1999). *Burra Charter*. Available at <http://australia.icomos.org/wp-content/uploads/BURRA_CHARTER.pdf.> (accessed November 4, 2011).

Kabeer, N. and Ramya, S. (eds) (1999). *Institutions, Relations and Outcomes: A Framework and Case Studies for Gender-Aware Planning*. London: Zed Books.

Kabeer, N. (1999). Introduction. From Feminist Insights to an Analytical Framework: An Institutional Perspective. In: Kabeer, K. and Subrahmanian, R. (eds), *Institutions, Relations and Outcomes: A Framework and Case Studies for Gender-Aware Planning*. London: Zed Books.

Kiefer, P. (2007). Woman Defies Venetian Tradition in Struggle to Pilot a Gondola. *International Herald Tribune*. Available at http://www.iht.com/articles/2007/05/10/news/journal.php (accessed June 8, 2012).

Kington, T. (2009). Female Gondolier Ends 900 Years of Venetian Discrimination. *The Guardian*, 26 June 2009. Available at <http://www.guardian.co.uk/world/2009/jun/26/venice-female-gondoliers.> (accessed June 26, 2011).

Labadi, S. (2007). Representations of the Nation and Cultural Diversity in Discourses on World Heritage. *Journal of Social Archaeology*, 4(7): 147–70.

Logan, W. (2007). Advice. E-mail (April 4, 2010).

McKenzie Gentry, K. (2007). Belizean Women and Tourism Work: Opportunity or Impediment? *Annals of Tourism Research*, 3(34): 477–96.

Moser, C.O.N. (1993). *Gender Planning and Development: Theory, Practice and Training.* New York: Routledge.

Pisa, N. (2010). Just One Trained Woman: Venice Finally Gets its First Female Gondolier. *The Telegraph*, 14 August 2010. Available at <http://www.telegraph.co.uk/travel/travelnews/7945750/Just-one-trained-woman-Venice-finally-gets-its-first-female-gondolier.html.> (accessed June 26, 2011).

Read, B. (1996). Historical Representations and the Gendered Battleground of the 'Past': A Study of the Canterbury Heritage Museum. *European Journal of Women's Studies*, 3(2): 115–30.

Richter, L.K. (1998). Exploring the Political Role of Gender in Tourism Research. In: Theobald, W.F. (ed.), *Global Tourism*, 2nd edn. Oxford: Butterworth-Heinemann, pp. 391–404.

Ruprecht, L. (2005). *Handbook for Gender Focal Points in UNESCO National Commissions*. Paris: UNESCO-BSP.

Saltmarsh, D. (2006). Celebrating Heritage and the Female Orphan School. *International Journal of Heritage Studies*, 6(12): 536–50.

Swain, M.B. (1995). Gender in Tourism. *Annals of Tourism Research*, 2(22): 247–66.

Theobald, W.F. (ed.) (1998). *Global Tourism*, 2nd edn. Oxford: Butterworth-Heinemann.

UNESCO (2000). *Gender Equality and Equity: A Summary Review of UNESCO's Accomplishments since the Fourth World Conference on Women.* Beijing: Unit for the Promotion of the Statutes of Women and Gender Equality.

UNESCO (2008a). *34 C/4 Medium Term Strategy 2008—2013.* Paris: UNESCO. Available at http://unesdoc.unesco.org/images/0014/001499/149999e.pdf (accessed June 20, 2011).

UNESCO (2008b). *Priority Gender Equality Action Plan 2008–2013.* Paris: UNESCO Division for Gender Equality. Available at http://unesdoc.unesco.org/images/0018/001858/185856m.pdf (accessed May 17, 2011).

Vernooy, R. (ed.) (2006). *Social and Gender Analysis in Natural Resource Management: Learning Studies and Lessons from Asia.* Canada: International Development Research Centre.

Waterton, E., Laurajane, S. and Campbell, G. (2006). The Utility of Discourse Analysis to Heritage Studies: The Burra Charter and Social Inclusion. *International Journal of Heritage Studies*, 4(12): 339–55.

Wilkinson, P.F. and Wiwik, P. (1995). Gender and Tourism in an Indonesian Village. *Annals of Tourism Research*, 2(22): 283–99.

Zerbe Enns, C. and Sincore, A. (2001). Feminist Theories. In: Worell, J. (ed.), *Encyclopedia of Women and Gender: Sex Similarities and Differences and the Impact of Society on Gender*, vol. 1. San Diego: Academic Press, pp. 469–80.

Chapter 9

The Local-to-Global Dynamics of World Heritage Interpretation

Noel B. Salazar

Introduction

Given the pervasiveness and local particularity of heritage, it is not surprising that heritage tourism is among those tourism niches growing most rapidly (Timothy and Boyd 2006). The money visitors spend on admission fees, souvenirs, transport, food and accommodation contributes billions every year to the global economy and employs millions of people directly and indirectly (Timothy and Boyd 2003). Apart from economic incentives, heritage tourism serves important political purposes. On the domestic level, cultural heritage is commonly used to stimulate pride in the (imagined) national history or to highlight the virtues of particular ideologies. In the supranational sphere, heritage sites are marketed and sold as iconic markers of a local area, country, region or even continent, and the journey abroad as an opportunity to learn about the "Other"—some go as far as promising a contribution to worldwide peace and understanding. At the same time, tourism is increasingly recognized and used as an agent of socio-cultural change. Cultural heritage tourism in particular has been advocated as an attractive alternative to mass tourism, providing sustainable livelihoods to small local operators, protecting and sustaining the cultural resources, and educating tourists and locals alike (NWHO 1999). Cultural heritage management is now commonly seen as a strategic tool to maximize the use of heritage within the global tourism market (Nuryanti 1997). However, the transformation of sites into destinations and cultural expressions into performances is seldom straightforward.

The mounting struggles over who controls heritage tourism reflect its growth and success (Porter and Salazar 2005; Salazar and Porter 2004). The process of "tourismification" of heritage confronts those stakeholders involved and communities affected with a whole set of complex issues, including authenticity, interpretation, heritage contestation, social exclusion, contested space, personal heritage, control and preservation (McKercher and Du Cros 2002; Timothy and Prideaux 2004). Conservation and safeguarding along with developing and managing visitation are major issues facing the cultural heritage tourism sector. In a tourism setting, heritage can be (mis)used in a variety of ways for a variety of purposes by a variety of stakeholders. Especially poor countries have a hard time achieving the international standards set by the tourism sector (Salazar 2010).

There are many issues in the less-developed world that create everyday obstacles to the sustainable development and management of heritage, including the role of local communities in decision making, sharing in the benefits of tourism development, empowerment and power, ownership of historic places and artefacts, lack of funding and skills and forced displacement to accommodate tourism growth (Hampton 2005). This chapter discusses some of the most pressing challenges that lie ahead in cultural heritage tourism and stresses the importance of heritage interpretation for its sustainable development. The case study of central Java, Indonesia, illustrates the general trends and shows the urgent need for more dialogue and collaboration between the fields of heritage management and tourism.

Interpreting Heritage for Local-to-Global Audiences

Although seldom acknowledged, the globalization of heritage through tourism can seriously influence its interpretation, both for locals and tourists. We should not forget that cultural heritage mainly has value because of the selective meaning that people ascribe to it, often through personal identification and attachment. The way people relate to a place is not so much caused by the specific site attributes but by the visitor's personal motivations and perceptions (Poria et al. 2003). Those who view a site as bound-up with their own heritage are likely to behave significantly differently from others. A single heritage site can provoke varied degrees of understanding—be it on a local, national, regional or even global scale. In fact, there is no heritage without interpretation, and the attached subjective meaning is always culturally (re)constructed and often contested, because "society filters heritage through a value system that undoubtedly changes over time and space, and across society" (Timothy and Boyd 2003: 2). As Adams writes:

> In today's context of international tourism, "heritage" and "tradition" become all the more intensely rethought, rearticulated, and recreated and contested, both by insiders and outsider packagers, politicians, and visitors. Tourism does not simply impose disjunctures between the "authentic past" and the "invented past," as earlier researchers suggested, but rather blurs these artificial lines, creating new politically charged arenas in which competing ideas about heritage, ritual, and tradition are symbolically enacted. (Adams 2003: 93)

As tourism construct, a wide variety of individuals and institutions attribute meaning and authenticity to heritage (Peleggi 1996).

The interpretation of heritage is important to defining, evoking and enhancing its meaning (Uzzell 1989). Making the different layers of multiple and shifting meanings and their dissonances accessible and understandable, for both local residents and tourists from varied backgrounds, requires carefully designed strategies of representation. Interpretative services are not a special favor to visitors; they are an essential part of the work of heritage management. As Moscardo argues, "successful interpretation is critical both for the effective management and conservation of built heritage sites and for sustainable tourism" (1996: 376). This is an extremely challenging task, because the desire to (re)present heritage for both domestic and international audiences often creates a tension around the selection of stories to be told and what is to be left untold (Salazar 2010). Moreover, "although the global heritage dialogue tends to present the built environment as an empty container, places of heritage remain places where real people live and where real conflicts may arise" (Al Sayyad 2001: 22).

What does the globalization of heritage do to its interpretation? Alternative readings of heritage as imbued with local values and meanings risk being subsumed, and thus erased, by the universalist assertions of global heritage tourism. When the interpretation of heritage crosses boundaries and becomes entangled in the complex web of global tourism, it can have the effect of disembedding local (or nationally) produced senses of identity. Local tour guides, therefore, play an instrumental role in mediating the tension between ongoing processes of global standardization and local differentiation. Paradoxically, they often seem to rely on fashionable global tourism tales to interpret and sell their cultural heritage as authentically "local" (Salazar 2007). This is partly because tourists appear to appreciate interpretations that combine narratives about the particularities of a destination with well-known tourism imaginaries that are circulating globally. In tourism to developing countries, for example, marketing has long capitalized on cultural economies of the exotic and the primitive, each of which are to be discovered in the pre-modern, traditional. However, this does not mean that local guides merely reproduce normative global templates. Guiding is always to some extent improvised, creative and spontaneous, in this way defying complete standardization. In the interaction with tourists, local guides become themselves creative producers of tourism rhetoric (Salazar 2010).

Highly trained heritage guides not only benefit tourists but also the local community, by preparing and instructing visitors to be more culturally sensitive and ethical, follow minimal impact or responsible behavior and encourage respect and proper consideration for local traditions and customs. As of lately, also the United Nations Educational, Scientific and Cultural Organisation (UNESCO) has become aware of the importance of professional tour guiding and the organization has taken a proactive role in benchmarking heritage interpretation, especially in Asia. Increased tourism activities at heritage sites tend to overlook the importance of transmitting knowledge about and learning the significance as well as the cultural value of such sites (Dioko and Unakul 2005). The UNESCO Asia and Pacific region office in Bangkok, Thailand, was among the first to acknowledge this. In 2005, it proposed, together with the Asian Academy of Heritage Management network, a regional-based program for heritage tour guide training (UNESCO 2005). The Macao Institute for Tourism Studies is the first institution to offer a "Cultural Heritage Specialist Guide Training and Certification Programme for UNESCO World Heritage Sites." The program aims to address several important challenges arising from the greater and more frequent interface between heritage and global tourism and how on-site tour guides specially trained in heritage guiding can play a central role in meeting these challenges. It is noteworthy that this is an example of a "regional standards of excellence" practice, rather than an attempt to create a global benchmark.

The Case of Central Java, Indonesia

Java is the fifth largest and most populated island of the Indonesian archipelago. The central region of Java comprises of two provinces: Central Java and the much smaller Yogyakarta Special Province. The earliest signs of habitation in this fertile volcanic area are prehistoric. From the seventh century, the region was dominated by Hindu and Buddhist kingdoms, giving rise to the eighth-century Buddhist shrine of Borobudur, the ninth-century Hindu temple complex of Prambanan, and many other temples. Islam, coming mainly via India, gained ground in the inner areas of the island during the sixteenth century. The Dutch began to colonize the archipelago in the early seventeenth century. The British established a brief presence on Java under Sir Thomas Stamford Raffles (1811–16), but the Dutch retained control until Indonesia's independence 130 years later. When the Dutch reoccupied Jakarta after the Japanese occupation of Java during World War Two (1946–49), Yogyakarta functioned as the stronghold of the independence movement by becoming the provisional capital of the newly declared Republic of Indonesia. In return for this unfailing support, the first Indonesian central government passed a law in 1950 granting Yogyakarta the status of Special Province and making its Sultan Governor for life.

Organized tourism to the center of Java first developed under Dutch colonial rule, mainly through the *Vereeniging Toeristenverkeer* (Association of Tourist Traffic of the Dutch East Indies), which opened an Official Tourist Bureau in Weltevreden (now Jakarta) in 1908. After independence, the new Indonesian government continued to promote international tourism, although President Sukarno's political rhetoric was markedly anti-Western. Under Major General Suharto's New Order government (1966–98), long-term planning and a relatively stable environment for business transformed the country's tourism, and Yogyakarta became a major gateway to central and east Java, both for international and domestic visitors. By the mid 1990s, tourism had become Indonesia's third most important source of foreign revenue and Yogyakarta the second most visited destination after Bali.

While central Java offers a whole range of touristic activities, the main product is cultural heritage. The three Indonesian cultural sites on UNESCO's WHS List—the Prambanan Temple Compounds (1991), the Borobudur Temple Compounds (1991) and Sangiran Early Man Site (1996)—are all located in central Java. Four others—the Yogyakarta Palace Complex, the Ratu Boko Temple Complex, the Sukuh Hindu Temple and the Great Mosque of Demak—are since 1995 on UNESCO's tentative list. The most common tour package includes visits to Borobudur, the Yogyakarta Palace and Prambanan. When time permits, tourists also have a chance to experience central Java's rich intangible cultural heritage, including performing arts (traditional court dances, Ramayana Ballet, shadow puppet plays and gamelan orchestra performances), traditional craftsmanship (woodcarving, batik design, the silverware from Kotagede and the pottery from Kasongan) and the occasional ritual or festive events (such as the annual Sekaten and Labuhan festivals).

As Dahles points out in her study on the politics of cultural tourism in Indonesia, "[T]he cultural heritage of the Yogyakarta area has shaped the (international) images of Indonesia, as government propaganda has used architectural structures like the temples and the sultan's palace and expressions of art like the Ramayana dance to promote Indonesian tourism world-wide" (Dahles 2001: 20). This kind of image building particularly happened during the New Order era, when the central government (led by Javanese) strongly favored central Java in their (re)invention of Indonesia, promoting it as the cultural heart of the nation. The current planning and development of heritage tourism in the area is in the hands of many authorities at various levels: city (Yogyakarta City Department of Tourism, Arts and Culture) and regency (Magelang, Sleman and Klaten Tourism Offices), provincial (Central Java and Yogyakarta Provincial Tourism Offices), Java (Jawa Promo), national (Ministry of Culture and Tourism), regional (ASEAN Committee on Trade and Tourism and APEC Tourism Working Group), and global (UNWTO and UNESCO) levels. Because policy makers at these different echelons have widely diverging interests, decisions taken at one level are often contested at another.

UNESCO has a long-standing history of involvement in central Java's heritage. In 1972, it launched a US$25 million safeguarding campaign to restore Borobudur, often listed as one of the seven forgotten wonders of the world. Concurrent with the elevation of Borobudur and Prambanan to WHS in 1991, UNESCO collaborated with UNDP and the former Indonesian Directorate General of Tourism in the ambitious 1991–94 "Cultural Tourism Development Central Java-Yogyakarta" project (UNESCO 1992). Since the May 2006 earthquake, UNESCO has been actively involved in the rehabilitation of the damaged Prambanan temple complex. Another influential global player in the area's heritage management is the non-profit World Monuments Fund, which listed Kotagede Heritage District in Yogyakarta on its 2008 World Monuments Watch list of 100 most endangered sites. Kotagede, which suffered severe damage after the 2006 earthquake, is also the current focus of the local Jogja Heritage Society.

It is no coincidence that sites such as Sangiran (prehistoric), Prambanan (Hindu) and Borobudur (Buddhist) appear on UNESCO's list of World Heritage, whereas Sukuh temple or the Sultan's palace are not (yet) included. After all, the central government in Jakarta proposes sites to UNESCO and it is in their strategic interest to nominate politically "safe" monuments. Sukuh temple, for instance is a beautiful Hindu temple tucked away in the highlands of Central Java. It is unique, not only in overall design, but also in decoration: it is the only known erotic temple on Java. Around the temple, statues and reliefs of erected male members abound. Given the moral sensibilities of the majority Muslim population (and the increasing power of fundamentalists), Sukuh is not a site the Indonesian government would want to promote. The Sultan's Palace, on the other hand, is Muslim (or, at least, partly) but a place where current politics are being played out instead of a "dead" heritage site, such as the Ratu Boko Hindu-Buddhist complex. The internationally little-known Mosque of Demak, the historical place from where Islam spread around Java, probably has more chance of being reclassified as world heritage than the Sultan's Palace. Such politics of heritage serve as a reminder that, ultimately, a WHS is the product of agency on the national level. Besides, the Indonesian government has its own national list of *cagar budaya* (heritage conservation).

Central Java is not only passively undergoing outside influences in its heritage management, but also acting as a symbolic location where broader heritage tourism agendas are being set. As a fashionable venue for conventions, Yogyakarta has had its share of key conferences in this domain. In 1992, for instance, the International Conference on Cultural Tourism led to the Yogyakarta Declaration on National Cultures and Universal Tourism. This was followed up in 1995 by an Indonesian-Swiss Forum on Cultural and International Tourism and in 2006 by an UNWTO-sponsored International Conference on Cultural Tourism and Local Communities, leading to the Yogyakarta Declaration on Cultural Tourism, Local Communities and Poverty Alleviation. In 1994, the city hosted the APEC Tourism Working Group meeting and, in 2001, it welcomed the East Asia Inter-Regional Tourism Forum. In 2002, Yogyakarta housed the ASEAN Tourism Forum.

During the last decade, central Java's tourism has suffered from a whole series of unfortunate events in Indonesia and the wider region (Salazar 2010). However, 2006 dealt a fatal blow to the already ailing industry. Between May and July of that year, the area had to endure numerous natural disasters, including multiple eruptions of Mt. Merapi (one of the most active volcanoes in the world), a minor tsunami (reminding Indonesians of the tragic 2004 tsunami in Aceh) and a major earthquake of 5.9 on the scale of Richter, killing around 6,000 people and leaving an estimated 1.5 million Javanese homeless. Tourists massively cancelled their trips to Java, exposing the fragility of the local tourism sector but also bringing to light the resilience of its workers. Prambanan was among those sites hit by the quake, along with parts of the Sultan's Palace. Borobudur did not suffer from the earthquake but had to be cleaned because the monument was covered under dark grey ashes from Mt. Merapi's eruptions.

The disasters disclosed some of the local-to-global politics driving heritage tourism. Although UNESCO rapidly sent experts to assess the damage, it took a long time before the people working at the site were informed about the recovery plans. After the assessment, a newly built viewing platform (very similar to the ones erected after September 11, 2001 around Ground Zero in New York) allowed tourists to see the main temple complex from a safe distance, without being allowed to enter them. PT Taman Wisata, the state-owned enterprise managing the park, decided not to lower the entrance fees (US$10 for foreigners). Anticipating tourist complaints, many local tour operators decided to suspend trips to Prambanan. The few tourists who still came to visit did not want the service of a local guide (approximately US$5 extra) because they knew that they could not get near the main temples anyway. This left the local guides in a very precarious situation. Some of the security guards in charge of protecting the site offered foreign tourists to enter the damaged main complex anyway, in exchange for sizeable amounts of cash. The on-site guides knew about these practices but preferred to keep quiet.

Interestingly, at a time when the economic value of Prambanan was dramatically affected, local tour guides felt the strong emotional need to change their usual interpretative narratives, hereby revealing the importance of some deeper cultural meanings attached to the site instead of merely recounting the facts and figures that they had learned through intense study when they were studying to become a professional guide. The calamities became the feeding ground for new interpretative narratives and imaginaries. The adversity precipitated a spontaneous revitalization of old Javanese myths and mystical beliefs, including the legend of Loro Jonggrang. According to local beliefs, the statue in the north chamber of the central Shiva shrine does not represent the Hindu goddess Durga but Loro Jonggrang (Javanese for slender virgin). Legend has it that she was a Javanese princess who agreed to marry a man she did not love if he could build her a temple ornamented with 1,000 statues, between the setting and rising of the sun. When the man was about to fulfil her demand, she tried to trick him. He was so furious that he petrified her and she became the last (and most beautiful) of the thousand statues. In the weeks following the earthquake, the Prambanan guides blamed UNESCO for keeping the main temples closed to the public (preventing them from earning their living). This translated in their narratives containing much fewer references to the organization or to the officially sanctioned interpretations of the WHS.

This tension also played out in the signage in front of the main temple complex. At the time of the earthquake, there were two signboards: an older "Candi Prambanan, World Heritage List number 642" and a newer "Candi Rara Jonggrang." This is a clear visual marker of conflicting meanings of the site. The placing of such signs is actually part of UNESCO's Operational Guidelines for the Implementation of the World Heritage Convention. Article 268 of that policy document states: "Properties inscribed on the World Heritage List should be marked with the emblem jointly with the UNESCO logo, which should, however, be placed in such a way that they do not visually impair the property in question" (UNESCO 2008: 69). With international tourists, guides will often stop at the sign for a photo opportunity, while using the information on the sign to reinforce their own tales. Bruner calls this strategy "dialogic narration" (2005: 169–88) because the guide's narrative is not just indexically referencing what is actually written—for instance that the Prambanan Temple Complex is a UNESCO World Heritage site—but takes account of all the stories tourists have heard, read or seen about other world heritage sites as well. Explicit comparisons with those other monuments are used to put the local site on an equal level of global value. By the time the restoration was over and the complex was opened again to the public, the letters on the "Candi Rara Jonggrang" signboard had been replaced with "Candi Prambanan."

Through initiatives such as the 2008 Prambanan Camp for World Heritage Volunteers, the negative perception of UNESCO in Prambanan was somewhat adjusted. This project, in collaboration with the Archaeology Department and Provincial Tourism Office of Central Java, enabled international volunteers to assist the experts with the restoration of the temple and to increase the heritage awareness of local youth. The example of Prambanan illustrates how, in times of change, the local meaning and function of heritage can change too. The growing supra-local interdependence of heritage tourism is irreversible but variously received (Salazar 2010). The global recognition by UNESCO, for instance, is used strategically when guiding for foreign tourists, but local guides clearly sensed and criticized the organization's "distance" in the period after the earthquake—not recognizing that, often, national instances were to blame rather than international ones.

Conclusion

As this chapter has illustrated, cultural heritage tourism is a double-edged sword. On the one hand, it can be a positive force to retain cultural values and to help mitigate threats. On the other hand, global tourism can become itself a menace to the sustainable management of heritage. Therefore, a good understanding of the tourism sector, its markets and trends is instrumental to sustainable heritage management. Those in charge of heritage sites clearly need to pay closer attention to reconciling the needs of the various parties involved, each with their own interests. Instead of one universally accepted meaning, the significance of heritage—be it natural or cultural, tangible or intangible—is characterized by pluriversality. Heritage interpretation is always enmeshed in complex webs of meaning, variously cherished and expressed by shareholders at different levels. Cultural heritage is, by nature, a unique and fragile resource. Although often heralded as a likely solution to conservation and community development challenges, local staff and communities in poor countries do not always have the resources, experience or training they need in order to use tourism as an effective instrument for protecting it. The tools to provide coherent and sustainable heritage management are yet to be fully developed or effectively applied. As I have argued, heritage interpretation and (re)presentation by local tour guides play a key role in this.

To make local heritage workers more competitive in the current landscape of international labor circulation, standardization seems to be the way to go. By studying the daily practices of local guides and the way they (re)present and actively (re)construct local culture for a diversified audience of global tourists, we can learn a lot about how processes of globalization and localization are intimately intertwined and how this glocalization is transforming culture—through tourism and other channels. Such studies bring to light that the processes of negotiation regarding the interpretation and (re)presentation of heritage is highly complex, multifaceted and flexible, owing to the involvement of various parties with different interests in these interactions. As global tourism continues to expand, heritage sites will be the source of historically unprecedented numbers of tourists. Most indicators suggest there will be a huge increase in tourism worldwide over the next 10 years, virtually doubling the current numbers. At any rate, the predicted growth of intraregional will seriously change the global tourism landscape. While the management of heritage is usually the responsibility of a particular community or custodian group, the protection, conservation, interpretation and (re)presentation of the cultural diversity of any particular place or people are important challenges for us all ...

References

Adams, K.M. (2003). The Politics of Heritage in Southeast Asia: Interplaying the Local and the Global. *Indonesia and the Malay World*, 31(89): 91–107.

Al Sayyad, N. (ed.) (2001). *Consuming Tradition, Manufacturing Heritage: Global Norms and Urban Forms in the Age of Tourism*. London: Routledge.

Bruner, E.M. (2005). *Culture on Tour: Ethnographies of Travel*. Chicago: University of Chicago Press.

Dahles, H. (2001). *Tourism, Heritage and National Culture in Java: Dilemmas of a Local Community*. Richmond: Curzon Press.

Dioko, L.A. and Unakul, M.H. (2005). The Need for Specialized Training in Heritage Tour Guiding at Asia's World Heritage Sites: Preliminary Findings on the Challenges and Opportunities. Paper presented at PATA Educator's Forum, Macao, April 16, 2005.

Hampton, M.P. (2005). Heritage, Local Communities and Economic Development. *Annals of Tourism Research*, 32(3): 735–59.

McKercher, B. and Du Cros, H. (2002). *Cultural Tourism: The Partnership between Tourism and Cultural Heritage Management*. New York: Haworth Hospitality Press.

Moscardo, G. (1996). Mindful Visitors: Heritage and Tourism. *Annals of Tourism Research*, 23(2): 376–97.

Nuryanti, W. (ed.) (1997). *Tourism and Heritage Management*. Yogyakarta: Gadjah Mada University Press.

NWHO (1999). *Sustainable Tourism and Cultural Heritage: A Review of Development Assistance and its Potential to Promote Sustainability*. Oslo: Nordic World Heritage Office.

Peleggi, M. (1996). National Heritage and Global Tourism in Thailand. *Annals of Tourism Research*, 23(2): 432–48.

Poria, Y., Butler, R. and Airey, D. (2003). The Core of Heritage Tourism. *Annals of Tourism Research*, 30(1): 238–54.

Porter, B.W. and Salazar, N.B. (eds) (2005). Heritage Tourism, Conflict, and the Public Interest, Theme Issue. *International Journal of Heritage Studies*, 11(5): 361–70.

Salazar, N.B. (2007). Towards a Global Culture of Heritage Interpretation? Evidence from Indonesia and Tanzania. *Tourism Recreation Research*, 32(3): 23–30.

Salazar, N.B. (2010). *Envisioning Eden: Mobilizing Imaginaries in Tourism and Beyond*. Oxford: Berghahn.

Salazar, N.B. and Porter, B.W. (eds) (2004). Heritage and Tourism, PIA and Global Interests, Theme Issue. *Anthropology in Action*, 11(2/3): 2–7.

Timothy, D.J. and Boyd, S.W. (2003). *Heritage Tourism*. Harlow: Prentice Hall.

Timothy, D.J. and Boyd, S.W. (2006). Heritage Tourism in the 21st Century: Valued Traditions and New Perspectives. *Journal of Heritage Tourism*, 1(1): 1–16.

Timothy, D.J. and Prideaux, B. (2004). Issues in Heritage and Culture in the Asia Pacific Region. *Asia Pacific Journal of Tourism Research*, 9(3): 213–23.

UNESCO (1992). *Cultural Tourism Development Central Java—Yogyakarta: Final Report*. Yogyakarta: UNESCO/UNDP/Directorate General of Tourism.

UNESCO (2005). *Heritage Tour Guide Training and Certification for UNESCO World Heritage Sites*. Bangkok: UNESCO Bangkok Office.

UNESCO (2008). *The Operational Guidelines for the Implementation of the World Heritage Convention*. Paris: UNESCO World Heritage Centre.

Uzzell, D.L. (ed.) (1989). *Heritage Interpretation*. London: Belhaven Press.

Chapter 10

Immediacy, Photography and Memory: The Tourist Experience of Machu Picchu

Sarah Quinlan Cutler, Sean Doherty and Barbara Carmichael

This chapter addresses the complex nature of the tourist experience at World Heritage Sites (WHSs), focusing on the use of different research methods in exploring encounters with sites of exceptional cultural and natural significance. Currently, little is known about immediate reactions to WHSs, the capturing of site images, or memories of the visit. This chapter will examine the experience of educational tourists at the Historical Sanctuary of Machu Picchu, Peru and discuss how WHSs can acquire more diverse information employing research techniques which have received little attention in World Heritage research.

Machu Picchu as a World Heritage Site

Machu Picchu is Peru's most popular destination due to its cultural importance, architectural significance, and the existence of rich flora and fauna within the surrounding natural area. In 1983, the 32,592 hectare site was designated as a WHS due to its outstanding cultural and natural value (UNESCO 2009). The ruins at Machu Picchu are thought to be a village or royal retreat occupied by the Incas in the 1400s and 1500s (WCMC 2008), which remained relatively undisturbed until 1911 when a local Peruvian, Melchor Arteaga, led archeologist Hiram Bingham to the area (Lumbreras 2005). Hiram recognized the archeological importance of the site and is often credited with its rediscovery.

Access to the site is relatively restricted; it can be reached by train from Cusco or Ollantaytambo to Aguas Calientes followed by a bus journey or hike to the site or by hiking the Inca Trail over 2–4 days. Despite its remote location, as of 2009 Machu Picchu received 815,268 visitors (MINCETUR 2011). This has numerous implications for conservation and site management but also impacts upon the tourist experience.

The Tourist Experience

Experiences occur within a person who is engaged with an event on an emotional, physical, spiritual, or intellectual level (Pine and Gilmore 1999). As an element of tourism, this involves everything that happens at a destination (Stamboulis and Skayannis 2003), indicating that the tourist experience is an intricate psychological process. In this chapter, the tourist experience is understood as the events and activities which take place during a tourism episode, the influences involved in shaping that episode, and the personal outcomes of that episode.

Researching the Tourist Experience at World Heritage Sites

Despite over three decades of research on the tourist experience, there are numerous gaps which should be addressed for a more comprehensive understanding of this area. More specifically, there is a lack of research on the experience of World Heritage Sites and how these are understood during the visit and remembered by the visitor. This research aims to address these gaps.

Immediacy

The immediate approach involves on-site, real time reactions, capturing raw emotions and thoughts which have not yet been contextualized within a whole travel event (S. Larsen 2007). Research involving immediacy has become popular in leisure studies, demonstrating that evaluations of experiences change over time (Lee et al. 1994). However, experiential data collection in tourism has mainly involved research relying on the recollection of experiences.

In leisure studies the Experience Sampling Method (ESM) is often used to capture immediate experiential data. This method is based on the repeated administration of self-reports designed to capture the perception of ongoing experiences by prompting subjects to answer questions at random points throughout a given time period within a natural setting when thoughts and feelings are fresh (Cerin et al. 2001; Feldman Barrett and Barrett 2001; Hektner et al. 2007; Larson and Csikszentmihalyi 1983). Previous studies have found that this approach can minimize memory distortions and allow for more in-depth examinations of experiences, relying on repeated measures throughout a prescribed time period rather than a single assessment (Cerin et al. 2001; Larson and Csikszentmihalyi 1983).

Recently there has been a move towards more computerized ESM data collection. Computerized procedures can allow for greater flexibility in question presentation, more precise control of timing, the ability to track compliance, and reduction in human error when managing data (Bolger et al. 2003; Feldman Barrett and Barrett 2001; Hektner et al. 2007; Stone et al. 1991). There is also opportunity for alternative types of data capture such as voice, picture, and video. In using this approach at sites with World Heritage status, it can capture raw responses to experiences during the experience itself, providing valuable data on the types of experiences, emotions, and learning opportunities taking place. This can provide insight into experiences that ultimately shape individual perceptions of WHSs and can also indicate areas that require attention. In this study immediate reaction data is capture using the Experience Sampling Method (ESM) modified for use on hand-held smartphones.

Photography

Photography and tourism share an intimate relationship. During a trip, the tourist selects images which will provide tangible evidence of his or her experience of a destination. After returning home, though the tourist experience has ended the photograph will still exist, giving these images and the event importance and immortality (Sontag 1978). Assessing the images which are chosen to preserve and narrate tourist experiences can illustrate the travel environment and help to further understand the experience itself.

There have been very few studies which empirically investigate tourist photography as experiential phenomena (Albers and James 1988; Larsen 2006; Markwell 1997). Research shows that there is a consumptive photographic pattern where tourists capture idealized images (Markwell 1997) and a focus on social relationships within tour groups (J. Larsen 2006). The lack of further research interest in this area seems odd as the relationship between photography and tourism has always been stressed as an important one (Albers and James 1988; Chalfen 1979; Sontag 1978). The integration of photography as a method of data collection in studies on WHSs is important as many of these sites involve highly aesthetic visual elements and iconic features which represent entire destinations (i.e., Stone Henge, Uluru, or the Egyptian pyramids). Static images provide information on the elements the tourists seek from the site and the attributes which are seen as important enough to preserve. They also act as a marker of the experience, showing the tourist standing within an interesting physical or cultural landscape. In this study, photographs taken by participants are analyzed for content, context, intention, and photographic density, and then related to photographer specific variables to explore the images of site experiences.

Memory

Memory is an important element associated with the tourist experience (Pine and Gilmore 1999). Svein Larson (2007) argues that memory could be the most influential aspect of tourism experiences, since memory will be what remains after the experience has ended and this can have a strong influence on the perception of destinations. Tung's (2009) study on memorable tourism experiences found that they are comprised of five dimensions: affect, intentionality, expectations, consequentiality and recollection, in the context of the destination. The importance of affect is reiterated by Trauer and Ryan (2005) who argue that emotional elements create memory and these memories can reinforce personal intimacies where places are seen as a center for emotional exchange. This idea of memorable information can be related to both positive and negative experiences. Therefore memories can be defined as filtering mechanisms which link the experience to the emotional and perceptual outcomes of a tourist event (Oh et al. 2007).

Though memory is seen as the outcome of experience, it can also be actively involved in the interpretation and transformation of experience through narration (Cary 2004; Selstad 2007). The narration of memory allows experiences to change, indicating that experiences are active items which continually evolve within tourist discourse.

Previous research measuring tourist experiences often involves post-travel questionnaires or interviews which ask subjects about their trip (Feldman Barrett and Barrett 2001). This can be problematic as memories and perceptions of sites can be inaccurate—fading, evolving, and changing over time (Feldman Barrett and Barrett 2001; Fridgen 1984). This emphasizes the importance of additional data collection, such as immediate reactions and photographs, to provide a more accurate understanding of site experiences. In this study, tourist memories of Machu Picchu are evaluated to better understand memorable aspects the site and to allow for the methodological evaluation of changes in experience perception over time.

Research Methods and Analysis

This research involved immediate data collection, photographic data collection, and recollection data. Immediate experience data was collected using In-Situ Tourist Experience Logging (ISTEL) software, a modified version of the Experience Sampling Method (ESM), deployed on a BlackBerry™ smartphone (model 8330), as shown in Figure 10.1. Each participant was given a smartphone with ISTEL software designed to alert participants approximately five times per day at random intervals via device vibration, prompting them to complete a tourist experience log. Each log involved a series of questions regarding their current experience which participants answered using a combination of pull-down lists and prompted voice recordings.

Photography data involved the collection of tourist photographs with their consent once participants returned from their trip. Participants were unaware of this element of the research during the trip so as to not bias individual choices in photography. All images were digital and subject to a process of visual analysis. Visual analysis involves a search for meaning and patterns through the examination of content and context of images which, in this case, reflect visual experiences (Collier 2001).

The collection of data on tourist memories of Machu Picchu was done using two different methods. In-depth interviews were conducted three to four months after the site visit, asking participants to reflect on their travel experience.

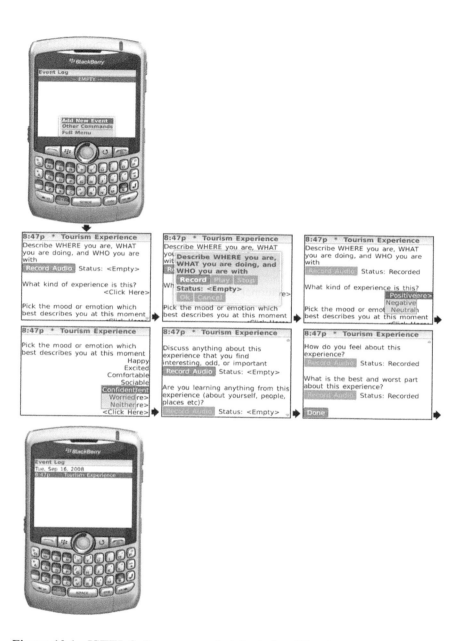

Figure 10.1   ISTEL Software snapshot depicting "Tourism Experience" randomly generated prompt

Trip participants were later sent an open-ended email survey 16 months after the site visit, again asking them to discuss their experience of the destination.

Immediate reactions and in-depth interviews were transcribed and imported into NVivo software along with email surveys to allow for computerized coding and content analysis. Content analysis evaluates the elements of human communication and is defined as a way to extract desired information from material through the systematic identification of specific characteristics, words, or meanings (Babbie 2001; Smith 2000). Once the data sets were coded, the analysis of themes, concepts, categories, and meanings were compared to examine immediate reactions and memorable experiences. Results were also used to further understand photographic relationships involved in the tourist experience which immerged from visual analysis.

The Tourist Experience of Machu Picchu

A purposive sample of 21 educational tourists from Canada participated in this study. The group consisted of 14 females and 7 males who travelled to Peru in August 2008. The Historical Sanctuary of Machu Picchu was accessed by this group in two different ways; 18 participants arrived after completing the Inca Trail hike and three participants arrived by train to Aguas Calientes and took a bus to the site. Both the hikers and day visitors were with guides and spent an equal amount of time at the site (approximately 2.5 hours) though the day visitors arrived earlier in the day and spent more time exploring the main ruin complex at a relaxed pace. Results indicate that Machu Picchu was an emotional, educational, and personal experience which became an image icon of Peru and a memorable event for many of the trip participants.

The Immediate Experience

Sixteen participants (13 hikers and 3 day visitors) produced 35 logs using the ISTEL software. The data does not include five participants due to lack of software prompting during this time and unexpected data corruption issues. Overall the descriptions of Machu Picchu tended to be very positive. Of the 51 references describing the site, only one was in a neutral tone. This indicates that in the moment, participants were having good reactions to the WHS. Participants also focused on learning, with one-third of participants discussing site history and Incan culture, and another third discussing learning about self and personal accomplishment. When asked about negative aspects of the experience, half of the participants mentioned having to go home or leave the site. There were three mentions of insects and four references to the trail regarding physical soreness or injury. Other mentions included weather, waiting, and missing certain people.

Hikers had more limited discussion on the historic qualities of the site compared to day visitors. Their discussion involved group pride and accomplishment in having completed the Inca Trail, revealing a shared experience of achievement with the site representing triumph over physical and mental challenges. The dialog was more emotional and personal than that of day visitors. This implies that immediate experiences of Machu Picchu are dependent upon the method of arrival, which has implications for site managers. If educating visitors about culture and history is a WHS priority, these lessons may be lost on hikers who, having battled fatigue and potential injuries, and consequently are not giving that their full attention. However, for hikers the site is discussed with greater emotional and personal emphasis, which could make it more memorable.

Photographing Machu Picchu

Eleven participants (7 females and 4 males) provided a full set of unaltered digital photographs, leading to a collection of 820 images taken during the Machu Picchu visit. On average, participants were taking 30 photographs per hour. This reveals the importance of photography as an on-site activity for visitors and also emphasizes the significance of the site visit for the individual. Table 10.1 shows the number of photographs taken and the main subjects by each participant.

Table 10.1   Total number and main subject of photographs taken by participant photographers at Machu Picchu

Participant*	# of photos taken	Subject of Photographs**			
		Ruins (%)	Social Setting (%)	Landscape (%)	Other (%)
Amber	257	48	21	16	–
Rachel	94	77	16	–	–
Matt	87	24	53	–	14 (plants)
Heather	79	68	10	9	–
Laura	78	50	32	13	–
Tom	72	58	25	–	6 (animals)
Michelle	55	53	36	6	–
Hannah	46	65	15	9	–
Blaire	26	75	8	8	–
Tyler	14	33	67	–	–
Sam	12	7	71	–	21 (animals)

Notes: *All names have been changed to protect the privacy of the participants of this research.**Only subjects constituting >5% of photos are listed here.

a) Example of ruins   b) Example of social setting

c) Example of natural landscapes   d) Example of individual experience

Figure 10.2   Representative examples of tourist photographs taken at Machu Picchu

Examples of photographs are provided in Figure 10.2. In examining the main subjects depicted in the photographs, over half are of the Machu Picchu ruins (52.8%). Though many ruins were photographed, few close shots were taken of Incan architectural features. This is interesting as Machu Picchu is protected as a site which exemplifies Incan building techniques.

The images also captured social settings (25.5%) and natural landscapes (9.2%). This demonstrates that the social group visitors arrive with is important as is the physical setting of the site. Results indicate that males took fewer photographs of landscapes (n=4, 2.3%[1]) and ruins (n=63, 35.6%) than expected, but much more of people (n=80, 45.2%), suggesting that Machu Picchu was a social experience. Females focused more on ruins (n=357, 57.8%[2]) and landscapes (n=69, 11.2%) with fewer social setting photos (n=123, 19.9%) than expected, signifying that the history and beauty of the area was important. However, in reviewing the people-centered photographs, males took more group

1   Percentage of total photographs taken by male subjects.
2   Percentage of total photographs taken by female subjects.

shots (n=56, 65.9%) than expected and fewer self-shots (n=4, 4.7%). Females took more self-shots (n=22, 16.1%) than expected and fewer group shots (n=53, 38.7%). This implies that males tended to frame Machu Picchu as a group experience, highlighting the importance of the people who came to the site with them. Females framed Machu Picchu as an individual experience, where they are standing alone in front of the ruins (see Figure 10.2). This reveals that, for the participants, encounters with this site were personal, involving the individual wanting to capture the intimate experience of self in place. This also suggests a need to demonstrate "I was here," having the photograph act as evidence of travel history and accomplishment.

In examining photographs it is important to note not only what is photographed but also what is not. There were few photographs of other tourists at the site outside of the group; therefore participants were limiting images to inanimate objects or known people. There were no photographs of transportation, tourist infrastructure, or tourist services outside of guides. The overall tendency was to capture ruins as if they were undisturbed and remote. This is similar to findings by Markwell (1997) who noted that tourists reinforce idealized images of the destination in pictures.

Memories of a World Heritage Site

In-depth interviews were conducted with all 21 participants three to four months after their visit. Overall, discussion of the site was positive, with Machu Picchu highlighted as a significant memory, the best part of the trip, or the image most associated with Peru. There were some negative associations with the site mentioned by six participants, mostly related to bug bites.

An email survey was sent out 16 months after the trip and was returned by 15 participants (71% response rate). Ten respondents used positive descriptions of the site such as amazing, impressive, and beautiful but six participants did mention negative attributes including insects or how the site was "just another ruin." Machu Picchu did feature strongly in the participants' memories of Peru. The site was a significant memory for nine respondents and an iconic image of Peru for eight respondents. Five respondents discussed the site as the best part of the trip and it features in stories that four respondents tell to others about their experience of Peru.

In comparing memories of Machu Picchu over time, responses indicate that memories on the whole became more positive. The site became more central to the experience, as part of stories told, the imagery of place, the best part of the trip, and as the most significant memory. Discussion of Machu Picchu is more frequent in the later survey with more mentions of specific positive and negative elements as well as more discussion on what was learned.

Examining Immediacy, Photography and Memory

Participants who discussed positive immediate experiences tended to discuss strong lasting, positive memories of the site in interviews and in surveys, whereas those with more neutral immediate reactions to the site had more neutral memories or mixed memories of Machu Picchu with both positive mentions (i.e., relating to accomplishment) and negative discussion (i.e., relating to bug bites). This demonstrates that trip memory changes over time, perhaps becoming more prominent due to the presence of photographs of the site or through the retelling of vacation details with friends and family. This confirms discussions by Selstad (2007) and Cary (2004) that tourists are involved in the production of trip meaning and the continual evolution of trip memory.

Results revealed a strong relationship between travel memory and photography. Those who remember Machu Picchu as the best part of their trip, a significant memory, or an iconic image of Peru were those who took more pictures of the site. This could indicate that memory is colored by the amount of photographs, with photographs acting as souvenirs of the trip and emphasizing that which was photographed over that which was not. There could also be other factors at play. If immediate experiences of a site are positive, individuals may take more pictures to capture this, and the on-site importance is what establishes travel memory, with photography acting as an indicator of immediate positive experiences. More research is needed to better understand this relationship.

One consistent element among all research methods has been the implications of hiking the Inca Trail on the understanding of the site. In immediate reaction data, the hike itself was given importance with many of the references to Machu Picchu describing it as a reward.

> I'm totally excited about this experience, this is the experience we've all been waiting for to reach the sun gate—to overlook Machu Picchu. It's great. This is definitely probably one of the climaxes of the trip. Although Machu Picchu was supposed to be amazing to see, I think the most exciting part is to see it from up here. (Olivia,[3] tourist experience log)

This links Machu Picchu to the Inca Trail and suggests that reaching the site is an important peak event but that the qualities of the site itself are not important. Day visitors referred to the site as awesome and interesting with no discussion of Machu Picchu as beautiful or as the best part of the trip, indicating that for them the qualities of the site were of interest, but it was not necessarily a peak event.

---

3   All names have been changed to protect the privacy of the participants of this research.

In photographs, hikers had many individual and group photographs taken when they first saw Machu Picchu. In the post trip interviews hikers discussed how the journey to Machu Picchu was important. The WHS became associated with personal achievement and overcoming difficulties experienced during the Inca Trail.

> I think finishing the Inca Trail and getting to Machu Picchu. And just standing there—well sitting there—of course. And just looking down at that, 3 days of hiking, 3 days of agony and finally gotten, like you're there, just knowing that if you push through even when you think that you can't that there's a reward at the end.
>
> (Michelle, post-trip interview)

> I play a lot of sports and I feel like I'm pretty physically fit and it [the trail] was pretty gruelling on me and then when you get to the top and you see Machu Picchu, it's pretty satisfying that you hike this whole trail and you get to see this ... this wonder of the world.
>
> (Alex, post-trip interview)

Though Machu Picchu was discussed as a highlight or an icon, it was a goal rather than a tourist destination. It marked the end of physical and mental testing. This was also evident in the post trip surveys, which reveals Machu Picchu as a lasting memory of accomplishment. This indicates that the method of arrival can impact on the experience of Machu Picchu. Hiking is the avenue of arrival for as many as 500 visitors per day so understanding how this shapes the experience of the site is important. Findings demonstrate that it can lessen the emphasis on Machu Picchu as a distinct experience, where visitors are not as concerned with the site history as they are with their own accomplishment. However, findings also indicate that this gives the site an aura of awe and amazement, promoting a more personal connection with the World Heritage area.

In comparing the various data sets, another interesting aspect emerges relating to social relationships. During the immediate experience of Machu Picchu, participants do not discuss other people as being the best part of the trip, but this was a major area of post travel discussion. The importance of the group was also demonstrated in the photographic data where a quarter of all photographs captured a people-centered experience, rather than a site-centered experience. This reinforces the importance of social aspects of travel and relationship formation within groups which has been discussed by other tourism researchers (see Selstad 2007; Trauer and Ryan 2005). It is important to note however, that as the Machu Picchu experience was at the end of the group trip, the data is indicative of relationship strengthening rather than formation.

Conclusion

The findings for Machu Picchu have implications for other World Heritage Sites. The ESM data collection method deployed on smartphones revealed complex visitor understandings of Machu Picchu. WHSs can benefit from this immediate approach and modify the questions to suit management goals. The software helped to isolate positive and negative experiences, allowing for site elements to be broken down and understood individually as well as within the context of the whole experience. These results can be used in planning and management to provide for better visitor experiences through reshaping interpretation programmes and in addressing more complex questions involved in managing on-site experiences.

This research demonstrates that photography is strongly related to WHS memories, indicating that site managers need a better understanding of photographic activity and images tourists seek to capture. As described by Tung (2009), planners and managers can identify and promote memory points in areas which house iconic features. At Machu Picchu, though participants photographed ruins, they did not specifically focus on architectural elements, and it did not feature in immediate reaction data or as a memorable aspect of the trip. If this is an element that managers wish to stress, interpretation services could be modified to better highlight this and representative examples of architectural techniques can be presented to visitors as a photographic opportunity.

The importance of social relationships emphasized in the data indicates that the site was a place where personal relationships within the group were reinforced. This presence of strong social elements is important for site managers to recognize. WHSs are not only important cultural or natural experiences but also social experiences. Managers can seek to augment this element, providing physical and temporal spaces for social interaction and inter-personal connections, which can help shape the on-site experience and augment site memory.

Overall, the findings of this research demonstrate that the tourist experience of WHSs is complex and cannot be fully understood using traditional recollection research methods. The ISTEL software and tourist photography data in combination with recollection methods allow for a more comprehensive and rich data set which highlights positive and negative site attributes, demonstrates important experiential site elements, and achieves a greater understanding of visitor experiences in sites of global significance. This understanding can be used to better direct World Heritage Site planning, policy, and management to augment the tourist experience and shape travel memory of these exceptional places.

Acknowledgments

We would like to thank Research in Motion (RIM) and Telus who donated the devices and service used for this research. We would also like to acknowledge that this project was financially supported by the Social Sciences and Humanities Research Council. We would like to thank Eric Sadowski and Luke Cwik, who aided in data collection and all subjects who willingly and openly participated in this study.

References

Albers, P.C. and James, W.R. (1988). Travel Photography: A Methodological Approach. *Annals of Tourism Research*, 15(1): 134–58.

Babbie, E. (2001). *The Practice of Social Research*. Belmont, CA: Wadsworth/ Thomson Learning.

Bolger, N., Davis, A. and Rafaeli, E. (2003). Diary Methods: Capturing Life as it is Lived. *Annual Review of Psychology*, 54(1): 579–616.

Cary, S.H. (2004). The Tourist Moment. *Annals of Tourism Research*, 1(31): 61–77.

Cerin, E., Szabo, A. and Williams, C. (2001). Is the Experience Sampling Method (ESM) Appropriate for Studying Pre-competitive Emotions? *Psychology of Sport and Exercise*, (2)1: 27–45.

Chalfen, R.M. (1979). Photograph's Role in Tourism: Some Unexplored Relationships. *Annals of Tourism Research*, 4(6): 435–47.

Collier, M. (2001). Approaches to Analysis in Visual Anthropology. In: Van Leeuwen, T. and Jewitt, C. (eds), *Handbook of Visual Analysis*. London: Sage Publications.

Crang, M. (1997). Picturing Practices: Research through the Tourist Gaze. *Progress in Human Geography*, 3(21): 359–73.

Feldman Barrett, L. and Barrett, D.J. (2001). An Introduction to Computerized Experience Sampling in Psychology. *Social Science Computer Review*, 2(19): 175–85.

Fridgen, J.D. (1984). Environmental Psychology and Tourism. *Annals of Tourism Research*, 1(11): 19–39.

Hektner, J.M., Schmidt, J.A. and Csikszentmihalyi, M. (2007). *Experience Sampling Method: Measuring the Quality of Everyday Life*. London: SAGE Publications Ltd.

Larsen, J. (2006). Picturing Bornholm: Producing and Consuming a Tourist Place through Picturing Practices. *Scandinavian Journal of Hospitality and Tourism*, 2(6): 75–94.

Larsen, S. (2007). Aspects of a Psychology of the Tourist Experience. *Scandinavian Journal of Hospitality and Tourism*, 1(7): 7–18.

Larson, R. and Csikszentmihalyi, M. (eds) (1983). *Naturalistic Approaches to Studying Social Interactions*. San Francisco: Jossey-Bass Inc.

Lee, Y., Dattilo, J. and Howard, D. (1994). The Complex and Dynamic Nature of Leisure Experience. *Journal of Leisure Research*, 3(26): 195–211.

Lumbreras, L. (2005). *Machu Picchu: About the Disoccupation when Discovered.* Available at <http://www.machupicchu.perucultural.org.pe/ingles/desarque. htm> (accessed April 28, 2010).

Markwell, K.W. (1997). Dimensions of Photography in a Nature-based Tour. *Annals of Tourism Research*, 1(24): 131–55.

Ministerio de Comercio Exterior y Turismo (MINCETUR) (2011). *Cusco: Llegada de Visitantes Al Santuario Historico De Machu Picchu, Enero 2004—Diciembre 2010.* Available at <http://www.mincetur.gob.pe/newweb/ portals/0/turismo/sitios%20turisticos/Cus_MAPI_LLeg_Nac_Extr.pdf> (accessed April 18, 2011).

Noy, C. (2007). The Poetics of Tourist Experience: An Autoethnography of a Family Trip to Eilat. *Journal of Tourism and Cultural Change*, 3(5): 141–57.

Oh, H., Fiore, A.M. and Jeoung, M. (2007). Measuring Experience Economy Concepts: Tourism Applications. *Journal of Travel Research*, November (46): 119–32.

Pine, B.J. and Gilmore, J.H. (1999). *The Experience Economy: Work is Theatre and Every Business a Stage*. Boston, MA: Harvard Business School Press.

PromPerú. (2009). *Nivel de Satisfacción del Turista Extranjero 2008*. Available at <http://www.peru.info/s_ftoPublicaciones.asp?HidAccion=Grupo&HidId= 2&ic=1&SubTipo_ZP=1> (accessed November 24, 2009).

Selstad, L. (2007). The Social Anthropology of the Tourist Experience. Exploring the "Middle Role". *Scandinavian Journal of Hospitality and Tourism*, 1(7): 19–33.

Smith, C.P. (2000). Content Analysis and Narrative Analysis. In: Reis, H.T. and Judd, C.M. (eds), *Handbook of Research Methods in Social and Personality Psychology*. Cambridge, UK: Cambridge University Press.

Sontag, S. (1978). *On Photography*, 3rd edn. Toronto: McGraw-Hill Ryerson Ltd.

Stamboulis, Y. and Skayannis, P. (2003). Innovation Strategies and Technology for Experience-based Tourism. *Tourism Management*, 1(24): 35–43.

Stone, A.A., Kessler, R.C. and Haythomthwatte, J.A. (1991). Measuring Daily Events and Experiences: Decisions for the Researcher. *Journal of Personality*, 3(59): 575–607.

Strauss, A.L. (1987). *Qualitative Analysis for Social Scientists*. New York: Cambridge University Press.

Trauer, B. and Ryan, C. (2005). Destination Image, Romance and Place Experience – An Application of Intimacy Theory in Tourism. *Tourism Management*, 4(26): 481–91.

Tung, V. (2009). Exploring the Essence of a Memorable Travel Experience. Unpublished Master's thesis, University of Calgary.

United Nations Educational Scientific and Cultural Organization (UNESCO) (2009). *Historic Sanctuary of Machu Picchu*. Available at <http://whc.unesco.org/en/list/274> (accessed November 24, 2009).

World Conservation Monitoring Centre (WCMC) (2008). *Historic Sanctuary of Machu Picchu Peru*, World Heritage Sites. Available at http://www.unep-wcmc.org/sites/wh/pdf/Machu%20Picchu.pdf> (accessed December 8, 2009).

Chapter 11

The Social Life of the Castles: Inclusion, Exclusion, and Heritage Sites in Ghana

Ann Reed

The title of this paper is inspired by Appadurai's (1986) work, *The Social Life of Things*, in which he suggests that commodities, like persons, can have social lives, and that economic things circulate under different "regimes of value" in space and time. This also holds true of World Heritage sites. I apply these ideas to show how Cape Coast Castle and Elmina Castle, two United Nations Educational, Scientific and Cultural Organisation (UNESCO) World Heritage sites in Ghana, have social lives of their own, as their significance to different human actors has changed over time and their purpose means different things to different people. In the discussion that follows, we might think about how dynamics of cultural desire, economic demand, and political power dominate the construction of heritage tourism sites, thereby overriding their other potential uses.

Since the early 1990s, stakeholders in Ghana's tourism industry have invested heavily in reconstructing Cape Coast and Elmina castles, which now attract thousands of visitors annually and contribute significantly to the national economy. This project has taken on material as well as metaphorical meaning if we consider how these structures have been rehabilitated physically with assistance from institutions such as the United Nations Development Program (UNDP), the United States Agency for International Development (USAID), and the Smithsonian Institution and have been recast from earlier historical and utilitarian roles to portray what tour guides there refer to as the "slave story." This chapter considers how these sites' use as pilgrimage tourism attractions focusing on the trans-Atlantic slave trade is not a foregone conclusion, but a deliberate choice by various social actors. This raises interesting questions about inclusion and exclusion. If tourism stakeholders are promoting a singular dominant use for the castles, what does that mean for the Ghanaians who live nearby? What is the relationship of local residents to these sites? Are they at risk of becoming alienated from historically significant places in their own neighborhoods as a result of the meanings and policies reinforced by the heritage tourism industry?

Elmina Castle and Cape Coast Castle started out as much more modest trading posts and have served a range of purposes over their long histories.

What eventually became Elmina Castle started out as São Jorge da Mina and was built by the Portuguese in 1482, in order to gain direct access to gold found in the region and to circumvent the trans-Saharan middlemen. Cape Coast Castle started out as the more modest Fort Carolusburg and was built by agents of the Swedish Africa Company in 1652. In the seventeenth and eighteenth centuries, both structures witnessed dramatic architectural transformations when European trading companies competed fiercely with one another to form trade alliances with local African populations and expand their commercial interests on the Gold Coast. The Dutch, English, Swedes, Danes, and Brandenburgers continued to secure gold, but beginning in the seventeenth century trade in slaves became increasingly important (Perbi 1992: 67), fueled by the plantation economy in the Americas.

Castles as Tourist Destinations

Before Cape Coast and Elmina castles were transformed into heritage tourism destinations in the 1990s, they were in a dilapidated state, underutilized, and mostly empty. A number of factors are responsible for the build-up to Ghana's heritage tourism. Institutions dedicated to historic preservation and conservation were part of the equation; economic development strategies centering on tourism were another part. In 1979, Ghana successfully secured UNESCO World Heritage status for its forts and castles; chief among them were Elmina Castle, Cape Coast Castle, and Fort St. Jago. The original rationale for inscription was that Ghana's forts and castles exhibited some of the most characteristic features of European fortified trade posts in the tropics and that Elmina Castle was exemplary for being "the most ancient and important in the world" (Ghana Museums & Monuments Board 2001: 4). The UNESCO World Heritage Committee continues to regard these sites as having outstanding universal value because of their unique architectural style and early evidence of joint activity between Africans and Europeans.

Since 1993, when the Ghana Ministry of Tourism (MOT) was founded, tourism has been central to state-based economic development efforts and has, indeed, been one of the fastest growing sectors of the economy. The MOT has noted in its development plan that diaspora Africans—and particularly African Americans—are an important niche market, as many of them consider Ghana or West Africa more generally to be their homeland. These economic directives have signaled an increasing need for tourism stakeholders to commemorate heritage sites significant in attracting these groups. The Ghana government sees tourism as an extremely important part of the national economy, contributing 6.2% to GDP and earning US$1.6 billion in 2009 and bringing in the fourth largest amount of foreign exchange after gold, cocoa, and remittances from Ghanaians living abroad. Ghana's tourism industry is also credited with creating 260,000 formal and informal jobs in 2009 (Ghana News Agency 2010). Approximately 700,000 tourists arrived in

Ghana in 2008 and the tourism economy is projected to grow at a rate of 4.1% annually for the next two decades (*Business & Financial Times* 2009).

From these figures, one might assume that international visitors dominate Ghana's tourism. Actually, the opposite is true. In 2007, residents of Ghana comprised 73% of the visitors to tourist sites, compared to 27% of non-residents. For the years 2005 and 2006, overseas Ghanaians ranked number one in international tourist arrivals, followed by Americans, Nigerians, and UK citizens (Ghana Tourist Board 2008: 1). Visitation to Cape Coast and Elmina castles reflects similar trends of dominant Ghanaian visitors which have been in place at least since the early 1990s. In 2004, 74% of total arrivals to Cape Coast Castle and 77% of total arrivals to Elmina Castle were Ghanaians (Ghana Tourist Board 2005: 1). After Ghanaians, the most likely visitors to the castles were North Americans (12%), Europeans (9%), and non-Ghanaian West Africans (3%). General admission to these castles has risen dramatically from approximately 7,900 in 1990 to 43,000 in 2004 (Ministry of Local Government & Rural Development 2006: 3; Ghana Tourist Board 2005: 1).

If Ghanaians are the most frequent visitors to the castles, then why are they marketed mainly to diaspora Africans? Financescapes provide us with part of the answer, as they have linked international donors—primarily in the US[1]—to Ghanaian state and regional development programs for some time now. In 1989, Regional Minister Ato Austin traveled to the United States to request money and expertise from US-based organizations towards the promotion of economic development in Ghana's Central Region. The effort resulted in a $5.6 million grant from USAID which was later increased to $7.8 million over a five-year period (Hyatt 1997: 31). United Nations Development Program (UNDP) provided an additional $3.6 million in technical assistance and the Ghana government added approximately $130,000 (Midwest Universities Consortium for International Activities 1994). The public and private sectors contributed $75 million towards infrastructure and tourism facilities (Hyatt 1997: 31). Altogether, nearly $90 million was invested by these groups located mostly outside of Ghana; the capital and expertise provided by them has recast Cape Coast Castle and Elmina Castle from earlier historical and utilitarian roles to portray what tour guides there refer to as the "slave story."

Sight Sacralization and the Commodification of Heritage

Dean MacCannell (1976) illustrates the first stage of what he calls sight sacralization in the process of naming a tourist sight. Here, the wider public recognizes the extraordinary status of a particular place. Ideally, people will forget about previous mundane uses of the place in question and focus their attention

---

1 The Netherlands government has invested in Ghana's heritage tourism more recently, particularly in relation to Elmina Castle and the Dutch Cemetery in Elmina.

on the newly projected meanings associated with the sight. A contemporary sign outside Cape Coast Castle proudly displays the fact that it is a UNESCO World Heritage site with notable features of interest; the Church of Jesus Christ of Latter Day Saints provided sponsorship for this sign which also serves as a meeting place for LDS members. Guides at Elmina and Cape Coast castles as well as Fort St. Jago introduce their tours by remarking on the destination's UNESCO World Heritage standing.

In 1994, a sign outside Elmina Castle read in English and Fante, "THIS AREA IS RESTRICTED TO ALL PERSONS EXCEPT TOURISTS" (Bruner 1996: 298). Elminans were prevented from entering the castle grounds and the message clearly prioritized tourists over locals in having access to the site. Ghanaian officials explained that this policy was meant to discourage locals from defecating in the area surrounding the castle and nearby beach and to guard against locals begging for handouts from tourists. Although this sign is no longer present, many of these policies are still in place. For example, security guards at both castles discourage locals from entering, unless as tourists, though this is less strictly enforced at Cape Coast than at Elmina. Sometimes, security guards will intervene if young men approach tourists asking for their addresses or make a pitch to them to raise funds for their school fees or football teams. Ghanaian stakeholders view this sort of interaction as harassment and want to minimize it to prevent negative impressions tourists may develop about Cape Coast or Elmina.

It is interesting to note that there are two different admission rates at the castles: Ghanaians pay the cedi equivalent to roughly US$1, whereas non-Ghanaians pay approximately US$5. This has been the subject of criticism in the visitor books to the castles; visitors often cite how in their host countries there would never be such a discriminatory policy charging nationals a different rate from foreigners. Another aspect of this criticism comes from diaspora Africans who in official Ghanaian discourse are being welcomed home as brothers and sisters in one breath and being told to pay the non-Ghanaian rate in the other breath. That some view Cape Coast Castle or Elmina Castle as being the last place where their ancestors were kept before embarking upon the middle passage leads some African Americans to complain about paying any admission fee.

They consider visiting these sites as something more spiritual, more sentimental and more personal than the mundane activities labeled tourism; for them, this experience should not be calculated in monetary terms but should exist in the realm of gifts. This is a good example of different regimes of value at work: should going to the castle be a gift or a commodity? The transfer of money becomes a moral issue in which some consider it wrong to be charged admission for visiting what amounts to a sacred site of pilgrimage. Instead of adding to the feeling of solidarity to Africa through diaspora connections to a homeland, the standardization of being charged admission fees as non-Ghanaians reminds visitors of their difference—that they are not Ghanaians and that they are recognized as tourists, just like anyone else who visits these sites.

Ghanaian officials justify their policy by stating that most foreigners can afford a five-dollar admission fee and that after all, they must maintain the sites, paint the castle walls white periodically, and pay workers their wages. At the same time, they want to encourage the local population to have a stake in their history and suggest that most Ghanaians would not be able to pay the $5 admission. In reality the $1 equivalent required for a guided tour is not something that the local fisher folk are likely to afford. Ghanaians who go on guided tours tend to have higher incomes, are more educated, and are conducted around on English-speaking tours, though they may also opt for tours in the local Fante language. It is not only the entrance fee that discourages local connections to these sites, but also the selective history as presented, which does not necessarily correspond to local memories of the castles.

In tours of Cape Coast Castle, visitors first descend into the dark, dank-smelling Male Dungeon, where guides recount the hardships endured by captives there. After the first chamber of the dungeon, visitors are told how human feces, blood, and decomposed bodies formed the floor and that captives lived in such crammed conditions for up to three months. Tour guides mention slaves being shackled together and fighting over the scraps of food that were thrown down to them through holes in the walls. Vivid descriptions—which are stressed by all of the tour guides—evoke an emotional reaction, haunting visitors and inviting them to imagine such torture. This account paints a dramatic picture but is complicated by excavations of Cape Coast Castle in which archeologists found no iron shackles, pins, stakes, or fixing points for chains that could be directly linked to the confinement of slaves (Anquandah 1999; Simmonds 1973). I do not wish to suggest that they had an easy life in the dungeons—only to underscore the tendency by tour guides to overly dramatize history and to play to the expectations of their audience at heritage tourism sites. James Anquandah, a Ghanaian archeologist and representative of the Ghana committee for the UNESCO Slave Route Project confirmed this perspective, adding that tour guides like the public to believe that that slaves went hungry but that the material evidence showed otherwise. In my interviews with tour guides, they admitted that they aim to deliver what those on tour anticipate. Some tourists may come for the architecture, others for the Akan aspects of the castles' history; however, most visitors are intent on hearing the "slave story," so interpreters do not want to disappoint. The danger of tour guides drumming up heightened emotions in the public is that negative acts or insulting remarks may result.

Remembering the Past: Visitors' Responses to Site Interpretations

An example of how visitors have responded to interpretations of history is that the message, "Death to the Oppressor," was etched into the wall of the Male Slave Dungeon at Cape Coast Castle. I have seen visitors spit on the grave of George Maclean, who was the president of the British company of merchants and oversaw local disputes at Cape Coast Castle. In the guest books, diaspora Africans have questioned why there is a marked grave for Maclean and two other non-Africans and not for the countless captives who perished before embarking upon the middle passage. Some have called for the removal of the graves, citing that it is insulting how Europeans are being valorized, which has led some Ghanaian guides to exclude from their tours with diaspora Africans any explanation of the marked graves at Cape Coast Castle. This is an example of how racial identity politics affects the scope and content of a tour. The content of a tour—what is both included and excluded—becomes the subject of vitriolic discussion which often reifies a master narrative essentially depicting Europeans as villains and Africans as victims in recounting the history of the slave trade. Interpreting these sites and reacting to what is recalled can have profound consequences. In 1994, a fight between African Americans and Europeans broke out which was reportedly sparked by the tour guide's lack of sensitivity in discussing slavery. Whether or not the tour guide was ultimately to blame in this instance, that conflicts still erupt between diaspora Africans and whites at Cape Coast and Elmina castles shows that people do care about identity politics, the way in which history is presented, and the standards for appropriate behavior associated with them.

Different groups of visitors have also been actively involved in alternatively memorializing individual Ghanaians or unnamed masses of enslaved Africans at Ghana's castles. For example, Philip Quaque was a Cape Coaster who had been educated in Britain through support from the Society for the Propagation of the Bible. After returning to the Gold Coast, Quaque became the first chaplain and schoolmaster of Cape Coast Castle in 1766. Local Ghanaians, particularly Anglicans, pay tribute to his missionization efforts today by placing wreaths at his grave and commemorating Philip Quaque Day every year. At the same time, some diaspora Africans critique the presence of his grave in close proximity to the marked graves of British individuals as a symbol of African complicity in the project of European domination. Many African Americans leave wreaths in the Condemned Cell, where tour guides relay that captives who resisted their confinement were sent to starve or suffocate to death. One wreath placed there was dedicated to "The Ancestors" from Crenshaw High School, a predominantly Black school in Los Angeles. These contrasting examples shows different regimes of value at work in practice: one a more salient diaspora African one with interests in remembering the slave trade, and the other a quieter local Ghanaian one with interests in paying tribute to someone credited with bringing Christianity to the Gold Coast. Different segments of the touring public each have their own people that they wish to remember by leaving wreaths, praying, rejoicing, and snapping photographs.

Sight sacralization relates to these acts, particularly for diaspora African visitors, by involving the mechanical reproduction of the sacred object and social reproduction. These stages are represented in Cape Coast Castle's Door of Return, which was officially named in 1998 during Ghana's first recognition of Emancipation Day, a Caribbean holiday honoring the abolition of chattel slavery in the British colonies. The remains of one African American man and one Afro Jamaican woman were brought through the Door of Return and reburied on African soil. Through this act, Ghana was marked as the Gateway to Africa and a homeland for diaspora Africans by pilgrimage tourism stakeholders. Today, Ghanaian tour guides recount this event and welcome home any diaspora Africans who may be on tour at Cape Coast Castle. The sacred nature of a new-found identity is mechanically reproduced when diaspora Africans take photographs at the Door of Return and recount the experience to friends and family back home.

An additional example of this phenomenon is found in the candlelight procession of diaspora Africans and Ghanaians through the principal streets of Cape Coast to Cape Coast Castle which is held annually on the eve of Emancipation Day. It is led by Rabbi Kohain Halevi, an outspoken African American resident in Ghana and includes not only a reverential walk, but also an array of speeches, performances, and rituals at Cape Coast Castle. The shrine housed in the Male Slave Dungeon of Cape Coast Castle is regularly looked after by a Ghanaian caretaker, and attracts numerous diaspora Africans during the Emancipation Day/PANAFEST (Pan-African Historical Theatre Festival) season. Emancipation Eve events culminate in a pilgrimage to the shrine, where mainly African American participants are encouraged to pray together, call out names of famous or personally known departed, and gain a new-found sense of African self. On official tours of the castle, guides will suggest that tourists may voluntarily contribute something to the maintenance of the shrine, as food and drink must regularly be offered to the deities as part of the traditional religious practice.

The Local Presence at Cape Coast and Elmina Castles

Even though the dominant messages at the castles recall the slave story and redemptive nature of re-claiming an African identity, there are other meanings visitors take away from their experience of touring these sites. Asantes and those interested in their history are attracted to Prempeh's Room in Elmina Castle. In 1874, the British drew up a treaty with the Asantehene (chief of the Asante), requiring the latter to hand over the southern portion of their empire, to open trade routes, to abolish human sacrifice, and to pay an indemnity of 50,000 ounces of gold (van Dantzig 1980: 78). The gold had still not been paid to the British by the 1890s, so the Asantehene, Nana Akwesi Agyeman Prempeh I, and members of his royal family were brought to Elmina Castle for punishment. They were imprisoned there for four years before being exiled to Sierra Leone and the Seychelles until 1931 (van Dantzig 1980: 78). Ghanaian tour guides at Elmina Castle include this history on all guided tours and generally interpret a much wider range of perspectives than their counterparts at Cape Coast Castle.

During my 2001–2002 fieldwork, I found that locals still utilize the castles for reasons other than tourism. The room resting above the Male Dungeon was once used as a church and a school; in more recent times, it was used controversially as a restaurant (local African Americans protested its presence in the midst of a graveyard), and now it is used as a children's library. During the 2002 drought in Cape Coast, people living nearby regularly collected water from cisterns found inside the castle. In my interviews with elderly Cape Coasters, individuals recalled Cape Coast Castle fondly as a place that housed the post office or where kids used to play games like hide-and-go-seek. Local residents regularly gather outside the castle by the ocean to converse and observe young men paddle out in their canoes to catch fish. These utilitarian purposes remain significant in the minds of everyday Ghanaians who live near to Cape Coast Castle, yet they remain largely hidden from the view of tourists and are deemed unremarkable and unprofitable by heritage tourism stakeholders.

Conclusion: Regimes of Value at Work in Heritage Tourism Sites

The above ethnographic examples illustrate how cultural desire, economic demand, and political power together produce regimes of value that direct the fundamental meaning of heritage tourism sites. Places like Cape Coast and Elmina castles are made into heritage sites simultaneously through the production of social identities and capitalism. Meanings related to heritage sites travel in increasingly efficient ways through local, national, and global networks to support the production of regimes of value (Myers 2001). Overriding regimes of value at Cape Coast and Elmina castles suggest that diaspora Africans have a special relationship with these heritage sites, as memorials for the trans-Atlantic slave trade and points of departure for re-claiming an African identity. At the same time, local Ghanaian identifications with these places produce altogether different cultural meanings, such as pride for a local man who brought Christianity to Cape Coast or reverence for an Asante chief who resisted colonial efforts at domination for which he and his family were punished. These varying memories of the same place remind us that heritage sites have their own social lives, whether they are made into tourist destinations or not.

Tourism stakeholders in Ghana have decided to largely ignore their Ghanaian market in favor of the African American one. The reason why tourism planners take this reductionist view of the diaspora is that African Americans are regarded as the wealthiest base with the most expendable income. The problem with this policy is the possibility of not only offending Ghanaians who patronize the castles and live nearby, but also alienating the very segment that tourism stakeholders are trying to attract. The danger in managing sites primarily for tourism is that we lose sight of diaspora visitors who resent the commodification of heritage, or Ghanaians who alternatively may be ignored local residents, those who cannot afford admission, or those that use or remember the castles for purposes other than their officially interpreted heritage. For any site that is developed for heritage tourism, we should consider its social life, what it means to different people, in the present as well as in the past, and recognize that the dominant meanings of heritage may be the most reified but are not necessarily the only ones worth remembering.

References

Anquandah, K.J. (1999). *Castles & Forts of Ghana*. Paris and Accra: Atalante and Ghana Museums and Monuments Board.

Appadurai, A. (ed.) (1986). *The Social Life of Things: Commodities in Cultural Perspective*. Cambridge: Cambridge University Press.

Bruner, E. (1996). Tourism in Ghana: The Representation of Slavery and the Return of the Black Diaspora. *American Anthropologist*, 98(2): 290–304.

Business & Financial Times (2009). Tourism in Ghana: 700,000 Tourists Arrived in 2008. *The Ghanaian Journal*. Available at <http://www.theghanaianjournal. com/2009/02/12/tourism-in-ghana-700000-tourists-arrived-in-2008/> (accessed July 27, 2010).

Ghana Museums and Monuments Board (2001). Periodic Reporting Exercise on the Application of the World Heritage Convention in the African Region: Section II. Available at <http://whc.unesco.org/:1–30> (accessed July 27, 2010).

Ghana News Agency (2010). Ghana Realised $1.6 bn from Tourism Last Year. *Business News*, 21 July. Available at <http://ghanaweb.com/GhanaHomePage> (accessed July 27, 2010).

Ghana Tourist Board (2005). Domestic Tourism Statistics 2002–2004. Available at <http://www.touringghana.com/.../DOMESTIC%20TOURISM%202002 –2004.pdf> (accessed July 27, 2010).

Ghana Tourist Board (2008). Tourism Statistical Fact Sheet. Available at <http:// www.touringghana.com/.../Facts.../Tourism_Statistical_FactSheet_070316. pdf> (accessed July 27, 2010).

Hyatt, V.L. (1997). *Ghana: The Chronicle of a Museum Development Project in the Central Region*. Washington, DC: Smithsonian Institution.

MacCannell, D. (1976). *The Tourist: A New Theory of the Leisure Class*. Berkeley, Los Angeles and London: University of California Press.

Midwest Universities Consortium for International Activities (1994). Brief on Natural Resource Conservation and Historic Preservation Project (Ghana), report. Cape Coast, Ghana, March 29.

Ministry of Local Government & Rural Development (2006). Cape Coast Metropolitan Tourism Attractions. *Maks Publications and Media Services*. Available at <http://www.ghanadistricts.com> (accessed July 27, 2010).

Myers, F.R. (ed.) (2001). *The Empire of Things: Regimes of Value and Material Culture*. Santa Fe: School of American Research Press.

Perbi, A. (1992). The Relationship between the Domestic Slave Trade and the External Slave Trade in Pre-colonial Ghana. *Institute of African Studies Research Review*, 8(1–2): 64–75.

Simmonds, D. (1973). A Note on the Excavations in Cape Coast Castle. *Transactions of the Historical Society of Ghana*, 14(2): 267–70.

United National Educational Scientific and Cultural Organization World Heritage Committee (1999). Convention Concerning the Protection of the World Cultural and Natural Heritage, report of the Twenty-second Session. Kyoto, November—December 1998. Available at <http://whc.unesco.org/archive/repcom98.htm#sc34> (accessed May 12, 2011).

van Dantzig, A. (1980). *Forts and Castles of Ghana*. Accra: Sedco Publishing Limited.

Chapter 12

Place Making and Experience in World Heritage Cities

Luna Khirfan

In this chapter I offer a comparative analysis of the management plans for two UNESCO World Heritage cities, Aleppo in Syria and Acre in Israel. These two cities share A third of the 12 criteria for inscription on the World Heritage List as they are considered to "bear a unique or at least exceptional testimony to a cultural tradition or to a civilization which is living or which has disappeared" (UNESCO 2008: paragraph 77). Additionally, Aleppo fulfils the fourth criterion, while Acre meets the second and fifth criteria (Table 12.1). Conforming with UNESCO's Operational Guidelines for the Implementation of the World Heritage Convention, the Syrian and the Israeli authorities developed a "comprehensive planning programme" for Aleppo and Acre (UNESCO 2008: article 5, i). Through managing the contemporary place making, both plans seek to preserve the "outstanding universal value" (UNESCO 1972) of Aleppo and Acre. I reveal however, how in the process, the two plans also influence how the users of these two World Heritage cities, whether residents or foreign tourists, experience their distinctiveness.

Table 12.1   The inscription criteria for Aleppo and Acre

Criterion #	Criterion details	Aleppo	Acre
ii	Exhibit an important interchange of human values, over a span of time or within a cultural area of the world, on developments in architecture or technology, monumental arts, town-planning or landscape design.		X
iii	Bear a unique or at least exceptional testimony to a cultural tradition or to a civilization which is living or which has disappeared.	X	X
iv	Be an outstanding example of a type of building, architectural or technological ensemble or landscape which illustrates (a) significant stage(s) in human history.	X	
v	Be an outstanding example of a traditional human settlement, land-use, or sea-use which is representative of a culture (or cultures), or human interaction with the environment especially when it has become vulnerable under the impact of irreversible change.		X

Source: Adapted from UNESCO 2008: paragraph 77.

The contemporary urban conservation of Aleppo begins with the controversies surrounding the Gutton Plan of 1954, which resulted in the demolition of significant parts of Old Aleppo's historic fabric. The Gutton Plan and similar other initiatives prompted local activists to lobby to halt them until their efforts eventually succeeded when Old Aleppo was designated in 1979 under the Syrian Antiquities Law. By 1986 Old Aleppo was inscribed on the World Heritage List, and then in 1992, the Syrian authorities signed an agreement with the German International Cooperation Agency (GTZ) to begin the Project for the Rehabilitation of the Old City of Aleppo (PROCA). The Old City Directorate was established in 1999 under the auspices of the Municipality of Aleppo to manage all aspects related to the rehabilitation initiative.

Around the same time Old Aleppo was designated, "Aitqot (the Israeli Antiquities Authority) also had designated Old Acre under its 1974 Antiquity Law." Atiqot had continuously performed archeological excavations since the 1950s to expose the Crusader remains of Old Acre (Hartal 1997; Kedar 1997; Kesten 1993). Realizing the city's tourism potential, the Israeli Ministry of Tourism commissioned several tourism development plans, beginning with the Kesten Plan of 1962 (Kesten 1993; Rahamimoff 1997). It also established the Old Acre Development Company (OADC) in 1967, a semi-private entity that was entrusted with converting Old Acre into "an international tourism city" (Kesten 1993; Old Acre Development Company). In 1993 the OADC proposed a $100 million Master Plan for Old Acre in anticipation of an international tourist influx in 2000 (Hecht 1997). The plan led to the inscription of Old Acre on the WHL in 2001 (UNESCO 2011).

In the first part of this chapter, I lay out the apparent differences and the inconspicuous similarities between the strategies and the tactics of Aleppo's and Acre's plans. In the second part I propose, then test a model that compares the experience of place for foreign tourists and for local residents in each city. My objective is to bridge the making of place through planning and management, and its experience by using a framework that addresses the question: how can the planning and management of a historic city sustain the qualities that contribute to its distinctiveness while concurrently ensuring a balance between the supposedly conflicting needs of local residents and of foreign tourists?

In order to analyze the processes of place making and experience, I traveled to both cities on separate trips between 2004 and 2006 and conducted in-depth interviews with nine planners in Aleppo and 11 in Acre. These interviews incorporated the different perspectives of government employees, private sector entrepreneurs and activists. I also carried out structured interviews in both cities with local residents who lived and/or worked within the areas where each project was implemented. I completed 36 structured interviews in Aleppo and 38 in Acre where each interview lasted anywhere between 45 and 90 minutes depending on the respondent's involvement. I also recruited foreign tourists near tourist attractions until 41 tourists in Aleppo and 28 in Acre completed a survey questionnaire.

Additionally, my personal observations of meetings, workshops, events and lived experiences, as well as my visual analyses of the built environment offered me in-depth insights of the two cities. I also used secondary sources such as planning documents; newspaper articles; journal publications; marketing and promotional materials; websites; and project documents and archives, all of which guided me as I constructed the bigger picture of each city.

Place Making: Two Divergent Plans

Urban heritage tourism triggers two inherent, contradictory and often mutually exclusive conditions. The first stems from the need to develop the historic city for tourism yet simultaneously preserve its distinctive identity (Chang et al. 1996), while the second results from the contradiction of tourism's global demand for distinctively local products (Harvey 2001). Given Old Aleppo's history with invasive contemporary development, it was not surprising that PROCA sought to avoid the challenges presented by these conditions through emphasizing the conservation of the historic urban fabric and the protection of its residential functions. PROCA not only resisted tourism, but altogether rejected it—the Development Plan, PROCA's main document, did not address tourism at all (Windelberg et al. 2001). Key decision-makers openly and adamantly opposed the infiltration of tourism-related services within the residential neighborhoods and introduced land use and licensing policies to restrain the uses that were deemed incompatible with the residential functions. These policies confined tourism services (e.g., cafés and restaurants) to the area around the Citadel of Aleppo, known as the Citadel Circle Road. Considered the city's primary tourist attraction, the Citadel of Aleppo itself was subject to a tourism development initiative under the Historic Cities Programme of the Aga Khan Trust for Culture. It underwent restoration and a new visitors center was introduced along with pathways and visitor management procedures (The Aga Khan Development Network 2007). The planners also emphasized the importance of infrastructure rehabilitation in extending the lifespan of Old Aleppo's historic fabric and considered this as the most significant achievement of PROCA. Infrastructure rehabilitation went hand in hand with urban design interventions such as the re-pavement of streets, sidewalks and public open spaces. Most importantly, PROCA amended Decision 39/1990, a legislation, which was perceived by planners as a "policy of control and regulation" that would "preserve the status quo" of the historic fabric by fending off contemporary development and thus preventing the occurrence of the aforementioned contradictory conditions (Windelberg et al. 2001: 13).

Contrary to PROCA, the Master Plan of Old Acre was driven purely by tourism development. Following UNESCO's selection of Acre among the sites that best represent medieval heritage (Torstrick 2000), and prompted by the anticipated influx of tourists to the Holy Land during the millennium celebrations, the OADC began work on the master plan in 1993. Planners realized early on that tourism development would incur high fixed costs for historic conservation, urban rehabilitation, tourism infrastructure and attractions development (Ashworth and Voogd 1990; Chang et al. 1996; Nuryanti 1996; Robinson 1999). Therefore, the OADC adopted an economically driven planning approach that used marketing to increase tourists' numbers, their length of stay and eventually, their spending (Ashworth and Tunbridge 1990: 73–6; Holcomb 1999; Holloway and Robinson 1995). Although researchers such as Kotler et al. (1993: 135) cautioned that such an approach considers the local residents as a liability to tourism development, several factors drove the planners of Old Acre to fall in this trap. Primarily, they perceived Old Acre as a major Arab stronghold within Israel, one that possessed an image of a drug infested and violent city (Galili and Nir 2001). They also considered Old Acre a national asset, because of its status as a World Heritage Site and the second most visited tourist destination in Israel after Jerusalem. The planners therefore, considered the Arab residents of Old Acre as a liability to tourism development and sought to transfer them to nearby towns in an attempt to create a "museum city" fit for international tourism (Hecht 1997; Kesten 1993: 6; Torstrick 2000). Local residents resisted the several attempts to transfer them until eventually the planners were compelled to focus on the rehabilitation of the entire infrastructure of Old Acre, and to design visitor management strategies that steered tourists away from the Arab residential neighborhoods. The Master Plan proposed trails that took tourists along the city walls, through the souq or marketplace and led them to the city's primary attractions. Urban design interventions endeavored to offer tourists a visually aesthetic experience throughout. Additionally, the Citadel of Acre underwent major restoration, and was equipped with a new visitors center and visitor management procedures. Meanwhile, the planners developed historic conservation policies that classified all the built structures according to their level of architectural and historic significance and then matched them with adequate conservation tactics.

Place Experience: The Physical and Non-Physical Constructs

Long before their inscription on the WHL, Aleppo and Acre have attracted international tourists. Traveling in the eighteenth century, Perry (1743: 141) offered a detailed description of Aleppo as 'a pretty large and well-built city; […] Its houses in common are large, built with a handsome sort of stone, and in a good taste. Some of its streets are spacious and handsome (a rarity in this country) and are well paved with flag stones.' Likewise, Rogers (1975: 73–4) described his arrival from the sea to Acre in 1880: "the external appearance of 'Akka is pre-eminently picturesque, […] No city in Syria or Palestine completely carries one back in fancy to Crusading and feudal times as does this city of 'Akka especially when thus beheld from the sea; if the tall minaret of the great mosque were not there to remind us of the local supremacy of the followers of the prophet Mohammed, we might easily imagine ourselves to be steering towards a stronghold still occupied by Crusading kings."

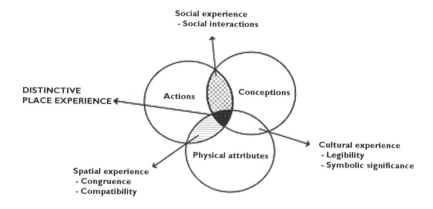

Figure 12.1   The proposed model for assessing the experience of place
Source: adapted from Canter 1977.

These accounts reflect the appreciation of the entire historic fabric, and not only its major monuments, for unlike confined sites and individual monuments, tourism to historic cities incorporates an experiential dimension (Chang et al. 1996; MacCannell 1999). While several disciplines such as geography, architecture, urban design and environmental psychology addressed the notion of place experience, it is the latter that avoided subjectivity by balancing the physical and the non-physical constructs of place (Arefi and Triantafillou 2005: 79; Groat 1995). David Canter (1977: 158) situated place at the center of a balanced interaction between the physical attributes of place, the activities of people within the place and the conception of the place. I propose that the interactions among Canter's three elements create spatial, cultural, and social experiences, each of which comprises of several variables and which collectively bestow a distinctive identity on the place (Figure 12.1). Throughout the remainder of this chapter, I test the ability of this new model to assess the experience of place in World Heritage cities as I apply it in Old Aleppo and in Old Acre.

The Spatial Experience

According to the proposed model (Figure 12.1), the interactions between the activities of people and the physical attributes of place produce a spatial experience that can be evaluated through compatibility and congruence. Compatibility refers to the suitability of the urban form for the functions and the activities undertaken by the users of the city (Lynch 1981). I use incompatibility as an indication of whether planning, driven by economic objectives, prioritized tourists by adopting urban design interventions that form the city according to the needs of foreign tourists rather than the needs of local residents (Boniface and Fowler 1993; Dahles 2001: 10;

Grunewald 2002). The analysis of compatibility revealed that not only in Acre, but also in Aleppo, both the residents and the tourists thought that the city was suitable for the needs of tourists more so than for the needs of residents (Figures 12.2 and 12.3). Understandably, these perceptions were triggered in Old Acre by the emphasis on tourism development but the unexpected finding in Aleppo may be attributed to residents' frustration with the policy of regulation and control imposed on them by Decision 39. The strict implementation of this regulation in commercial areas forced shop owners to modify the façades of their property to comply with pre-set design standards (Figure 12.4). According to Dahles (2001), while such standardization establishes quality control, it also leads to Disneyfication.

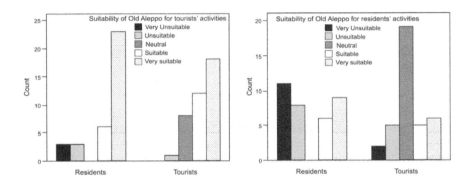

Figure 12.2   A comparison between residents' and tourists' perceptions of the suitability of Old Aleppo for tourists' activities and for residents' activities

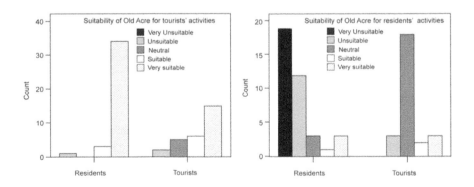

Figure 12.3   A comparison between residents' and tourists' perceptions of the suitability of Old Acre for tourists' activities and for residents' activities

**Figure 12.4   The standardized façades of a commercial street in Old
Aleppo that had to comply with the building regulations of
Decision 39/1999**

Congruence assesses the extent to which the image of the urban form represents
societal processes such as the balance between the city as a living place and as
a tourist destination (Lynch 1981). A lack of congruence entails legitimization,
which tips this balance in the favor of tourism by transforming the local
representations in the urban fabric into the comprehensible and acceptable images
for the consumption of the foreign tourists who come from diverse backgrounds
(Dahles 2001). For example, legitimization occurs when planning emphasizes
the conservation of monuments at the expense of ordinary buildings, and when
it prioritizes tourism-related services over social infrastructure. Indeed, there was
consensus among the residents and the tourists in both cities that planning bestowed
more care on monuments than on the ordinary buildings that are used by local
communities (Figures 12.5 and 12.6). Furthermore, local residents complained
from the lack of social infrastructure especially, clinics and schools. Old Acre's
residents repeated the phrase "the project invests in stone not in people"—eluding
to the project's emphasis on the visual experience of the tourists instead of the
much needed social infrastructure of the local residents. Similarly, by 2005 and
more than 10 years after it had started, PROCA provided only one health unit for
the 110,000 inhabitants of Old Aleppo.

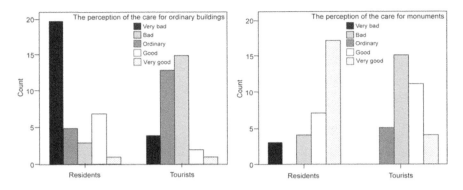

Figure 12.5   A comparison between residents' and tourists' perceptions of the level of care of ordinary buildings and monuments in Old Aleppo

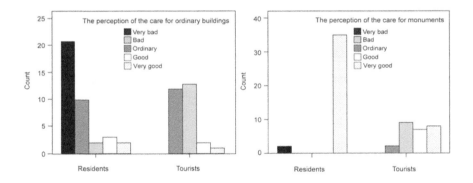

Figure 12.6   A comparison between residents' and tourists' perceptions of the level of care of ordinary buildings and monuments in Old Acre

Disneyfication and legitimization have imposed irreversible changes on the historic fabric in Aleppo and in Acre, and have yielded homogenized urban spaces that lack distinctiveness (Beriatos and Gospodini 2004; Boniface and Fowler 1993). They have influenced the spatial experience of the historic city and have consequently, jeopardized its distinctive identity—the very quality that attracts tourists (Ahn et al. 2002; Bryden 1996; Nasser 2003).

The Cultural Experience

The proposed model recognizes that a cultural experience stems primarily from the intersection of the physical attributes of the historic city and the users' conception of these attributes and includes indicators such as legibility and significance. Legibility indicates users' understanding and interpretation of the place's physical attributes (Lynch 1981; Moughtin and Mertens 2006). The lack of legibility is manifested in residents' inability to mentally represent and communicate information about the historic city such as its monuments, nodes, paths, districts, and edges and was evaluated among local residents through simple cognitive mapping and verbal descriptions. As for the cultural significance of place, ICOMOS Australia (1999: paragraph 1.2) considers that it extends beyond its architectural, historic and aesthetic values to include "the place itself, its fabric, setting, use, associations, meanings, records, related places and related objects." Tourists seek to experience those qualities that contribute to the cultural significance of historic cities in general, and to the outstanding universal value of World Heritage cities in particular. A lack of consensus about what is culturally significant in the historic fabric combined with a lack of legibility indicate a decreased understanding of the relation between the city's physical attributes and their historic and contemporary values (Lynch 1981; Moughtin and Mertens 2006).

Surprisingly, only one of the residents who were interviewed in Aleppo was able to describe the physical layout of the city, while the rest almost unanimously identified only the Citadel of Aleppo but were unable to offer more. In contrast, all the residents who were interviewed in Old Acre revealed a clear legibility of their city and offered detailed visual descriptions of its layout and its relationship to the Mediterranean. They also linked the physical attributes of Old Acre to historic events such as, the city's walls and Napoleon's siege. Also, while the residents of Aleppo chose the citadel as the most distinctive urban element, the residents of Acre chose the entire city. The tourists however, had a different view and chose the traditional souq in both Aleppo and Acre because for them it represented a distinctive aspect of local life (Table 12.2).

By emphasizing the Citadel of Aleppo, planning actually met the expectations of Aleppo's residents of a cultural experience. Conversely, planning in Old Acre perceived the historic city as a national asset and excluded local residents from identifying its cultural significance. The Master Plan of Old Acre considered that the city's distinctiveness, or its Unique Selling Preposition (USP) in marketing terms (Holloway and Robinson 1995; Kotler et al. 1993; Kotler et al. 1999; alWard 1998), lies in its Crusader urban form and history.

Table 12.2   The ranking of the distinctive urban elements of Aleppo and Acre

As a tourist/resident in this city, can you list what you think are the most distinctive elements in it?	Tourists' Percentage		Residents' Percentage	
	Aleppo	Acre	Aleppo	Acre
Souq	47	24	3	0
Citadel	24	20	88	3
Historic fabric	15	16	9	40
City walls (in Acre)	N/A	12	N/A	24
People	6	8	0	3
Baha'i palace (in Acre)	N/A	8	N/A	0
Traffic congestion	6	–	–	–
Religious buildings	0	0	0	11
Harbor and fishermen	N/A	4	N/A	13
Bathhouse (in Acre)	N/A	4	N/A	0
Museum	3	0	0	5
Khan el-Umdan (the Caravanserai of the Pillars in Acre)	N/A	0	N/A	3
Total	100	100	100	100

Interestingly though, what is imaged in marketing as a Crusader city is in reality an eighteenth-century Ottoman construction that follows, to a certain extent, the layout of the Crusader remains beneath it (Philipp 2001). The exclusion of Acre's residents from the commodification of their cultural heritage has alienated them from the place making process, and eventually from its experience (Boniface and Fowler 1993; Graham et al. 2000; Robinson 2001). As Robinson (1999: 11) has argued, such alienation occurs because the commodification of cultural heritage entails, in addition to the city's physical attributes the "ways of life, traditions and the complex symbolism which supports these, are imaged and transformed into saleable products."

The Social Experience

Referring back to Figure 12.1, the social experience of the historic city bridges the users' actions and their conception of the city's physical attributes. Social interactions therefore, are the formal (e.g., active, planned) or informal (e.g., casual, unplanned) social opportunities in which the users of the same place interact together (Kim and Kaplan 2004). I employ the difference in the perception of social interactions between the local residents and the foreign tourists as an indicator of the differences in the social experience of place. When the tourists were asked about their opinions of their interactions with local residents, most of them in both cities considered these interactions as an important part of their social experience of the historic city (Table 12.3). As for the residents of Aleppo, their opinions were divided—while 56% expressed their interest in having more tourists, 44% had reservations against tourism. The latter based their opinions on the social differences between them and the foreign tourists primarily, in terms of dress code, alcohol consumption and cross-gender interactions. Unlike their counterparts in Aleppo, 81% of Old Acre's residents thought that tourism was not foreign to their local culture and actually welcomed tourists and considered their presence as an opportunity to improve their image along with their economic situation. An Old Acre resident said "[we] happily receive tourists and help them whether they were Jewish or foreigners. It is in our best interest to increase tourism in this city." These perceptions of the residents and the tourists contradict with the trails of Old Acre's Master Plan, which steer the tourists away from the local residents.

Table 12.3   Tourists' perception of their interactions with local residents

The interactions I had with local residents are an important part of my experience of this city as a tourist	Aleppo	Acre
	Percentage	Percentage
Disagree / Strongly disagree	11.4	32.1
Neutral	17.1	21.4
Agree / Strongly Agree	71.5	46.4
Total	100.0	100.0

Concluding Remarks: Two Divergent Plans yet Two Similar Approaches

Notwithstanding the differences in their objectives, the analysis revealed that the plans of Aleppo and Acre employed similar place making strategies that emphasized conservation regulations and land use policies. Both plans also adopted identical place making tactics that depended on infrastructure rehabilitation, urban design interventions and tourism management procedures. Therefore, not surprisingly, the two projects were yielding place experiences that had more in common than their seemingly divergent plans endeavored. The local residents and the foreign tourists concurred that place making in both cities produced urban environments that suited tourists more than residents. The policy of control and regulation in Aleppo was as exclusionary of local residents as was the marketing of a Crusader image for Acre—both were formulating an urban environment that alienated local residents.

Furthermore, tourists' preference of the souqs of Aleppo and Acre confirmed findings such as Echtner and Prasad's (2003) of foreign tourists' stereotypical images of historic cities that are static in past times (also see Galani-Moutafi 2000). Simultaneously, local residents valued certain physical elements in their city and considered that their shared perceptions and experiences of these elements bound them together like Anderson's imagined communities (1991). The findings also revealed that the two projects were not inclusive of local residents' perceptions of symbolic significance in the urban landscape. Likewise, both projects gave precedence to the provision of tourism infrastructure and to the conservation of monuments and tourist attractions more so than the provision of social infrastructure and the conservation of ordinary buildings (Pendlebury 2009).

Finally, it is important to emphasize that my intent in this chapter is not to criticize the two projects. Rather, my objective is to propose and test a model that links place making and place experience in World Heritage cities in particular. The proposed model provides a framework that may guide the various stages of the planning process from the initial data collection phase, to the implementation and finally, to the on-going evaluation. Because it stipulates that the historic city is the interface between the place experience of foreign tourists and of local residents, and because it distinguishes between the three types of experiences, the proposed model holds the potential to transform the management plans of World Heritage cities from initiatives that only address the Outstanding Universal Value notion, with its emphasis on the intrinsic values of heritage (i.e., physical attributes), to ones that account for the activities within, and the conceptions of the World Heritage city (i.e., non-physical constructs) (Arefi and Triantafillou 2005). Most importantly, the model is by no means final or conclusive and further research and testing in other cities will help to refine, modify and add to its proposed variables.

References

Ahn, B. Yong, Lee, B. and Shafer, C.S. (2002). Operationalizing Sustainability in Regional Tourism Planning: An Application of the Limits of Acceptable Change Framework. *Tourism Management*, 23(1): 1–15.

Alexander, C., Ishikawa, S. and Silverstein, M. (1977). *A Pattern Language: Towns, Buildings, Construction*. New York: Oxford University Press.

Anderson, B. (1991). *Imagined Communities: Reflections on the Origin and Spread of Nationalism*. London and New York: Verso.

Arefi, M. and Menelaos, T. (2005). Reflections on the Pedagogy of Place in Planning and Urban Design. *Journal of Planning Education and Research*, 25(1): 75–88.

Ashworth, G.J. and Tunbridge, J.E. (1990). *The Tourist-Historic City*. London and New York: Belhaven Press.

Ashworth, G.J. and Henk, V. (1990). *Selling the City: Marketing Approaches in Public Sector Urban Planning*. London: Belhaven Press.

Beriatos, E. and Aspa, G. (2004). "Glocalising" Urban Landscapes: Athens and the 2004 Olympics. *Cities*, 21(3): 187–202.

Boniface, P. and Fowler, P.J. (1993). *Heritage and Tourism in the Global Village*. London: Routledge.

Bryden, D. (1996). Capacity Compromised. *Interpretation*, December: 10–12.

Canter, D. (1977). *The Psychology of Place.* New York: St. Martin's Press.

Chang, T. C., Milne, S., Fallon, D. and Pohlmann, C. (1996). Urban Heritage Tourism: The Global–Local Nexus. *Annals of Tourism Research*, 23(2): 284–305.

Dahles, H. (2001). *Tourism, Heritage and National Culture in Java: Dilemmas of a Local Community.* Richmond, Surrey: Curzon Press.

Echtner, C.M. and Pushkala, P. (2003). The Context of Third World Tourism Marketing. *Annals of Tourism Research*, 30(3): 660–82.

Galani-Moutafi, V. (2000). The Self and the Other: Traveler, Ethnographer, Tourist. *Annals of Tourism Research*, 27(1): 203–24.

Galili, L. and Ori, N. (2001). From the Hebrew Press. *Journal of Palestine Studies*, 30(2): 97–106.

Graham, B., Ashworth, G.J. and Tunbridge, J.E. (2000). *A Geography of Heritage: Power, Culture and Economy.* New York: Oxford University Press.

Groat, L. (1995). Introduction: Place, Aesthetic Evaluation and Home. In: Groat, L. (ed.), *Giving Places Meaning.* London: Academic Press, pp. 1–25.

Grunewald, R. de A. (2002). Tourism and Cultural Revival. *Annals of Tourism Research*, 29(4): 1004–21.

Hartal, M. (1997). Excavation of the Courthouse Site at 'Akko: Summary and Historical Discussion. *'Atiqot*, XXXI: 109–14.

Harvey, D. (2001). The Art of Rent: Globalization and the Commodification of Culture. In: Harvey, D. (ed.), *Spaces of Capital: Towards a Critical Geography.* New York: Routledge.

Hecht, E. (1997). A Sinking City. *The Jerusalem Post.* Jerusalem, October 31: 14.

Holcomb, B. (1999). Marketing Cities for Tourism. In: Judd, D.R. and Fainstein, S.S. (eds), *The Tourist City.* New Haven and London: Yale University Press, pp. 54–70.

Holloway, J.C. and Robinson, C. (1995). *Marketing for Tourism.* Singapore: Longman Group Limited.

ICOMOS Australia (1999). The Burra Charter: The Australia ICOMOS Charter for the Conservation of Places of Cultural Significance. ICOMOS Australia.

Kedar, B.Z. (1997). The Outer Walls of Frankish Acre. *'Atiqot*, XXXI: 157–80.

Kesten, A. (1993). *The Old City of Acre: Re-Examination Report 1993.* Acre: The Old Acre Development Company.

Kim, J. and Kaplan, R. (2004). Physical and Psychological Factors in Sense of Community: New Urbanist Kentlands and Nearby Orchard Village. *Environment and Behavior*, 36(3): 313–40.

Kotler, P., Bowen, J. and Makens, J. (1999). *Marketing for Hospitality and Tourism.* Upper Saddle River, NJ: Prentice-Hall, Inc.

Kotler, P., Haider, D.H. and Rein, I. (1993). *Marketing Places: Attracting Investment, Industry, and Tourism to Cities, States and Nations.* New York: The Free Press, Macmillan, Inc.

Lynch, K. (1960). *The Image of the City.* Cambridge: The MIT Press.

Lynch, K. (1981). *Good City Form.* Cambridge: The MIT Press.

MacCannell, D. (1999). *The Tourist: A New Theory of the Leisure Class*. Berkeley: The University of California Press.

Moughtin, C. and Mertens, M. (2006). *Urban Design: Street and Square*. Oxford: The Architectural Press.

Nasser, N. (2003). Planning for Urban Heritage Places: Reconciling Conservation, Tourism, and Sustainable Development. *Journal of Planning Literature*, 17(4): 467–79.

Norberg-Schultz, C. (1991). *Genius Loci: Towards a Phenomenology of Architecture*. New York: Rizzoli.

Nuryanti, W. (1996). Heritage and Postmodern Tourism. *Annals of Tourism Research*, 23(2): 249–60.

Old Acre Development Company (2010). Old Acre. Available at <ttp://www.akko.org.il/English/main/default.asp> (accessed September 10, 2010).

Orbaşli, A. (2000). *Tourists in Historic Towns: Urban Conservation and Heritage Management*. New York: E. & F.N. Spon.

Pendlebury, J. (2009). *Conservation in the Age of Consensus*. New York: Routledge.

Perry, C. (1743). *A View of the Levant: Particularly of Constantinople, Syria, Egypt, and Greece*. London: T. Woodward.

Philipp, T. (2001). *Acre: The Rise and Fall of a Palestinian City, 1730–1831*. New York: Columbia University Press.

Rahamimoff, J. (ed.) (1997). *Arie Rahamimoff: Architect & Urbanist*. Jerusalem: A.S.R.

Relph, E. (1976). *Place and Placelessness*. London: Pion Limited.

Robinson, M. (1999). Cultural Conflicts in Tourism: Inevitability and Inequality. In: Robinson, M. and Boniface, P. (eds), *Tourism and Cultural Conflicts*. Oxon and New York: CABI Publishing.

Robinson, M. (2001). Tourism Encounters: Inter- and Intra-Cultural Conflicts and the World's Largest Industry. In: AlSayyad, N. (ed.), *Consuming Tradition, Manufacturing Heritage: Global Norms and Urban Forms in the Age of Tourism*. New York: Routledge.

Rogers, M.E. (1975). Acre, the Key of Palestine. In: Wilson, C.W. (ed.), *The Land of Galilee & the North: Including Samaria, Haifa, and the Esdraelon Valley*. Jerusalem: Ariel Publishing House, pp. 73–90.

The Aga Khan Development Network (2007). Syria: Revitalising Historic Sites. In: Aga Khan Trust for Culture: Historic Cities Programme: The Aga Khan Development Network. Available at <http://www.akdn.org/hcp/syria.asp> (accessed April 16, 2011).

Torstrick, R. (2000). *The Limits of Coexistence: Identity Politics in Israel*. Ann Arbor, Michigan: The University of Michigan.

Tuan, Y. (1990). *Topophilia: A Study of Environmental Perception, Attitudes, and Values*. New York: Columbia University Press.

UNESCO (1972). *Convention Concerning the Protection of the World Cultural and Natural Heritage*. Paris: UNESCO.

UNESCO (2008). *Operational Guidelines for the Implementation of the World Heritage Convention*. Paris: World Heritage Center.

UNESCO (2011). The World Heritage Center. Paris. Available at <http://whc.unesco.org/> (accessed April 16, 2011).

Ward, S.V. (1998). *Selling Places: The Marketing and Promotion of Towns and Cities: 1850–2000*. New York: Routledge.

Windelberg, J., Hallaj, O.A.A. and Stürzbecher, K. (2001). *The Development Plan*. Deutsche Gesellschaft für Technische Zusammenarbeit (GTZ) and Aleppo's Old City Directorate.

Chapter 13

Le Morne Cultural Landscape Heritage Site: Its Different Senses of Attachment and Contestation

Chaya Hurnath and Priscilla Sambadoo

Traditionally, developing tropical islands such as Mauritius have concentrated their promotional efforts on boosting their tourism economies via the Sun, Sea and Sand (three Ss). However, with the realization that cultural heritage is a resource for tourism; many traditional beach destinations are refocusing their planning and marketing efforts to include heritage attractions (Bennet 1993; Dallen and Nyaupane 2009; Luxner 1999; McCabe 1992). Due to the perceived potential of increasing tourism revenues through world recognized United Nations Educational, Scientific and Cultural Organisation (UNESCO) Heritage Sites; many countries are vying to have their own sites inscribed. However, this tacit assumption has not been substantiated so far according to Hall and Piggin (2007) and for Li et al. (2008).

Heritage sites, as well, are being increasingly endowed with new sets of tasks and responsibilities, few of which can be reconciled (Ashworth et al. 2007). From having economic functions to political ones of nation-building, without forgetting its cultural roles of producing collective identities or creating cultural boundedness, heritage in general is becoming an organizing topic in academia. However, the processes of heritagization of sites are inherently fraught with conflicts, conflicts of meaning and territorial conflicts. This is demonstrated by Hall (1997: 61) who states *"It is us—in society, within human culture who make things mean, who signify. Meanings, consequently, will always change, from one culture or period to another."* Management of heritage sites and the various systems of meanings attributed to these sites inevitably imply some levels of conflict among different groups with attachment to the heritage sites (Kaltenborn and Williams 2002; Mêlée 2003). These conflicts can best be envisaged through the premise of place attachment to heritage sites. Much of the literature on place resource conflict is studied through the "insider-outsider distinction," thereby giving rise to irreconcilable visions of the way place ought to be used, developed and managed (Chang 2000).

After reading different local newspapers, the authors embarked on this exploratory research to understand the current situation at the World Heritage Site of Le Morne Cultural Landscape (LMCL). Indeed fears that the inscription will be removed have brought about fundamental questions regarding the need and reasons for its very existence amongst various stakeholders in Mauritius.

Hence, the objective of this chapter is to assess the varying degrees of place attachment of stakeholders from the prism of "insider-outsider" dichotomy. This is done at two levels. Firstly, the important aspects of the heritage site and its associated senses of attachment are looked at. Secondly, it is to examine the emerging territorial claims and conflicts due the heritage site. In this respect, armed with an interview guide measuring six dimensions of place attachment, face-to-face interviews were conducted (Hurnath and Sambadoo 2010).

The chapter begins with an overview of the conceptual underpinnings of place attachment from a human geography perspective. Relph's model (1976) of "insideness-outsideness" dichotomy is introduced along with other supporting concepts. The substantive part of the chapter discusses three different relationships between insider-outsider groups of old-time and new residents, Creoles and non-Creoles and hoteliers (users) and planners of the heritage site. Discussions will eventually end with the support for heritage sites and the level of place attachment.

The Concept of Place Attachment

In the humanistic and phenomenological tradition within geography, place refers itself to the locales in which people find themselves live, have experiences, interpret, understand and find meanings (Peet 1998). Indeed, places are not only the physical location in space as per the positivistic view of the 1960s but they are defined according to the sets of practices and behaviors, social interactions and representations that people assign to them. The related academic literature on the associations between place and people can be subsumed under a plethora of classifications: rootedness (Hummon 1992), topophilia (Tuan 1974), sense of place (Hay 1998; Relph 1976), place attachment (Altman and Low 1992; Williams 2002) and place identity (Barth 1969; Beheldi 2006; Bonnemaison et al. 1999; Cuba and Hummon 1993; Debarbieux 2006; Di Meo 2004; Guerin-Pace and Guermond 2006; le Bosse 1999).

In his book, Mêlée et al. (2003) identified different groups of people who possess divergent territorial claims on a place and in our case, on a heritage site. Firstly, he mentions conflicts or oppositions between inhabitants, users and public actors. The nature of their oppositions can be in terms of the choice of implantation of a structure, conflicts in terms of perceived potential impacts of a territorial project or in terms of environmental concerns of an existing activity. Picon (1988) on the other hand contends that conflicts over place can occur between the inhabitants themselves while Ripoll and Veschambre (2002) analyses social and political conflicts under their spatial and territorial dimensions. These works echo an important theme relevant to the study of LMCL Heritage Site—that is territorial conflicts are derived primarily from divergent spatial ideologies best conceived in terms of insider-outsider disparities, first conceived by Relph's (1976: 49) "insideness-outsideness" distinction (see Table 13.1).

The "inside-outside" dialectic is conceptually useful to interrogate territorial conflicts as it tells us that spatial conflicts arise from ideological differences. A number of other conceptual viewpoints can be further studied as a way to deepen Relph's spectrum while throwing more light on the issue of territorial struggle (Chang 2000).

Table 13.1   Relph's Model of Insideness-outsideness

MODES OF INSIDENESS and OUTSIDENESS
1. EXISTENTIAL INSIDENESS
A situation involving a feeling of attachment and at-homeness. Place is "experienced without deliberate and self-conscious reflection yet is full with significances." One feels this is the place where he or she belongs. The deepest kind of place experience and the one toward which we probably all yearn.
2. EXISTENTIAL OUTSIDENESS
A situation where the person feels separate from or out of place. Place may feel alienating, unreal, unpleasant, or oppressive. Homelessness or homesickness would be examples. Often, today, the physical and designed environments contribute to this kind of experience *unintentionally*—the sprawl of suburban environments, the dissolution of urban downtowns, the decline of rural communities.
3. OBJECTIVE OUTSIDENESS
A situation involving a deliberate dispassionate attitude of separation from place. Place is a thing to be studied and manipulated as an object apart from the experiencer. A scientific approach to place and environment. Ironically, the approach to place often taken by planners, designers, and policy makers.
4. INCIDENTAL OUTSIDENESS
A situation in which place is the background or mere setting for activities—for example, the landscapes and places one drives through as he or she is on the way to somewhere else.
5. BEHAVIORAL INSIDENESS
A situation involving the deliberate attending to the appearance of place. Place is seen as a set of objects, views, or activities. For example, the experience we all pass through when becoming familiar with a new place—figuring out what is where and how the various landmarks, paths, and so forth all fit together to make one complete place.
6. EMPATHETIC INSIDENESS
A situation in which the person, as outsider, tries to be open to place and understand it more deeply. This kind of experience requires interest, empathy, and heartfelt concern. Empathetic insideness is an important aspect of approaching a place phenomenologically.
7. VICARIOUS INSIDENESS
A situation of deeply-felt secondhand involvement with place. One is transported to place through imagination-through paintings, novels, music, films, or other creative media. One thinks, for example, of Monet's paintings of his beloved garden Giverny or of Thomas Hardy's novels describing nineteenth-century rural England.

Source: Seamon 1996.

Cresswell's (1996) notion of being in place as opposed to "out of place" can be also relevant. According to the author, feelings of "displacement" or "out of placeness" arise when individuals fall short of the rules and regulations governing society. Hay (1998) has differentiated differing degrees of insideness from the superficial sense of place among tourists and transients, the partial sense of place among long-term visitors and holiday home owners, the personal sense of place typical of residents, to ancestral and cultural sense of place. According to him, the high level of residential mobility in modern society encourages the development of partial or personal sense of place, noting that *"those with superficial connections to place do not develop the strong attachment that is often found among insiders raised in the place"* (Hay 1998: 5).

The insider-outsider cleavage is also well captured by Lefebvre's (1991) distinction between "representational spaces" and "spaces of representation." While the first refers to spaces that are used in everyday life by the lay person, the latter refers to the planned or controlled spaces of the powerful members of which include planners, architects and technocrats. Where the behavior of the lay person coincides with the "rule of behavior" as prescribed by planners, tensions are diffused. Conversely, conflicts occur when different stakeholders have divergent perspectives on the way space ought to be used and developed, contrary to government planning ideals. In urban planning, the state works from a functionalist perspective as an "outsider," holding such values such as pragmatism and rationalism. This posture demands that *"planners separate themselves emotionally from the places which they are planning and to restructure them according to principles of logic, reason and efficiency"* (Relph 1976: 52).

While humanistic geographers have focused on the experience of insideness, for critics the nature and desirability of insideness is contested and problematic. According to Giuliani and Feldman (1993), the humanistic tradition has focused on the negative consequences of outsideness and placelessness, the sense of decline in community and neighborhood and concerns over high residential mobility. Thus, while strong place bonds are seen as having a positive effect on psychological wellbeing from the humanistic perspective, such bonds may be mal-adaptative as low mobility is strongly associated with low economic and social well-being.

To understand the current nature of place attachment, support or conflict at the LMCL Heritage Site, it was imperative that we acknowledge the many stakeholders involved and their relationship with each other in the forms of outright conflicts or subtle negotiation. Hence, three types of interpersonal relationships were interrogated: old and new residents' relationship to Le Morne Village, interethnic ties and lastly hoteliers' (users) and planners' dynamics to the heritage site.

Background of Le Morne Cultural Landscape (LMCL)

Currently, Mauritius has two inscribed UNESCO World Heritage Sites and despite their universal values, both of them are clearly associated to two prominent ethnic groups at a national scale. The mountain, Le Morne Brabant (see Figure 13.1) was officially inscribed on the UNESCO list in July 2008.[1] A few years prior to the designation of the site, heated debates on the position of Creole history and identity were unleashed throughout the country. Nevertheless, according to Boswell (2006), these debates have generated very few reflections on the ramifications of the UNESCO designation on the development of the area. Though the Management Plan of LMCL contains a local development plan for the inhabitants of Le Morne village,[2] the Village Chief claims that none of the promises (employment creation, increased facilities) made to them prior to designation have been concretized. As a result, support for the heritage site seems to be diminishing and territorial contestation is increasing.

Has the inscription as UNESCO Heritage Site changed the perspectives of the inhabitants? In return, has their sense of attachment to the place and their own identity evolved as well? As this heritage site is mostly associated with the Creoles, do local people of other ethnic groups feel left out? Has this modified their relationship with the Creole community? What are the reactions of the planners in face of the claims of the Chief of the village? As this designation which has limited their tourism activities in the core and buffer zones, how are hoteliers reacting? To what degree are there conflicts and complementarities between various stakeholders and the heritage site? These are some guiding questions that steered this exploratory research.

---

1 It has long occupied a space of importance in Mauritian mythology and history as it was used as a refuge for slaves who managed to escape from brutal conditions on sugarcane plantations elsewhere on the island. Universally, the heritage site symbolically represents the resistance of mankind to slavery as it is said that the runaway slaves preferred to throw themselves from the top of the mountain rather than be brought back in captivity.

2 This region of Mauritius is not well developed. In fact, due to its topography of mountain ranges, the peninsula and neighboring villages have remained quite remote compared to other places in Mauritius. These were the very conditions that enabled the settlement of runaway slaves. Even after the abolition of slavery; the freed slaves chose this area to live in self-sufficiency based on fishing and maize cultivation. Until 1979, the village of Le Morne was situated on the slope of the Mountain but the local people were displaced further away by a rich, Franco-Mauritian landowner who converted the land into a deer grazing pasture. Road access, access to potable water, electricity, schools and other public institutions were still very limited in 2000. In fact, according to the Central Statistical Office report, it is considered as one of the poorest area and the Region Development Index (RDI, as per Figure 13.2) is less than 0.499. Together with low development, this area registers low economic performance and high social problems such as alcoholism, low literacy level and poor access to jobs.

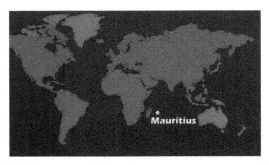

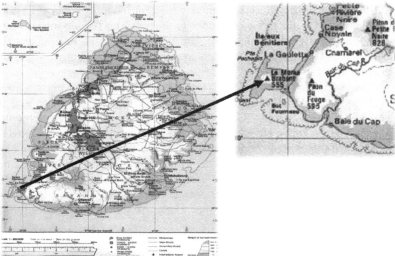

Figure 13.1   Geographical position of Mauritius and LMCL Heritage Site
Notes: Core Zone: 349 hectares; Buffer Zone: 2,407 hectares; 5 hotels on the Morne Peninsula; 50,000 tourists per year.
Source: Management Plan of LMCL, 2008.

Le Morne Cultural Landscape: An Increasingly Contested Place

The Long-Time—New Residents Dichotomy

The results show that long-time residents tend to have a very strong feeling of at-homeness and attachment to their village and area. For R11, *"being cut from other villages by rivers in the southern part and mountains on the East, the sea on the west and little road access on the North have created a cocoon in which they live and interact."* Despite the determinism implied, these residents have had to adapt themselves to their environment. As R2 says,

If I don't have money to buy food, my father dives to get fish from the sea, we can use the wood from the mountains for fire and we can eat it with a bit of green chili. I do not travel much to go elsewhere because it costs a lot to take the public bus. I have never wanted to leave this place to go elsewhere, some persons did so but they have returned after a few years. They went to Quatre Bornes (the nearest town) to find jobs. I did not want to go because I feel free here. I am proud that we have been able to build a concrete house compared to others. Now, with Mama's association of Old Citizens, we are trying to help others to uplift themselves as well. The village is slowly changing, more and more residents are building concrete houses by following our example.

From this, we can infer that this is the strongest sense of place experience in what Relph termed as "existential insideness."

On the other hand, two types of reactions could be studied from the residents who settled in Le Morne Village quite recently. Hence, R7 moved to the village since the designation in order to set up a guesthouse and *table d'hôte*. Though motivated by financial strategies at the beginning, R7 reckons that

We are slowly starting to understand the mindset of the people here. Alongside, we have discovered that there is a strong solidarity between them, traditional values of neighborhood keeps the cohesion of this village. When we announced to our friends that we were moving to Le Morne, they were very apprehensive because of the reputation of the village. But I am happy that we did it.

Conversely, also motivated by economic strategies, R10's view on the village is quite different. She moved to the Morne village after hearing that the State was regularizing the situation of squatters, occupying state land illegally. She settled in the part of the village called, *Dilo Puri* (literally meaning rotten water). For R10,

… my family was not welcomed in this village. We don't have access to fresh water nor to electricity. Our children don't go to school either. We just wanted to have a place of our own.

As per Relph's model, these two reactions could be classified as that of "empathetic insideness" for R7 and "behavioral insideness" for R10.

The Creole–Non Creole Interaction

According to Chang (2000), the insider-outsider dichotomy may also be dissected along ethnic lines. As mentioned earlier, despite the universal value of LMCL, it is strongly associated with the Creole community nationally. Two Hindus, also living in the village of Le Morne were interrogated for this purpose along with the Creoles. At a local level, both groups of people displayed existential insideness to the village.

The User-Planner Dichotomy

Conflicts can occur between these two sets of planners and users in terms of values attached to the heritage sites. In the case of LMCL, different types of reactions from the hoteliers and planners could be observed. The planners of LMCL are natives of the village of Le Morne and are employed by the Morne Heritage Trust Fund (MHTF). An interesting reaction is that with the diminishing support of the villagers to the heritage site, there are increasingly feelings of resentment against the latter. For R9,

> The other fellow villagers have started to view my presence with suspicion and wariness. Before, they were very proud of me but now, I feel that they are wary of me as the promises made to them have not yet been concretized. We are slowly working towards achieving the goals set in the management plan. We are planning to train locals to become tour guides in the near future. At the same time, we try to support a local who has opened a guest house as the experts of ICOMOS stay at her place.

It seemed that the site officer had moved from existential insideness to existential outsideness from the villagers' perspectives.

Concerning the hotel operators, three respondents displayed different types of insideness-outsideness to the heritage site. For R13 and R15,

> ... the hotel has been the first beach resort to be developed on the island in the 1970s and since then, has been renovated several times. The sense of attachment of the repeat customers (30 percent) to this hotel and place is very strong.

In this sense, they displayed characteristics of "behavioral insideness." On the other hand, for R14,

> The concept of the hotel club is similar to that of Club Med whereby tourists come on all-inclusive packages and stay within the premises of the hotel. The main aim of the tourists to come here is to have fun. The heritage site is a mere backdrop for the tourists as they are basically not cultural tourists.

According to Relph's model (1976), this would be classified as incidental outsideness.

In the second part of the research, the interviewees were asked their opinions since the inscription of the site.

Critical Issues Leading to Potential Territorial Conflicts

The following issues emerged in the research relating the perception and image of the site and, to the ownership of the site.

Tendency to Essentialize the Site to an Ethnic Group

Sources of conflicts are not arising between Creoles and non-Creoles but they do bring to light the delicate nature of interethnic relations. The mountain has become a *"duty of recollection for the Creoles"* but the non-Creoles claim that they have also guarded over the mountain and that they also have attachments to it. As R4 says, *"when you are poor, you do not think of your ethnic community."* This sentiment is confirmed by R1, herself a Creole. As she describes the hardships experienced by the villagers, she refers to the strong sense of interdependence with non-Creoles. Food shortages meant that Creole locals had to depend on maize cultivated by the Hindus. A local Chinese shopkeeper owned the maize mill and R1 worked for him to crush the maize in flour, hence demonstrating the strong inter-ethnic contact and exchange in the village. However, these relations are not showcased nor valorized in the heritagization process of the site. Focus is on the lives of the slaves and not on that of their descendents and the inherent ingenious cooperation between the locals. In a multicultural country like Mauritius, cultural boundedness and absence of inter-ethnic links could have had significant impacts on the efforts of nation-building.

When interrogated about the designation, most of the respondents claimed that they were happy to have finally come out of anonymity [*"at last we were on the world map,"* R16]. However, when probed further, local people displayed a tendency to equate conservation of the site as backwardness and perceived it as antithetical to modernity. While the site is universally recognized as a symbol of resistance against human domination, for them, it is a site that is reminiscent of their humble past. As Timothy (1999) says, conservation is seen as standing still, in opposition to progress and development.

Another significant reaction to note is that of the Creoles of the village against those from the rest of the country. A national day of Commemoration of Slavery has been designated every 1st February. This is the occasion whereby the Creole Community from across the country is invited to celebrate this day at the LMCL site. Apart from the traditional formal commemoration ceremony, a cultural show is also programmed. The interrogated respondents felt that there was a strong cleavage between them and the 'other' creoles. As R16 says,

> For these people, it is an occasion to come and enjoy themselves by the beach. They throw lots of litter, get drunk and fight in between themselves. Whatever respectability we had obtained from the designation is destroyed as these people create more problems. Finally, this impacts on the image of our village and we get a bad reputation.

Feelings of Alienation from the Territory

The heritagization process has created a sense of unease regarding the value of the mountain itself amongst the villagers. According to Boswell (2006), the villagers, whose memory, myths and storytelling endowed the mountain with significance, have been for a long time the informal guardians of the site. Now the site has come under the formal management of the Morne Heritage Trust Fund. Long-time residents (irrespective of ethnic belonging) who experience an existential insideness to the area, have a strong feeling of alienation from the site that has been part of their identity as well as a source of sustenance for a long time.

Feelings of Deprivation from Their Source of Sustenance

Indeed, since the villagers have been for a long time marginalized from the rest of the island, they have developed ingenious ways of livelihood by making use of resources available from the mountain and its surroundings. According to Boswell (2006), their settlement on the mountain slope had already been displaced in 1979 by a land exploiter for deer raising purposes. With the designation, they are now being deprived of their source of sustenance without any compensation in return. Indeed, though the Management Plan (2008) makes a provision to bring about local development, the villagers have not seen any improvement in their living conditions, as R10 says "they [site officers from the MHTF] come to talk to us but it is only talk. We have not seen anything yet. Instead, we can't go to the mountain anymore. They told us that they will give us a piece of land on the mountain but we are still waiting. Again what would we do with this land if we cannot develop anything on it?"

Skepticism towards the Economic Value of the Designation

The designation has also changed their perception of the site from an everyday, ordinary landscape to an economic resource and the villagers would like to reap the benefit in terms of development and modernization. As Dallen and Nyaupane (2009) say, nearly always, public opinions about heritage in less developed countries are based on its perceived economic value and there will be little support for it unless residents can connect to it economically (Cohen 1978; Timothy 1999). This according to Feilden (1993) is understandable because in places where health care, food and education are in short supply and where people go hungry, conservation of the tangible environment is unlikely to be high on their list of priorities. This is illustrated by R12 who says, "Can you eat heritage [ou capav manz patrimoine ou]?"

Disputed Rights to Financially Exploit the Site

Another source of conflict could arise, between long-time and new residents. As mentioned earlier, the new residents settled in the village for economic reasons, R7 by setting up a tourism business and R10 to have a piece of land property. Long-time residents feel they are the ones who are more entitled to reap the benefits of the designation since they have living in the village for a long time rather than by the new residents. However, according to the site planner R3,

> ... the guest house operator (R6) can barely read or speak properly and has a lot of difficulty to interact with potential tourists. We try to give them as much support but since they are not educated even to a basic level, they cannot find jobs in hotels or operate businesses.

The Conservation vs. Development Dilemma

Since the designation, conservation around the buffer zone has become stricter. Hoteliers, who have a long-term vision for their properties, view conservation positively as it means that development for new hotels and risks of competitors is minimized. At the same time, conservation means that the surrounding environment will be maintained, as such safekeeping the very reasons that loyal customers choose to come back to these resorts. However, the contribution of the hoteliers in supporting the MHTF is very minimal.

A major conflict between the MHTF and the potential developers of an Integrated Resort Scheme project[3] (IRS) is taking place, henceforth re-launching the question of conservation or development of the site. In 2004, the director of the Societe Morne Brabant (SMB) initiated an IRS project on the Morne Peninsula and was granted approval in 2005. However, with the designation of the LMCL in July 2008, this project has been frozen by the MHTF as it falls right into the core zone of the site. The SMB is now suing the Mauritian State and has even gone to the UNESCO Commission in Paris to complain about the imposed conservation. The problem is even more compounded by the fact that the villagers would have preferred to have the IRS project built as it would have meant that jobs would have been created. As per the Environmental Impact Assessment Report of the IRS project (2006), 2–3 people would have been employed per villa constructed.

---

3   IRSs are exclusive second-residences that are aimed at foreign purchasers and who are given permanent residence permits in Mauritius.

Conclusion

Employing Relph's (1976) concept of insideness-outsideness, this chapter has focused on the sense of attachments and ensuing conflicts arising from differences of values between three different groups in the area of LMCL. The fluidity of the insider-outsider boundary is re-emphasized as who constitutes an insider and who represents the outsider is open to negotiation. Moreover, it has been argued that landscape contestation is a highly dynamic process and some issues of territorial struggle on the LMCL were discussed. In Mauritius, not everyone agrees on how to manage the cultural heritage of Le Morne. The local villagers, who have been the guardians of the memory of the site, have expressed pride to be finally connected to the rest of the country and to the world. They have also expressed wishes to have more employment and to have community development in terms of education, poverty eradication, a decrease in social problems and more amenities in the village. At the same time, it has been demonstrated that interethnic dependence coexists in the village and that the association of the site to a specific ethnic group is creating cultural boundedness and alienation. Though the Management Plan of the LMCL includes a chapter on a Local Development Plan, it is not clear whether the plans proposed or even the IRS proposers will achieve the cherished goals of the villagers. Hence, there seems to be a growing sense of dissatisfaction among the local people and their initial support to the nomination dossier is dwindling. This brings us to reflect upon the representations, values and hopes that different sets of players project on a given territory. How the concerned authorities will balance the needs of the heritage management and economic growth of this particular area needs to be studied more profoundly in order to bring light to heritage and their sustainability in postcolonial developing countries. This can be done by using the concept of "sense of place attachment" to bring light to territorial representations and conflict.

References

Altman, I. and Low, S.M. (1992). Place Attachment: A Conceptual Inquiry. In: Altman, I. and Low, S.M. (eds), *Place Attachment: Human Behaviour and the Environment*. Advances in Theory and Research, 12. New York: Plenum Press, pp. 1–12.

Ashworth, G.J., Graham, B. and Tunbridge, J.E. (2007). *Pluralising Pasts: Heritage, Identity and Place in Multicultural Societies*. London: Pluto Press.

Barth, F. (1969). *Ethnic Groups and Boundaries*. London: Georges Allen & Unwin.

Beheldi, A. (2006). Territoires, appartenance et identification. Quelques réflexions a partir du cas tunisien. *L'Espace Géographique*, 35(4): 310–16.

Bennet, J. (1993). *Travel to Europe … in the Caribbean*. Europe, pp. 19–22.

Bonnemaison, J., Calbrezy, L. and Quinty-Bourgeois, C. (1999). *Les Territoires de l'identité. Le Territoire lien ou frontière?* Tome I. Paris: L'Harmattan.

Boswell, R. (2006). Heritage Tourism and Identity in the Mauritian Villages of Chamarel and Le Morne. *Journal of Southern African Studies*, 2(31): 283–95.

Chang, T.C. (2000). Singapore's Little India: A Tourist Attraction as a Contested Landscape. *Urban Studies*, 2(37): 343–66.

Cohen, E. (1978). The Impact of Tourism on the Physical Environment. *Annals of Tourism Research*, 5(2): 215–37.

Cresswell, T. (1996). *In Place/Out of Place: Geography, Ideology and Transgression*. Minneapolis, MN: University of Minnesota Press.

Cuba, L. and Hummon, D.M. (1993). A Place to Call Home: Identification with Dwelling, Community and Region. *The Sociological Quarterly*, 34(1): 111–31.

Dallen, T.J. and Nyaupane, G.P. (2009). *Cultural Heritage and Tourism in the Developing World: A Regional Perspective*. New York: Routledge.

De Cauna, A. (2006). Le Multiculturalisme à l'île Maurice, pour une lecture géographique. *Géographie et Cultures*, 58(1): 23–45.

Debarbieux, B. (2006). Prendre Position: Réflexions sur les ressources et les limites de la notion d'identité en géographique. *L'Espace Géographique*, 35(1): 340–54.

Di Méo, G. (1995). Patrimoine et territoire, une parenté conceptuelle. *Espaces et Sociétés*, 78(3): 15–34.

Di Meo, G. (2004). Composantes spatiales, formes et processus géographiques des identities. *Annales de Géographie*, 638–9(July–October): 339–444.

Eriksen, T.H. (1998). *Common Denominators: Ethnicity, Nation-Building and Compromise in Mauritius*. Oxford: Berg.

Feilden, B.M. (1993). Is Conservation of Cultural Heritage Relevant to South Asia? *South Asian Studies*, 9(2): 1–10.

Guerin-Pace, F. and Guermond, Y. (2006). Identité et rapport au territoire. *L'Espace Geographique*, 4(35): 289–90.

Guiliani, M.V. and Felman, R. (1993). Place Attachment in a Developmental and Cultural Context. *Journal of Environmental Psychology*, 13(3): 267–74.

Hall, C.M. and Piggin, R. (2001). Tourism and World Heritage in OECD Countries. *Tourism Recreation Research*, 1(26): 103–5.

Hall, S. (ed.) (1997). *Representation: Cultural Representations and Signifying Practices*. London: Sage/Open University.

Hay, R. (1998). Sense of Place in Developmental Context. *Journal of Environmental Psychology*, 21(1): 5–16.

Hummon, D.M. (1992). Community Attachment: Local Sentiment and Sense of Place. In: Altman, I. and Low, S.M. (eds), *Place Attachment*. New York: Plenum, pp. 253–78.

Hurnath, C. and Sambadoo, P. (2010). *Le Morne Cultural Landscape Heritage Site: Its Different Senses of Attachment and Support*. 2010 Conference World Heritage and Tourism, June 2–4, Quebec City, Quebec, Canada (refereed proceedings).

Kaltenborn, B.P. and Williams, D.R. (2002). The Meaning of Place: Attachments to Femundsmarka National Park, Norway among Tourists and Locals. *Norwegian Journal of Geography*, 56(3): 189–98.

Le Bosse, M. (1999). Les Questions d'Identité dans la Géographie Culturelle: quelques aperçus contemporains. *Géographie et Cultures*, 31: 31–8.

Lefebvre, H. (1991). *The Production of Space*, translated by D. Nicholson-Smith. Oxford: Basil Blackwell.

Li, M., Wu, B. and Cai, L. (2008). Tourism Development of World Heritage Sites in China: A Geographical Perspective. *Tourism Management*, 29(1): 308–19.

Luxner, L. (1999). Reviving Haiti's Paradise. *Americas*, 4(51): 48–54.

McCabe, C. (1992). The Carribean Heritage. *Islands*, 4(12): 62–76.

Mêlée, P., Larrue, C. and Rosemberg, M. (2003). *Conflits et Territoires*. Presses Universitaires Francois-Rabelais, Maison des Sciences de l'homme 'Villes et Territoires.'

Peet, R. (1998). *Modern Geographical Thought*. Oxford: Blackwell.

Picon, B. (1988). *L'espace et le temps en Camargue*. Arles: Actes Sud.

Relph, E. (1976). *Place and Placelessness*. London: Pion.

Ripoll, F. and Veschambre, V. (2002). Face à l'hégémonie du territoire: éléments pour une réflexion critique. In: Jean, Y. and Calenge, C. (eds), *'Lire les territoires,'* Villes et Territoires, 3: 261–88.

Seamon, D. (1996). A Singular Impact: Edward Relph's Place and Placelessness. *Environmental and Architectural Phenomenology Newsletter*, 7(3): 5–8.

Timothy, D.J. (1999). Built Heritage, Tourism and Conservation in Developing Destination. *Journal of Sustainable Tourism*, 1(61): 52–68.

Tuan, Y.F. (1974). *Topophilia. A Study of Environmental Perception, Attitudes and Values*. Englewoods Cliffs, New Jersey: Prentice Hall.

Williams, D.R. and Vaske, J.J. (2003). The Measurement of Place Attachment: Validity and Generalizability of a Psychometric Approach. *Forest Science*, 49(6): 6–18.

Chapter 14

Expectations and Experiences of Visitors at the Giant's Causeway World Heritage Site, Northern Ireland

Kevin R. Crawford

Introduction

Understanding and conceptualizing tourist experiences has been a key research issue since the 1960s (Uriely 2005). Even after more than 40 years, the nature of contemporary tourist experiences continues to be an important research focus amongst tourism researchers. Examples of such work can be found in Ryan (2002) and Sharpley and Stone (2010). Today the focus of research into tourists' expectations and experiences largely examines and explores the concept of postmodern (or post-mass) tourism (Uriely 2005) and responses to transformations in the dynamic socio-cultural world of tourism (Sharpley and Stone 2010). One area where this has particular resonance has been in world of heritage tourism. Studies into visitor experiences and expectations at cultural heritage settings have been a key research focus in heritage tourism studies since the early 1990s. In many cases, this has focused on improving the understanding of tourists' experiences, motivations and expectations, for example, in early studies such as Pocock (1992), Parrinello (1993) and Light (1995a) and more recently in Poria et al. (2006a, 2006b), Mason and Kuo (2008), de Rojas and Camarero (2008), and Chen and Chen (2010). In addition to this, the nature of the interpretation provided plays a key role in the tourist experience of heritage sites (Poria et al. 2006a, 2009) and can contribute to a memorable experience (Gilmore et al. 2007). Gilmore et al. (2007) further state that interpretation affects the satisfaction derived from a visit by adding value and meaning thereby helping visitors appreciate the site. Interpretation can also be a tool to attract visitors to a site especially if there is competition between sites and tourist attractions (Poria 2010).

Literature on interpretation at heritage settings commonly involves studies on the content of the interpretation, the display, or the educational contribution, rather than on the tourists' expectation of interpretation (Poria et al. 2006a, 2009; Poria 2010). This has been particularly true in studies that have taken place in geological heritage settings. Most published work relating to interpretation at geological heritage sites (geosites) focuses on raising awareness and understanding of geological information e.g. Burek and Davies (1994), Dias and Brilha (2004), Hose (1996, 1997, 2006) and Pralong (2006). These authors mainly report on engagement of the general public with the geological heritage or the development of interpretation rather than on studies associated with expectations and experiences of the on-site interpretation. These studies are important, since from a geological perspective, raising awareness is a key requirement of any visit to a geosite given that public understanding of geology and geological heritage issues is generally poor and most people are unfamiliar with geological knowledge (Dias and Brilha 2004). Hose (1996, 1997, 2006) indicates that appropriate geological interpretive provision is important in not only informing visitors about geosites but can also ensure that they will understand and recall the information relating to the geosite. Pralong (2006) explores this further by indicating that on-site interpretation at geosites needs to be more adapted to the visitors' expectations and more striking and original ways of communication have to be developed in order to improve their overall experience of the site.

In order to explore many of the points highlighted here, a case study on tourists' expectations and experiences of a key geological heritage site in the UK; the Giant's Causeway and Causeway Coast World Heritage Site is presented and discussed. Given the gap in heritage tourism literature pertaining to geological heritage sites and the paucity of information on tourists' expectation of interpretation, the survey findings presented here may help to reduce the gap and add to the research in the area of geological heritage interpretation.

Giant's Causeway and Causeway Coast World Heritage Site

The Giant's Causeway and Causeway Coast World Heritage Site has an area of 71 hectares and occupies a thin, approximately 5 km strip of coast, between Causeway Head and Benbane Head on the north coast of County Antrim in Northern Ireland. The main Giant's Causeway feature is owned by the National Trust (a charitable NGO) who first acquired it in 1961. Doughty (2008) states that the name "Giant's Causeway" derives from a local Irish legend that the causeway was built by a giant named Finn MacCool. Although having cultural mythological significance, the Giant's Causeway name also reflects the nature of the geological features contained within the site. The geology of the Giant's Causeway itself (Causeway Stones) consists of approximately 40,000 basalt columns which were formed 60 million years ago during a series of intense volcanic eruptions that were linked to the opening of what is now the North Atlantic Ocean (Lyle 1996, 2002; Smith 2005; Tomkeieff 1940). International acknowledgement of the geological importance of the Giant's Causeway (and Causeway Coast) came in 1986 with its inscription on the World Heritage list as a natural site under the World Heritage Convention.

The National trust owned part of the World Heritage Site is a popular tourist attraction with over 750,000 people visiting each year (based on 2008 visitor numbers) and is actively promoted and marketed as Northern Ireland's top tourist attraction (Boyd and Timothy 2006). As a result, it has become a "must-see" tourist attraction for anyone visiting Northern Ireland. This popularity as a tourist attraction presents significant challenges to the site not only in terms of the management of large numbers of visitors and the visitor experience (Cochrane and Tapper 2006) but also in its conservation.

The visitor experience has been based around temporary on-site visitor facilities since a fire all but destroyed the visitor center in 2000. The facilities are jointly managed by the National Trust and the local authority (Moyle District Council) and include a car park, visitor information center, shop selling literature on the site, and a café. It has been acknowledged in the Giant's Causeway and Causeway Coast World Heritage Site Management Plan (Environment and Heritage Service et al. 2005) and by Gilmore et al. (2007) that the temporary facilities are inadequate for a World Heritage Site. It is anticipated that this will be addressed when a new visitor center is opened in summer 2012. Possibly as a consequence of the temporary facilities, Doughty (2008) feels that there are unresolved issues at the site particularly in the lack of geological information on the approach to, and at, the Causeway Stones.

Aim and Methodology

The aim of this case study is to provide some evidence of visitor's opinions on the current on-site interpretation and what they feel could be added to improve their understanding and experience of the site. The aim is not to comment on the content of the interpretation but to determine whether the current interpretation meets the expectations and needs of the visitors.

In order to meet the aim, a face-to-face interview and questionnaire survey with members of the public visiting the National Trust owned part of the World Heritage Site was conducted on 20–21 October 2007. This survey was undertaken in order to explore issues associated with geoconservation and geotourism in addition to investigating the promotion of the site as a World Heritage Site. Visitors were approached and invited to participate in the survey and as the survey was undertaken outside the peak summer tourist season, it is not aimed to be representative of the full profile of visitors to the Giant's Causeway but provides an insight into visitor expectations and experiences. The data were analyzed using the statistical computer program SPSS. Significance values pertaining to the chi-square test of association are included where they particularly highlight something of note. The results are presented as percentage values (rounded to one decimal place) and in the tables as both the number of interviewees and the percentage values. Additional data in the form of unattributed quotes from the interviewees are included to illustrate the nature of the comments expressed during the interviews.

Results

A total of 150 visitors were interviewed, of which 91 were male and 59 female. All interviewees were over 18 years old, with 72.0% aged 18–35 (full age profile is presented in Table 14.1). In addition to age, other socio-demographic details were collected. In terms of educational qualifications, just over 97% had secondary or tertiary level educational qualifications. Of these, nearly 59% were university degree level educated. The highest educational qualifications held by the interviewees are presented in Table 14.2. It is interesting to note here that the educational profile of the visitors surveyed closely resembles the common adult geotourist characteristic identified by Hose (1997, 1999) in that, at specifically geological attractions, they are above the national average for educational attainment. The majority (71.0%) of interviewees were employed either in full- or part-time employment and 22.0% belonged to an environmental or other similar organization such as the National Trust. Nearly all the interviewees (82.7%) were visitors from either the United Kingdom or the Republic of Ireland.

Table 14.1   Age profile of interviewees

Age Group	Number	%
18–25	56	37.3
26–35	52	34.7
36–45	9	6.0
46–55	12	8.0
56–65	13	8.7
Over 65	8	5.3

Note: *n* = 150.

Table 14.2   Highest educational qualifications held by interviewees

Education Qualification	Number	%
GCSE (Secondary School)	6	4.0
A-level (Secondary School)	33	22.0
Diploma (Secondary School)	19	12.6
Bachelors Degree (University)	37	24.7
Higher Degree—Masters or PhD (University)	51	34
Other	4	2.7

Note: *n* = 150.

Opinions on the Current On-Site Interpretation

The survey was designed to gauge visitor opinions on the quality of the current on-site interpretation (interpretation/information panels at selected locations around the site plus some free leaflets providing general site information) and whether it met their expectations and needs.

Firstly, the survey asked whether the interviewees had noticed any interpretation panels during their visit to the site; whether they had gained any new information from the interpretation; and what information had they gained from the interpretation.

48.0% of interviewees had noticed the interpretation panels, with 52.0% not noticing anything on the site. There was a clear relationship between age and noticing the panels ($p<0.001$). Fewer than expected 18–25 year olds and more than expected interviewees aged 56 and over noticed the interpretation panels.

With regard to gaining any new information from the interpretation, 58.7% of interviewees stated that they did not feel they had learnt anything new, and of these, 50.0% were aged 18–35. Again, there was a clear age relationship ($p<0.001$), with fewer than expected 18–25-year olds and more than expected interviewees aged 56 and over feeling that they had learnt something from the information provided on the site. The interviewees indicated that the main information gained related to the geology/rock features and the formation of the causeway (38.0%). Other cited examples were the work of the National Trust and conservation (16.0%); health and safety on the site (11.0%); erosion of the site's coastal path (9.0%); myth of Finn MacCool (8.0%); or information on a range of other aspects of the site and surrounding area (18.0%). From these responses, it is worth noting that age seems to be important in noticing interpretation panels and learning something new from interpretation. This seems to support the findings of Light (1995b), who indicated that there is a tendency for older visitors to make greater use of interpretation to improve their understanding and for those aged under 30 to engage less with interpretation.

Secondly, interviewees were asked to comment on the quality of the interpretation and if it met their needs and expectations. Presentation was a key consideration in the survey. Only 38.0% of interviewees agreed that the interpretation was well presented. Educational level had a strong relationship ($p<0.001$) with how the interviewees felt the material was presented. Lower levels of agreement was associated with interviewees who had tertiary level educational qualifications (degree level and above). In terms of meeting needs and expectations, interviewees were asked to consider whether the interpretation could be better presented and what they would like to see included that would improve their experience of the site. 35.0% of the interviewees agreed that the interpretation could be better presented. The remaining 65.0% disagreed or did not know if it could be better presented. Further analysis determined that age ($p<0.01$) and education ($p<0.05$) were significant with regard to agreement. Interviewees aged 36–45, and those with tertiary level qualifications had higher levels of agreement.

When asked if there was anything they had wanted to know that was not on the information boards, 26.0% said yes and 74.0% no or do not know. Those most in agreement were interviewees with higher degree qualifications. Light (1995b) had similar findings and stated that there is a tendency for better educated visitors to seek out information during their visit. Particular aspects highlighted by the interviewees included more information of the mythology/legend of the site, more information on the geology and formation of the site, explanation of red horizons (laterite palaeosol) between the lava layers, and more general information on the surrounding nature and features.

A key focus of the survey was to determine if the visitor's informational needs were being met by the current on-site interpretation. In particular, if they receive sufficient information on how the Giant's Causeway was formed and if this information is explained in a way they could understand. On the presentation of the geological information relating to the formation of the Giant's Causeway, 58.7% of interviewees agreed that it had been explained in a way they could understand but 41.3% felt that it had not. Responses by those not in agreement included "it wasn't clear enough," "it was too technical" and "needs more general information." This is an interesting finding since Hose (1997) indicates that visitors to geosites least access geology interpretive panels when they are in competition with other subject matter. The survey findings also reiterate the observation by Poria et al. (2006a, 2009) in that the nature of the interpretation plays a key role in the tourist experience of a site. This may also help to explain the significance of belonging to an environmental or similar organization (p<0.001) with regard to interviewees feeling that they had not received enough information. The previous experiences of interviewees at other heritage sites, for example, those owned by an organization such as the National Trust, may lead to higher levels of expectations.

With regard to the level of information received from the interpretation material, 35.3% agreed that they had received sufficient information but 64.7% felt that they had not. Most comments related a general lack of availability of information both on-site and in the free leaflets. The provision of detailed information was also a commonly cited reason by interviewees. In particular, detailed information on the geological features of the site as a whole, and on the geological significance of the site as a World Heritage Site. The provision of someone to talk to help their knowledge of the geological features of the site was stated by three interviewees. There was a clear relationship with age (p<0.01) and agreement, with fewer than expected 18–25-year-olds and more than expected interviewees aged 56 and over feeling they had received enough information for them to understand the geology and rock formations on the site. Education level (p<0.001) was also significant in terms of agreement. Interviewees with tertiary level educational qualifications (degree level and above) had lower levels of agreement.

The last part of the survey aimed to determine from the interviewees, what they would like to see on the site in order to improve their learning experience.

In addition to verbal responses, they were asked to choose up to three options from a list of examples of ways that could improve their experience. The top four choices were the provision of rangers/people to explain the features on the site, provision of guided walks, more information boards and the provision of an audio guide to the site. Table 14.3 presents the percentage responses cited by the interviewees. These results would seem to match the findings of Hose (1997) in that guided walks and accompanied field excursions are very popular amongst geotourists as ways of enhancing their experiences of geosites.

Table 14.3   Information improvements to the learning experience cited by interviewees

Information Source	%*
Rangers/Person to explain	23.3
Guided walks	15.3
Audio guide	14.0
More information boards	14.0
Free detailed leaflet	8.7
Detailed booklet to buy	8.7
Detailed map	6.0
Detailed leaflet to buy	2.0
Other	8.0

Note: * % calculated on multiple answers cited by interviewees (*n*=150).

Discussion: Visitor Opinions on the On-Site Interpretation

The results of the survey revealed a level of dissatisfaction amongst interviewees with regard to the current on-site interpretation. Interviewees expressed difficulties in finding information appropriate to their needs. Actually noticing the interpretation panels at key locations on the site was identified as an issue. With regard to the quality of the interpretation, the survey highlights that interviewees had key concerns with the presentation of the information and in it being at the right level to give them sufficient understanding of the site features. These are significant concerns and must be addressed in order to improve the visitor experience. One solution to the problem of finding information might be for the site managers to think about the location of the interpretation panels. Key considerations should relate to the most appropriate locations to maximize their impact, and to ensure that they can be seen or found when there are large numbers of visitors. Provision of information relating to the location of the panels such as on a site map or on a leaflet may improve visitor engagement with the site features and could contribute to improving the visitor experience of the site.

The quality of interpretation panels in terms of meeting the needs and expectations of the visitors was highlighted through the survey. The format (rotating hexagonal columnar drum), size, content and presentation were all commented on by the interviewees. The interpretation panels provided for their basic needs by giving general information to aid a broad understanding of the site features and how the Giant's Causeway was formed but interviewees indicated there was some room for improvement. Stated was a need for the information to be informative for all levels of understanding and interest through the provision of different age group or knowledge level information e.g., leaflets for children or for those with a specialist geological interest. This is in agreement with the findings of Pralong (2006) who stated that different targets groups, such as seniors and schools, should be considered as specific markets for interpretation materials. If such materials were to be developed at the Giant's Causeway then this may help address some of the age and education level differences found in the survey question responses. In addition, the lack of information in languages other than English was highlighted by international visitors. The interviewees were generally disappointed by the presentation of the on-site interpretation; many had higher expectations of the quality of the information. More discerning visitors expected the use of modern technology to add to their experience. Examples stated included the provision of audio guides, downloadable podcasts (mp3 downloads), or SMS (text) information.

In order for the previous comments to be addressed, thereby improving the visitor understanding and experience of the site, then an overhaul of the site interpretation needs to be undertaken. From the interviewee responses, the interpretation should contain more specific information on the Giant's Causeway itself and the significance of the site as a World Heritage Site. This would seem to be a vital development since Pralong (2006) highlights that the demand for explanatory commentaries is important for natural sites and landscapes with Earth science features of interest. It is anticipated that the new visitor center (due to open in summer 2012) will contain this information as part of the new interpretative media given that it is being designed to give a world-class visitor experience at the site offering state of the art visitor facilities, state of the art interpretation and enhanced trails on site (National Trust 2010).

The interpretation should be designed not only to meet the needs and expectations of the visitors but also to accommodate the nature of the site. The suggestion by Hose (2005, 2006) of adopting an interpretative strategy such as geotourism may help to meet these two aspects. Hose (2005: 28) states that "Such a strategy depends upon identifying and promoting its physical basis, knowing and understanding its users and developing effective interpretation materials." In undertaking this approach, then both the tourism and conservation requirements of the site could be accommodated.

Hughes and Ballantyne (2010) outline the process of developing interpretive plans and signage for geotourism attractions and provide examples of good practice in this area. If the interpretation contains an appropriate level of geological information, then the visitors should better understand the nature of the site and thus improve their experience. They should also be better able to understand and recall the information relating to the geosite, which Hose (1996, 1997, 2006) states to be a key issue for visitors to geosites.

Improving the Visitor Experience

The survey reveals that there are opportunities to enhance the overall visitor learning experience of the site in order to meet visitor expectations. The survey shows that the experiences and expectations of the interviewees are not being entirely met by the current on-site interpretation materials or services. Interviewees indicated that more interpretation in the form of boards, leaflets or audio guides that highlight, locate, and describe the key features of the site, or provide more information highlighting the significance of the Giant's Causeway and its designation as a geological World Heritage Site, would meet their basic informational needs. This interpretation would need to accommodate all levels of understanding and interest plus be available in multiple languages so that the visitors can fully enjoy and understand the Giant's Causeway.

The survey also highlights that a key requirement would be to provide more human interaction. Provision of on-site rangers/guides was considered by interviewees as a good way of improving their experience. Having rangers available to answer questions, give guidance on what to see/visit on the site, or to give guided walks would greatly improve the visitor understanding and experience of the site. They are also much appreciated by geotourists (Hose 1997) and improve the learning experience (Hose 2006). The ranger services could be linked to other forms of interpretation to provide an integrated approach to enhancing the visitor experience.

A significant improvement to the visitor experience would be the development of a more co-ordinated information/visitor center or a "gateway" to the site. This has previously been highlighted as an issue by Smith (2005), Wilson and Boyle (2006) and Gilmore et al. (2007). The lack of cohesion in the visitor facilities and possible lack of co-operation between operators and stakeholders (National Trust and Moyle District Council) may be affecting the quality of the visitor experience. The temporary visitor facilities are disjointed and on arrival, visitors do not really know where to go, what to do, or what to find on the site. This lack of co-ordination may also be having an effect on the quality of the on-site interpretation and on meeting many of the visitor management and experience objectives detailed in the site management plan (Environment and Heritage Service et al. 2005). For example, the provision of good interpretation facilities on the site, as detailed in objective 21, is key to giving a good tourist experience. The development of the new visitor center should provide visitors with sufficient information for them to fully engage with, and understand, the site features. By providing a good experience, the visitor concerns and issues raised during the survey should hopefully be addressed.

Conclusions

The visitor survey revealed that the current on-site interpretation does not fully meet the needs and expectations of the visitors. Clear improvements need to be made to both the interpretation and infrastructure in order to improve the visitor experience of the site. When re-designing the on-site interpretation or visitor facilities, it would be beneficial to determine visitors' opinions on what they would like to see included so that they are provided with the best on-site experience. Healy and McDonagh (2009) see it as essential that visitor infrastructural planning take on board visitor views prior to any development to ensure visitor satisfaction with the development.

Finally, the survey results have some implications for the management of the World Heritage Site. Although some progress has been made on the actions detailed in the site management plan, there still seems to be some way to go before the visitor management and experience objectives and actions are fully addressed from a visitor's perspective.

References

Boyd, S.W. and Timothy, D.J. (2006). Marketing Issues and World Heritage Sites. In: Leask, A. and Fyall, F. (eds), *Managing World Heritage Sites*. Oxford: Butterworth-Heinemann, pp. 55–68.

Burek, C.V. and Davies, H. (1994). Communication of Earth Science to the Public—How Successful Has It Been? In: O'Halloran, D., Green, C., Harley, M., Stanley, M. and Knill, J. (eds), *Geological and Landscape Conservation*. London: Geological Society, pp. 483–6.

Chen, C.-F. and Chen, F.-S. (2010). Experience Quality, Perceived Value, Satisfaction and Behavioural Intentions for Heritage Tourists. *Tourism Management*, 31(1): 29–35.

Cochrane, J. and Tapper, R. (2006). Tourism's Contribution to World Heritage Management. In: Leask, A. and Fyall, F. (eds), *Managing World Heritage Sites*. Oxford: Butterworth-Heinemann, pp. 100–109.

Dias, G. and Brilha, J. (2004). Raising Public Awareness of Geological Heritage: A Set of Initiatives. In: Parkes, M.A. (ed.), *Natural and Cultural Landscapes –* Dublin: The Geological Foundation, Royal Irish Academy, pp. 235–8.

Doughty, P. (2008). How Things Began: The Origins of Geological Conservation. In: Burek, C.V. and Prosser, C.D. (eds), *The History of Geoconservation*. London: The Geological Society Special Publications 300, Geological Society, pp. 7–16.

Environment and Heritage Service, National Trust and Moyle District Council (2005). *Giant's Causeway and Causeway Coast World Heritage Site Management Plan*. Available at <http://www.ni-environment.gov.uk/whs_final_draft_man_plan.pdf> (accessed April 26, 2011).

Gilmore, A., Carson, D. and Ascenção, M. (2007). Sustainable Tourism Marketing at a World Heritage Site. *Journal of Strategic Marketing*, 15(2/3): 253–64.

Healy, N. and McDonagh, J. (2009). Commodification and Conflict: What Can the Irish Approach to Protected Area Management Tell Us? *Society and Natural Resources*, 22(4): 381–91.

Hose, T.A. (1996). Geotourism, or Can Tourists become Casual Rock Hounds? In: Bennett, M.R., Doyle, P., Larwood, J.G. and Prosser, C.D. (eds), *Geology on Your Doorstep: The Role of Urban Geology in Earth Heritage Conservation.* London: Geological Society, pp. 207–28.

Hose, T.A. (1997). Geotourism—Selling the Earth to Europe. In: Marinos, P.G., Koukis, G.C., Tsiamaos, G.C. and Stournass, G.C. (eds), *Engineering Geology and the Environment.* Rotterdam: A.A. Balkema, pp. 2955–60.

Hose, T.A. (1999). How Was It for You? Matching Geologic Site Media to Audiences. In: Oliver, P.G. (ed.), *Proceedings of the First UKRIGS Conference.* Worcester: Worcester University College, pp. 117–44.

Hose, T.A. (2005). Geotourism—Appreciating the Deep Time of Landscapes. In: Novelli, M. (ed.), *Niche Tourism.* Oxford: Elsevier Butterworth-Heinemann, pp. 27–38.

Hose, T.A. (2006). Geotourism and Interpretation. In: Dowling, R. and Newsome, D. (eds), *Geotourism.* Oxford: Elsevier Butterworth-Heinemann, pp. 221–41.

Hughes, K. and Ballantyne, R. (2010). Interpretation Rocks! Designing Signs for Geotourism Sites. In: Newsome, D. and Dowling, R.K. (eds), *Geotourism: The Tourism of Geology and Landscape.* Oxford: Goodfellow Publishers Ltd, pp. 184–99.

Light, D. (1995a). Heritage as Informal Education. In: Herbert, D.T. (ed.), *Heritage, Tourism and Society.* London: Mansell, pp. 117–45.

Light, D. (1995b). Visitors' Use of Interpretive Media at Heritage Sites. *Leisure Studies*, 14(2): 132–49.

Lyle, P. (1996). *A Geological Excursion Guide to the Causeway Coast.* Northern Ireland: Environment and Heritage Service.

Lyle, P. (2002). The Volcanology of the Tertiary Lavas of the Giant's Causeway, Co. Antrim. In: Knight, J. (ed.), *Field Guide to the Coastal Environments of Northern Ireland.* Coleraine, Northern Ireland: University of Ulster, pp. 172–7.

Mason, P. and Kuo, I.-L. (2008). Visitor Attitudes to Stonehenge: International Icon or National Disgrace? *Journal of Heritage Tourism*, 2(3): 168–83.

National Trust (2010). *Giant Development for World Heritage Site.* Available at <http://www.nationaltrust.org.uk/main/w-global/w-localtoyou/w-northern ireland/w-northernireland-news/w-northernireland-news-giants_causeway_ update.htm> (accessed April 26, 2011).

Parrinello, G.L. (1993). Motivation and Anticipation in Post-industrial Tourism. *Annals of Tourism Research*, 20(2): 233–49.

Pocock, D. (1992). Catherine Cookson Country: Tourist Expectation and Experience. *Geography*, 77(3): 236–43.

Poria, Y. (2010). The Story behind the Picture: Preferences for the Visual Display at Heritage Sites. In: Waterton, E. and Watson, S. (eds), *Culture, Heritage and Representation: Perspectives on Visuality and the Past*. Aldershot: Ashgate, pp. 217–28.

Poria, Y., Reichel, A. and Biran, A. (2006a). Heritage Management: Motivations and Expectations. *Annals of Tourism Research*, 33(1): 162–78.

Poria, Y., Reichel, A. and Biran, A. (2006b). Heritage Site Perceptions and Motivations to Visit. *Journal of Travel Research*, 44(3): 318–26.

Pralong, J.-P. (2006). Geotourism: A New Form of Tourism Utilising Natural Landscapes and Based on Imagination and Emotion. *Tourism Review*, 61(3): 20–25.

de Rojas, C. and Camarero, C. (2008). Visitors' Experience, Mood and Satisfaction in a Heritage Context: Evidence from an Interpretation Center. *Tourism Management*, 29(3): 525–37.

Ryan, C. (2002). *The Tourist Experience*, 2nd edn. London: Continuum.

Sharpley, R. and Stone, P. (2010). *Tourist Experience: Contemporary Perspectives*. London: Routledge.

Smith, B.J. (2005). Management Challenges at a Complex Geosite: The Giant's Causeway World Heritage Site, Northern Ireland. *Géomorphologie: Relief, Processus, Environnement*, 3: 219–26.

Tomkeieff, S.I. (1940). The Basalt Lavas of the Giant's Causeway District of Northern Ireland. *Bulletin Volcanologique*, 6(1): 89–143.

Uriely, N. (2005). The Tourist Experience: Conceptual Developments. *Annals of Tourism Research*, 32(1): 199–216.

Wilson, L.-A. and Boyle, E. (2006). Interorganisational Collaboration at UK World Heritage Sites. *Leadership & Organization Development Journal*, 27(6): 501–23.

Chapter 15

Demolition of Tangible Properties as an Intangible Practice

Ayako Fukushima

Introduction

Catholic churches built around 1900 AD exist on islands in Western Japan. For various reasons local Catholics have carried out intangible practices of dismantling, demolition, relocation, reuse and/or recycle of some of those church buildings. Architectural historical studies in the 1970s and 1980s have revealed the physical architectural characteristics (Kawakami and Tsuchida 1983; Maekawa 2003). However, those studies paid little attention to the intangible aspects of church buildings. The recent research by Kikata et al. (2010) has relevance to intangible aspects. They have revealed traditional methods and practices to maintain churches by the local Catholic congregation as well as factors to enhance or hinder participation of non-Catholic residents in church maintenance.

There has been no previous research into the value and meaning of intangible practices of dismantling/demolition/relocation/recycle/reuse of churches. It is not appropriate to label any demolition practices as vandalistic without any assessment because the associated community has specific reasons to conduct those intangible practices, and possibly social or religious meanings as well. Any heritage value assessment should be based on the examination of both the tangible and intangible elements. Conservation management plans as well as tourism management should be derived from such a heritage value assessment. This study set out to establish two major points: first, to evaluate the values of intangible practices of dismantling, demolishing, relocating, reusing and recycling churches; second, to suggest a conservation policy for conservation management planning based on the identified values.

Materials and Methodology

The major methodology used in this study was interviews conducted by the author with Catholics who have been involved in maintenance, dismantlement, demolition, relocation and/or recycle of churches. The core principles on which this study stands are the concept of "conservation process" including the five values defined in "the Burra Charter" created by Australia ICOMOS and the concept of "authenticity" defined by "the Nara Document on Authenticity."

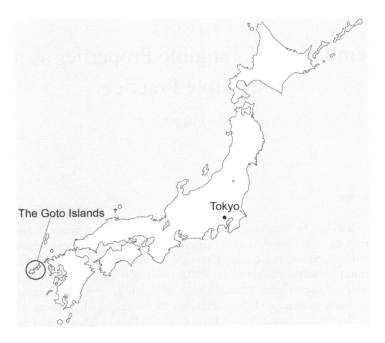

Figure 15.1   Location of Goto Islands

Case Studies and Background History

The case studies consisted of Catholic churches on the Goto islands in Kyushu Region, Japan (Figure 15.1).

Background History

The Kyushu region is the area where Catholicism was introduced in the sixteenth century. It became the center of Catholicism with a number of proselytized Japanese Catholics and foreign missionaries. However, in the seventeenth century, the Edo government officially imposed a ban on Catholicism that lasted until 1873 AD. Missionaries were expelled, and Japanese Catholics were severely persecuted. Around 1800 AD, many Catholics who resided in the mainland Kyushu emigrated to the Goto islands in order to avoid persecution, and also to secretly practice their faith by living in remote and rural areas. They found places to establish their villages where there were no native residents and thus most of the Catholic villages are located on the periphery of the islands where living conditions are worse than other areas. In 2010 there were 20 Catholic churches still in use in the lower Goto islands (Figure 15.2). Eight churches other than the existing ones have been closed and/or dismantled because of the decrease in Catholic population.

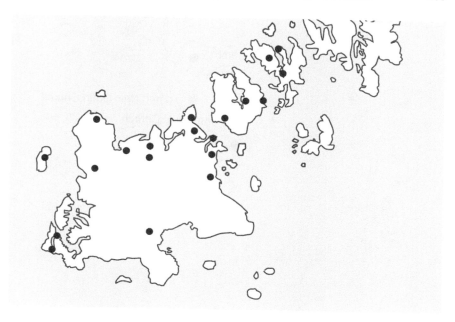

Figure 15.2   Locations of Catholic Churches in use in the lower Goto Islands

Case Study 1: Egami Church

Egami Church, located on Naru Island, was built in 1918 (Figures 15.3 and 15.4). It is a wooden structure and has a double roof. The floor plan consists of a nave with aisles on both sides, and a rib-vaulted ceiling that creates a greater sense of space. In 2008, it was designated by the national government as an "Important Cultural Property."' The church is still owned and managed by the Catholic Archdiocese of Nagasaki, with the Naru Parish responsible for maintenance. Local Catholics in Egami village provide daily maintenance. However, Egami and the surrounding areas are extremely depopulated, and only three aged Catholics attend mass at the church, which is held once a month. Only one of them is physically able to carry out maintenance such as cleaning. The upkeep by the local congregation became unsustainable; therefore, around 2007, the local congregation considered closing and dismantling the church.[1] However, the heritage designation of the church was decided in 2008 between the national government and the archdiocese without sufficient consultation with the local congregation. Consequently, the plan to close and dismantle had to be canceled.

---

1   Interview with Naru Parishioners, Fukue, May 25, 2008.

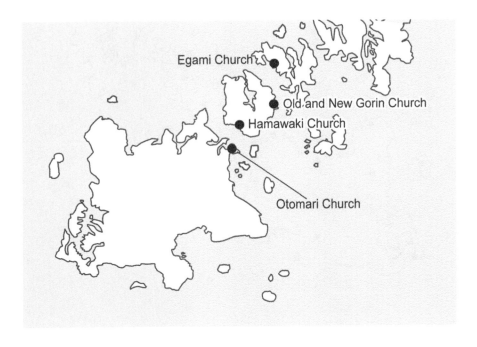

Figure 15.3   Locations of case studies

Figure 15.4   Egami Church

The local congregation explained the reason behind their plan to close down the church, "For local Catholics, the most inacceptable thing is to allow the church to decay with no one to take care of it. It is rather appropriate and responsible treatment of a church to close it down and dismantle it when the congregation becomes incapable to maintain it."

Case Study 2: Ohtomari Church

Ohtomari Church, which existed on Fukue Island (Figure 15.3) was closed and dismantled in 1969. The exact architectural design is unknown because archival records are missing. However, we know that the church was a wooden structure with a residential quarter for a priest, and another building that stood next to it. They were built in the late nineteenth century, but had become too decayed to maintain by the 1960s. Typhoons often damaged the church and the adjacent buildings, which caused serious financial burdens on the local congregation to repair.[2] In the late 1960s, a new church intended as a mother church in the parish, was planned to be built in a nearby village. All the parishioners were required to make financial contributions for its construction. It was too difficult for Catholics in Ohtomari to be financially responsible for both the Ohtomari church and the new mother church. As a result of this and other factors, the local congregation in Ohtomari village decided to decommission and dismantle the church building. Dismantling was decided to be implemented because it was inappropriate for the local congregation to leave and allow the closed church, which was the House of God, to decay. For them, treating the church with respect and dignity meant dismantling it.[3]

After dismantling, the building materials such as wooden beams and pillars were recycled by some local Catholics into their cowsheds and barns. The cleared site of Ohtomari Church was then refurbished as Ohtomari Catholic Cemetery (Figure 15.5). The Old Catholic Cemetery in this village was located on the top of a high hill, which made it difficult to carry wooden coffins in a funeral, or to visit family members's tombs, especially as local Catholics became aged. Therefore, it was decided to relocate the cemetery to the lower location, the former site of Ohtomari Church, where access was relatively easy.

---

2   Interview with Fujio Hamaguchi, Fukue, March and May 2009.
3   Interview with Fujio Hamaguchi, April 18, 2011.

Figure 15.5   Ohtomari Catholic Cemetery

Case Study 3: Gorin Church

The Gorin Church was originally built in 1881 as Hamawaki Church in Hamawaki Village, a mother church of the Hisaka Parish on Hisaka Island (Figure 15.3). It is a wooden structure with roof tiles and a gabled roof. It belongs to the oldest group of church architecture whose characteristics include columns connected with exposed beams. The ceiling is a rib vault with wooden boards. The floor plan consisted of a nave with aisles on both sides (Kawakami and Tsuchida 1983; Maekawa 2003) (Figure 15.6).

When the congregation grew, the parish decided to replace the old church with a new concrete structure in 1931 (Figure 15.7). The old church was dismantled and relocated to Gorin village where Catholics in the village were longing for a church because it was in an extremely remote area, which made it difficult for members to go to another church for Sunday mass (Figure 15.8). In 1931, the old Hamawaki Church was reassembled and reused as Gorin Church.

Fifty years later in the 1980s, the local congregation had difficulties meeting the repair costs due to water damage from a leaky roof. Therefore, the local congregation decided to dismantle the old church and replace it with a concrete block structure.

Figure 15.6   Old Gorin Church after relocation (originally Hamawaki Church)

Figure 15.7   Hamawaki Church and Hamawaki village

Figure 15.8   Gorin village

The construction cost was estimated to be lower than repairing the severely decayed church and the maintenance was estimated to be much easier than keeping the old church.[4] When the local congregation was about to begin dismantling it in 1985, a local journalist informed the local government about the dismantling plan. The local government responded by telling the local Catholics not to dismantle the church while it considered the possibility of saving the structure as a historical site. Negotiations were carried out in great haste among the local congregation, the parish priest, the local municipal government, the prefectural government, and scholars in architectural history. Finally it was agreed by all parties to do *in-situ* conservation of the church structure. A new church was erected at a nearby location in the village to be the new Gorin Church (Figures 15.9 and 15.10). The old church was deconsecrated, and the ownership of the building was transferred from the Nagasaki Archdiocese to the local government. The old church became a municipally designated "Cultural Property" without any religious practices or any particular activities or use inside; whereas, the new Gorin Church nearby became consecrated to conduct all the religious practices. The old Gorin Church was designated as an "Important Cultural Property" by the national government in 1999.

---

4   Interview with Hideo Sakatani and Mitsuru Kojima, Hisaka, August 23 and November 3, 2009.

Figure 15.9 Old and new Churches of Gorin

Figure 15.10 New Gorin Church

Even though it is not currently a religious facility, the local government has entrusted the daily maintenance to local Catholics such as cleaning and unlocking/locking when visitors wish to get inside.

The negotiation process in 1985 to conserve the old Gorin Church focused solely on *in-situ* physical conservation and lacked assessment of intangible heritage value as well as authenticity in religious value. No discussion or examination were given on whether it was appropriate to conserve only the "shell" of the church without any living spirit.

Nowadays, the Gorin village has only three Catholic families consisting of six people. Fewer than 20 Catholics come to the new Gorin Church for Sunday mass, which is held once a month. Maintenance of both the old and new churches is not sustainable in terms of human resources for the long term, as the next generation is unlikely to come back to the village to live. Therefore, the village might be unpopulated in several decades. In such a case, not only the new church, but also the old "heritage" church will have no one on site to maintain them.

Assessment of Heritage Values of Intangible Practices

Churches are, in principle, living religious sites unless they are closed, demolished, or converted into another use. Herb Stovel states that "understanding living religious heritage requires recognizing that the intangible significance of tangible religious objects, structures, and place is the key to their meaning. The tangible and intangible cannot be separated since all cultural materials have intangible value" (Stovel 2005: 9). Gamini Wijesuriya states that religious heritage has been born with its values in place. Therefore, a question the conservator has to ask in order to define religious heritage value is: what values are already recognized by the religious community? (Stovel 2005: 2).

There is a discussion of "pious vandals" introduced by Wijesuriya (2001). According to him, "pious vandals" refers to pious and well-meant devotees who carry out non-scientifically planned repairs and restorations to religious places. Those devotees conduct rebuilding and restoring of the worship places because they firmly believe such practices to be one of their prime tasks. From the scientifically-oriented conservation viewpoint, restorations by "pious vandals" leads to the loss of documentary value. However, as Wijesuriya also argued, restorations by "pious vandals," in another word "built-in continuity," actually secure and enhance spiritual value (Wijesuriya 2005). Practices such as dismantling a church could be defined as the last action of "pious vandals" to be taken by the associated community when they decided to end "built-in continuity."

Article 11 of "Nara Document on Authenticity" states as follows:

All judgments about values attributed to cultural properties as well as the credibility of related information sources may differ from culture to culture, and even within the same culture. It is thus not possible to base judgments of values and authenticity within fixed criteria. On the contrary, the respect due to all cultures requires that heritage properties must be considered and judged within the cultural contexts to which they belong. (Nara Conference 1994)

Cristina Carlo-Stella of the Pontifical Commission for the Cultural Heritage of the Church in Roman Curia addresses that "the material cultural heritage of Church always reflects and should communicate the essential immaterial heritage, in other words the traditions of spirituality (the religious and devotional traditions, customs and practices of worship). This immaterial heritage should be considered to be the major reason behind the efforts to conserve and enhance the material forms" (Carlo-Stella 2005: 108).

To summarize, living religious heritage has, in nature, a different set of values from secular heritage. Authenticity is culturally dependent in nature. Therefore, assessment of values and authenticity needs a set of criteria specifically catered for each living religious heritage. Particular attention should be paid to intangible aspects and values of the associated community. The Vatican shares the same view regarding value and authenticity.

Assessment of Values in Intangible Practices

It is necessary to identify what factors, concepts, or motivations make the associated community engaged in intangible practices as dismantling, and what values those practices embody. The value which has been derived from religious heritage is spiritual value resulting from a particular belief system or religion. Other values could be identified in intangible practices. Table 15.1 summarizes intangible practices observed in the case studies along with the reasons behind them and the type of value.

Table 15.1   Value assessment of intangible practices

		Intangible Practices	Reason	Type of Value
Case 1	Egami Church	Dismantling	Death with dignity	Spiritual
Case 2	Ohtomari Church	Dismantling	Death with dignity	Spiritual
		Recycle of materials	Economic	Historic
Case 3	Gorin Church	Construction (re-assembling)	Desire to have a local church	Spiritual
		Dismantling, relocation and reuse of the whole building	Economic	Historic

In the Egami Church, though it was not actually carried out, dismantling of the church was about to be implemented because the shrinking congregation thought that it was the proper way to be responsible for their own church, and to treat the sacred church with dignity. It may be called "death with dignity" of a church. The value of this practice is identified as "spiritual" since the practice is driven primarily by a spiritual reason. It should be noted that, for the associated community, dismantling was not "optional," but rather a "must", in order to treat the church to be decommissioned as the local Catholics had clearly expressed.

As for the Ohtomari Church, dismantling was carried out for the same reason as Egami. Therefore, value is identified as spiritual. However, recycling of church building materials that followed after the dismantling was carried out for economic and practical reasons. Such a practice to recycle building materials has been a common and shared practice all over Japan, as new building materials are generally expensive; whereas, recycled materials cost less. Hence, this practice has historic value as it is a long-established method in the wooden architecture building system (Sakurai 1997; Sato et al. 2001). Recycling was an optional practice rather than indispensable, and not derived from spiritual grounds. Furthermore, this practice was not exclusively performed by the associated community, but commonly practiced by anyone, for any type of building, in any region of Japan.

Regarding Gorin Church, construction of a church in Gorin village was in itself supported by a pure spiritual desire by members to have a church in their own village. Therefore, the value is spiritual. However, the dismantling, relocation, and reuse of the former Hamawaki Church into Gorin Church were the consequences of economic and practical reasons, as seen in the Ohtomari Church. Such a process was optional rather than a spiritual necessity because the associated community would have built a new church with new materials if they had enough money to do so. Relocation and re-use of a building has also been a popular approach for wooden architecture in general. Hence, the value is identified as historic.

Based on this analysis, Figure 15.11 illustrates how values and authenticity were split when the Gorin Church was deconsecrated and became a cultural property. When the church was still in use, elements of "congregation," "religious practices" and "management practices" by the congregation were present. Spiritual and social values were embodied because of their presence. The church building itself possesses aesthetic and historic values. All those values bare authenticity. Once the church fell into disuse after the ownership was transferred to the local government, the spiritual and social values were lost as the congregation, religious practices, and congregational management were removed. Accordingly, authenticity was reduced or lost completely. The historic and aesthetic values, which the old Gorin Church had possessed, have not been obtained by the new church. Here again, authenticity is lost or reduced partially. Such a split of values has occurred because the negotiation for conservation totally lacked the examination of heritage values, both tangible and intangible, and conservation management planning based on identified values.

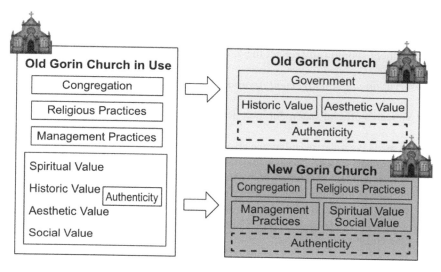

Figure 15.11   Split values of Gorin Church

Value-Based Conservation Management Policy

The three case studies show the shrinking of congregation and management abilities led to two approaches: 1) close down and dismantle a church or; 2) handover ownership and management administration of the church to a government. These approaches have not gone through the proper value assessment.

Conservation Management Approaches by Conservation Professionals

Article 8 of "Nara Document on Authenticity" states that "responsibility for cultural heritage and the management of it belongs, in the first place, to the cultural community that has generated it, and subsequently to that which cares for it" (Nara Conference 1994).

Stovel addresses that the care for living religious heritage is primarily the responsibility of the religious community for whom this heritage has importance, and the fullest respect should be paid for the practices and values which sustain faith in the religious community that may involve restrictions, rules, and exclusions regarding what conservation treatment may be appropriate (Stovel 2005: 10).

Wijesuriya states that "when dealing with the conservation of sacred heritage, the more familiar top-down process of decision-making was changed to a bottom-up approach, placing priority on inherent values and the voice of the associated communities." He also clearly addresses that "religious values govern conservation decisions" (Wijesuriya 2005: 37, 42).

To sum up, living religious heritage should be maintained, in the first place, by the associated community or religious community. Decisions on conservation management should fully reflect the value system of the associated community.

Conservation and Management Approaches by the Religious Communities

The Vatican's official statement includes the following:

> ... some decisions regarding the alienation of the immovable heritage should not be taken in haste. Rather, one should take into account the purposes assigned to each building in an effort to maintain integral its original aim, especially in the case of liturgical centers. ... they should be made available, if possible, for social and cultural activities in favor of the people with whose help these works were built in the past. (Pontifical Commission for the Cultural Patrimony of the Church 1994)

This statement is important as it stresses the conservation of original use, yet at the same time, indirectly permits the adaptive re-use of churches for compatible uses.

A Proposal of Policies for Conservation Management of
Catholic Churches in Disuse

Figure 15.12 illustrates four different types of conservation management policies and how values can be retained accordingly. Among different values identified in intangible practices, spiritual value is given the prime importance here for conservation management purpose because the heritage has been born with it in place; whereas, other values were attained much later as historical results. The best way to retain the spiritual value at the highest possible degree is "*in-situ* re-use" of the church meaning that a church once disused may be used again as a church on the same site. This policy does not affect the spiritual value as well as the setting. This approach is also desirable because when a church in a village totally loses followers, there may still be a chance that some followers who currently live outside of the village, may move back to the village, and attend the church after they retire. Therefore, a disused church need not be demolished in haste.

The second best way is "relocation and re-use" as a church in a different setting. As the case studies show, the associated community embraces the relocation and re-use of a church, and it does not harm the spiritual value. Another justification is that most Japanese churches do not have any location meaning like many European churches, which are often built on burial sites of saints or places of other monumental events. Therefore, relocation of a church in Japan does not undermine the spiritual value although it affects the historic value to some extent. If the church is reused again as a church, the religious value will be secured.

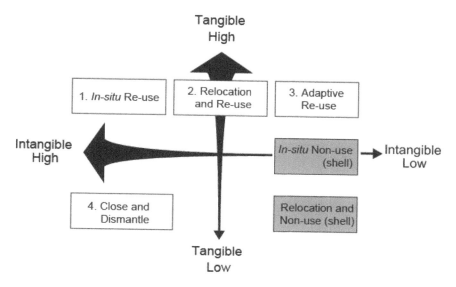

Figure 15.12   Four approaches of conservation

The third best policy is "adaptive re-use" of a church building. As the Vatican states, adaptive re-use is acceptable when there is no way to keep using it as a living church. Followers have respect and attachment towards a church building that are partially based on spiritual reasons. Adaptive re-use can possibly secure it if the building is properly converted while paying respect to the tangible and intangible evidence and values. Therefore, this policy can partially retain the spiritual value although it is reduced once a building has become deconsecrated. Values such as historic, aesthetic and social values will be retained, or could possibly be strengthened by obtaining a new use.

The fourth policy is to allow the associated religious community to dismantle and close down a church as they did in the past. Needless to say, it will diminish the aesthetic, historic and social values, as well as the physical embodiment of the spiritual value. However, as dismantling and closing down themselves possess a spiritual value for the associated community to treat their own church with dignity, this practice of "death with dignity" itself should not be ruled out as an option. This traditional approach secures the spiritual value in the intangible act itself, yet weakly as a tangible one.

The decision for conservation management policy should be made based on thorough discussion on how many resources can be available by the associated community as well as conservation professionals in order to conserve the spiritual value at the highest possible level. Due consideration and justification should be given if either the "*in-situ* re-use" or "relocation and re-use" are not chosen.

Conclusion

This chapter has examined the value of intangible practices to dismantle, demolish, relocate, recycle or re-use church buildings. The spiritual value is identified in dismantling. Relocation, recycling and re-use are identified as having no spiritual value, but rather historic significance. Based on this value assessment, four policies for conservation management of disused churches are proposed: "*In-situ* re-use" and "relocation and re-use" are the more desirable approaches to sustain spiritual value at a high level; whereas, "adaptive re-use" and "dismantling"' are also acceptable only when other better approaches are not possible.

Modern conservation tends to overemphasize the physical evidence of heritage value and neglect the intangible significance, which is particularly important in living religious heritage. Any conservation efforts should be based on strong research of the meaning and value of intangible practices in order to avoid mere conservation of a "shell" without any spirit. It should be noted that the four proposed policies may not be applicable to Catholic churches in other regions with different historical and social contexts where social or locational values may have strong presence and importance to be taken into consideration for conservation.

Acknowledgment

A part of the materials used in this study is obtained through the Project for Conservation of Cultural Landscape funded by the municipal government of Goto in which the author participated.

References

Bøytler, J. (2005). Christianfeld: A Religious Heritage Alive and Well. Twenty-first Century Influence on a Late Eighteenth–Early Nineteenth Century Moravian Settlement in Denmark. In: Stovel, H., Stanley-Price, N. and Killick, R. (eds), *Conservation of Living Religious Heritage*. Papers from the ICCROM 2003 Forum on Living Religious Heritage, Conserving the Sacred. Rome: ICCROM, pp. 19–30.

Carlo-Stella, C. (2005). Religious Heritage as a Meeting Point for Dialogue. In: Stovel, H., Stanley-Price, N. and Killick, R. (eds), *Conservation of Living Religious Heritage*. Papers from the ICCROM 2003 Forum on Living Religious Heritage, Conserving the Sacred. Rome: ICCROM, pp. 107–12.

Kawakami, H. and Tsuchida, M. (1983). On the Process of Development of the Architectures of Churches in the Region of Nagasaki Prefecture (in Japanese). *Transactions of the Architectural Institute of Japan*, 346: 155–63.

Kikata, J., Fukushima, A., Takao, T. and Shibata, H. (2010). A Study on Spatial Management Activities in Christian Village in Islands of Kyushu Region –Towards a Sustainable Management System for Cultural Landscapes in Depopulated Villages. *Journal of Housing Research Foundation*, 36: 71–82.

Maekawa, M. (2003). *Kyokai Kenchiku Ronsou* (Studies on Church Architecture). Chuo Kouron Bijutsu Shuppan.

Nara Conference (1994). *The Nara Document on Authenticity*. Nara.

Pontifical Commission for the Cultural Patrimony of the Church (1994). The Cultural Heritage of the Church and Religious Families. Available at <http://www.vatican.va/roman_curia/pontifical_commissions/pcchc/documents/rc_com_pcchc_19940410_religious-families_en.html> (accessed April 24, 2011).

Sakurai, T. (1997). Kodai ni okeru Kenchiku no Yukue (Treatment of Buildings in the Ancient Times). *Journal of Architecture and Building Science*, 1401(112): 34–5.

Sato, S., Konishi, T., Masuda, Y., Nakamura, S., Kaneko, K. and Liu, L. et al. (2001). Recent Development of Minka Recycling and Value of Used Timber (in Japanese). *Summaries of Technical Papers of Annual Meeting*. Architectural Institute of Japan, pp. 687–88.

Stovel, H. (1995). Considerations in Framing the Authenticity Question for Conservation. In: *Proceedings of the Nara Conference on Authenticity in relation tothe World Heritage Convention*. UNESCO WH Centre – Agency for Cultural Affairs (Japan) – ICCROM – ICOMOS, pp. 393–8.

Stovel, H. (2005). Introduction. In: Stovel, H., Stanley-Price, N. and Killick, R. (eds), *Conservation of Living Religious Heritage*. Papers from the ICCROM 2003 Forum on Living Religious Heritage, Conserving the Sacred. Rome: ICCROM, pp. 1–11.

Wijesuriya, G. (2001). "Pious Vandals": Restoration or Destruction in Sri Lanka? In: Layton, R., Stone, P. and Thomas, J. (eds), *The Destruction and Conservation of Cultural Property*. London: Routledge, pp. 256–63.

Wijesuriya, G. (2005). The Past is in the Present: Perspectives in Caring for Buddhist Heritage Sites in Sri Lanka. In: Stovel, H., Stanley-Price, N. and Killick, R. (eds), *Conservation of Living Religious Heritage*. Papers from the ICCROM 2003 Forum on Living Religious Heritage, Conserving the Sacred. Rome: ICCROM, pp. 31–43.

Chapter 16

The Ethics of Landscape: Discourses of Cultural and Environmental Sustainability in the Heart of Neolithic Orkney World Heritage Site

Angela McClanahan

Introduction

This chapter sketches out a particular case in which the "values" of a World Heritage Site (WHS) in Scotland became entangled in competing discourses relating to political and moral economies in the context of a case around cultural and historic "sustainability." In a number of public meetings, media statements and during an official Scottish Government inquiry in 2008, different social and cultural groups debated whether to approve or deny a planning application to construct a wind farm that would provide a substantial output of renewable energy, but which would be sited within view of the Heart of Neolithic Orkney (HONO) WHS, inscribed by the United Nations Educational, Scientific and Cultural Organisation (UNESCO) in 1999. Utilizing ethnographic approaches drawn from material culture studies in anthropology and archeology, I examine the ways in which social actors on both "sides" of the conflict articulated arguments about its value as a community "commons" and the ways in which it could provide forms of social capital for Orkney communities, both in relation to its "aesthetic" properties as an authentic cultural landscape, and as a potential site for the symbolic and actual production of a form of sustainable energy.

Exploring these threads, and the way they are negotiated and used to inform social action in the present, adds to our understanding of how the management of World Heritage Sites play an active role in using the past to help shape moral codes and visions of "the future" within contemporary societies.

Context

The Heart of Neolithic Orkney (HONO) World Heritage Site (WHS), is a spectacular collection of 5,000-year-old henge monuments, a settlement site and passage tomb, located in the Western half of the largest island in the Orkney archipelago, around seven miles north of the tip of the Scottish Mainland. It is lauded in heritage management terms for its high levels of "authenticity" and preservation, as well as its significance in relation to existing bodies of archeological evidence that trace the origins and cultures of some of the first settlers in the British Isles, and Northwest Europe more generally (Historic Scotland 1999, 2002, 2004, 2008). It is also celebrated both historically and contemporarily for the famed aesthetics of its landscapes, their "dramatic," windswept, treeless, "Northern" settings, and the iconic status of its Neolithic monuments within archeological history, which also tend to be viewed as symbols that are associated with the myths and origins of Scottish nationhood.

In 2001–2, I undertook one year of ethnographic research that examined how communities living amongst the HONO, as well as visitors from outside Orkney, used, understood and made meaning from their engagement with the various monuments that constitute the site. The resulting insights gained from that research included specific understandings of how power relationships between different heritage organizations and local communities were acted out in the context of the heritage management process, the ways in which the management of the fabric and aesthetics of the site impacted on visitor engagements with it, as well as how the site is used by various social groups for sociocultural, political and economic purposes in the present (McClanahan 2006a, 2006b, 2007).

In the succeeding years since the publication of much of this research, a private land owner living near the HONO site submitted a planning application to the Orkney Islands Council in 2007 that outlined plans for the construction of a wind farm in the Merranblo region of the Orkney Mainland. The landscape where the site would be situated was within view of the three of the WHS monuments, including the Ring of Brodgar (Figure 16.1). The developer, along with a Scottish renewable energy firm, proposed that the enterprise would be partially community-owned, in that 10% of profits from the eco-efficient energy generated by the three large white, 900KW turbines would go to the community immediately surrounding the site. Objectors to the development of the site, including local, national and international cultural and natural heritage conservation agencies and organizations (including UNESCO), as well as local authority and academic archeologists and community interest groups, argued that such a development would threaten the very "values" upon which the site was inscribed. The aesthetics and authenticity of the monuments, they claimed, would be destroyed if the turbines were to be erected.

This conflict generated highly contentious arguments amongst all interested parties, and was steeped in moral rhetoric on both "sides" from the outset about what the priorities of "conservation" should be within a contemporary society that is concerned both with its history and heritage, but also the well-being of its future inhabitants. The various "values" the site is claimed to embody in terms of its narrative worth to human history and origins, and its "value" as a generator of tourism within the Orkney community (boosted by World Heritage status), were publicly set against arguments about the role and "moral" responsibility that

Figure 16.1   Visitors at the Ring of Brodgar

both the Orkney community and the Scottish nation should have in promoting and providing resources for renewable energy, how the economic future of the community and "culture" could be ensured (and indeed, "conserved") through the profits generated by the wind farm, and the role its members should play in deciding what happened to the development in the consultation process. The planning application for the Merranblo project was eventually rejected by the Orkney Islands Council, owing to the disruption that such a material intervention would cause to the WHS, which, according to conservations specialists from the International Council on Monuments and Sites, would potentially put the WHS status of the HONO under threat.

Building on my understanding of these ethnographic contexts, gained through original research, as well as my ongoing familiarity with the interests of the parties involved in the management of the Orkney WHS, I engaged in qualitative research relating specifically to the Merranblo development conflict by adopting a strategy for "following" various arguments as they were publically articulated in forms of mass media, in particular, Orkney newspapers, as well as internet forums, local government websites, community interest "blogs" that related to heritage and renewable energy, and official government documents like planning applications and reports about them. Such reflexive strategies, as outlined by ethnographers and other qualitative researchers in recent years (see especially Aull-Davies 2008; Marcus 1998), require the researcher to "connect" and "follow" discourses about the phenomenon under scrutiny, in order to gain a layered, dynamic and multifaceted understanding of it. I paired this research with an approach that included gaining an understanding of the moral ideals bound up with "commons" resources, as discussed below, in order to understand how both sides appealed to different kinds of ethical arguments about the benefits of accepting or rejecting the Merranblo project.

Historic Sites as Cultural "Commons"

I argue here that heritage sites have become a kind of contemporary "commons" that, it is often argued, can be used for the positive benefit of communities of people. I propose this in two senses. First, heritage sites are very much seen as cultural "resources" that contribute to the common good of humankind. Indeed, the lexicon adopted in North American and Australian contexts explicitly refers to historical and archeological remains as "resources" that can be physically depleted; a kind of material form that can provide the means for the production of wealth for those who live amongst them (Nonini 2007: 1). This understanding of the commons is very much in line with the ways in which anthropologists and cultural ecologists have tended to discuss and analyze "commons" resources since Garrett Hardin's famous thesis on *The Tragedy of The Commons* in 1968.[1]

On the other hand, the idea of heritage sites as a particular form of "commons" is also compatible with other more recent definitions of the kind of resources that have been developed by social scientists and historians of science in the examination of new technologies like the internet, that are said to be a kind of "information" commons that benefit humankind through mass access; that is, *"the more they are used, the more valuable they become"* (Nonini 2008: 71, emphasis mine).

This double-notion of the commons, though contradictory in several senses (the fact that the material fabric of historic sites can be depleted and destroyed through "use," but that their value lies in the information they can provide about past societies to future populations) is useful to apply to the Merranblo case, as it helps us to understand some of the contradictory and competing claims in the way that the social actors involved in the case articulated their arguments, and thus, how discourses of heritage management are constantly negotiated, contested and in tension.

---

1   Garrett Hardin's classic 1968 paper "The Tragedy of the Commons" proposed that resources held in common for the benefit of human populations, such as parcels of land that were jointly farmed by members of communities, were in danger of being depleted in the absence of structures implemented to "manage" their conservation. Some use this work as an example of how/why "commons" should be "enclosed" or privatized to protect them, whilst others argue that commons should be held in trust by governments for the benefits of their populations. Both kinds of solutions are inherently contentious, and the application of the idea of these concepts to "heritage" sites, in particular "World Heritage Sites" is useful in debating their role in contemporary societies and political structures in the postmodern, globalized world.

Ensuring "Cultural" Conservation: "Development" vs. Preservation

Drawing on the idea that WHS's are often used, appropriated and represented as a kind of "commons" that can be used to impact on the lives of those who live amongst them, I want now to discuss how heritage managers, community groups, archeologists and developers argued for and against the rejection or acceptance of the project.

Because of the high profile of the case, various community interests, and the public outcry involved in the submission and review of the Merranblo project planning application, an official public inquiry was launched by the Scottish Government to examine the arguments outlined in relation to the case in January, 2008. Throughout the course of the inquiry, community members, heritage managers and agencies, members of local government, and, of course, the developers of the proposed windfarm site, aired their views to a public audience. Specialists from ICOMOS UK were brought in to defend the values of the WHS, as were academic archeologists from universities around the UK. Specialists from renewable energy companies, local community members, as well as heritage "experts" also defended the morality of placing a development that would benefit both the local community in terms of wealth generation through profit-making from "selling" the energy, as well as humanity at large in the longer term, in Orkney. All of the arguments, whether for or against the development, had interesting points in common; that their invocation of the kinds of social capital described related to the common good. How, then, were these arguments (and the way they are publicly, discursively contested) tied to ideas about community, society and culture, in particular?

Those in favor of the development used the economic benefits of "community" wealth generation and hybrid "ownership" via the social capital generated largely by private enterprise which would ensure community cooperation and potential growth. The developer, speaking in the local newspaper *The Orcadian*, said:

> Orkney has a tremendous wind resource. We are trying to do it as a local developer keeping the revenue within Orkney to help the Orkney economy. You have to look at the balance of economic benefit, community benefit and the visual impact.

Those against the project argued against it, invoking the highly rhetorical lexicon of UNESCO policy and analysis, including that any development that threatened the aesthetic, "universal value" of a public (government owned) commons which attracts tourism and profit should be rejected on the basis that common good is under threat. A letter to another local paper, *Orkney Today* (2007), reads:

> Some people don't seem to realize that given current form, the people of Orkney and all businesses that benefit from our vital tourist industry in particular, have more to lose than gain. For example, do we want to risk having the World Heritage Site designation stripped from the Heart of Neolithic Orkney? Surely not.

Such arguments were also posed by ICOMOS UK, in a statement submitted to the inquiry outlining its position on how the wind turbines might impact upon the setting of the WHS. Discussing the site's "universal values" in overtly humanist terms, Denyer (2008: 10) argued that "[t]he monuments of Orkney .... Encapsulate ... the ability of the visual attributes of the landscapes to have 'profound effects on psyche and disposition.'"

Arguing for a more overtly utilitarian approach to cultural conservation—that is, arguing for ensuring the "sustainability" of the Orkney community via financially securing its financial future, those in favor of the project argued that profit generated for the Orkney community via the Merranblo development argued that the project would keep the "community" profitable, modern, alive and dynamic in the face of collapsing traditional industries like agriculture and fishing; that it boosts the role of Scotland as a nation and "a people!" in the burgeoning "sustainable energy industry" in Late Capitalist Society; and that it demonstrates Scotland's environmental awareness, concern and compassion in a within a globalized world threatened by climate change. Arguing as a "heritage consultant" and appealing to sentiments relating to Lynn (2007) argued in a consultation document submitted to Historic Scotland:

> At the Stenness consultation event, a venerable and respected Orcadian with an immense pride in their heritage and no windfarm involvement whispered to me that the colonial imperialists had returned again. My impression is that this is an opinion held by many Orcadians in relation to the WHS proposals, and it should be treated as a serious message to avoid any possible future backlash against the continuation of the WHS from the people whose lives would be affected by its implementation.

Those categorically against the project argued that it: threatens conservation of historic, aesthetic authenticity, historical continuity, tradition, and traditional values in an increasingly globalized world; threatens the role of Scotland on "World Culture" stage; shows Scotland's important role in creating new aesthetically inspired artists; threatens Scotland's role in creating new scientific knowledge about human origins through WHS-encouraged European Union money to fund new excavations.

Community, Authenticity and Loss

Yet another strand of arguments featuring in the Merranblo case are appeals to differing notions of "authenticity" and "identity," concepts that are central to and valued highly by both heritage organizations like UNESCO and ICOMOS, as well as featuring as a theme in what many visitors seemed to say about the HONO. In "After Authenticity at an American Heritage Site," the now-classic work based on ethnographic work at the Colonial Williamsburg site in the US, Handler and Gable (1996: 568) claims that:

Heritage is one form of cultural salvage. A "lost world" or a world about to be lost is in need of "preservation" and the museum or heritage site bills itself as the best institution to perform this function .... They are also objective manifestations of cultural, ethnic, or national identity, which outside the museum is often perceived as threatened by collapse and decay.

Handler and Gable suggest here that the morality of identity and loss is often articulated and legitimated through official heritage policy and discourse. In cultural contexts where the past is employed to legitimate cultural histories and practices in the present, people are encouraged to hold sentimental attachments to material things that invoke collective, shared histories. Such sentiments have been explored extensively over the last two decades, and indeed came up time and again in my own interviews with visitors to the HONO, particularly at the henge monuments. The material past is something to be experienced in a pure, unmediated way, separate from the trappings of modernity. The following comment from my research illustrates this, in that the visitor wants to experience the HONO monuments without the visibility of the present:

> It [power lines] seems to destroy the natural setting of the site in a way. I mean its, you know, you're standing here looking at things that are thousands of years old, and then you've got the wires, the telephone wires, you know, and you're surrounded by the modern, you've got all this modern stuff. (Respondent SoS-8, *Monuments in Practice* (McClanahan 2006))

In defense of a similar view of heritage and embodied experience of the HONO WHS, one of the heritage professionals also defended the idea of unmediated encounters with the past. In *The Orcadian* (2007), the individual notes that "Visitors today value the open, natural, setting of these sites. Comparison with Stonehenge is often made, with many visitors commenting that they prefer the lack of development in the Orkney landscape."

Supporting such sentiments, an individual who identified themselves as members of Orkney's artistic community, also ardently defended this position in similar terms, invoking a number of themes to situate the case in relation to how identity is constructed around the material world, the power relations involved in development processes, as well as contesting the ways in which "developers" as a sociocultural group are categorized as wishing to industrialize (and perhaps thereby commodify) a landscape that instead has 'intrinsic' rather than utilitarian value. One respondent (Anonymous 2010) to the Scottish Government consultation on Merranblo argued that:

> ... current forms of consultation are being latched onto by self-interested developers in an extremely disproportionate manner. This has also been true in local Council consultations where renewables developers and their paid consultants actually respond far more actively than the general public who are

suffering from consultation/volunteer fatigue, apathy of course and a distinct lack of spare time. There is also a silent majority who still naively believe that SNH, SEPA and planning legislation look after all interests in a dare I say it—even and democratic manner. From what I have seen this simply is not the case. At Merranblo Public Inquiry we saw how private developers with full backing of the local councilors were quite happy to challenge, and lose if necessary, Orkney's Neolithic World Heritage Status for the sake of three badly sited wind turbines .... Orkney's west coast has provided Orkney with everything from official council logo, official Orkney "The Brand" imagery, dozens of Orkney Business brochure covers and nearly every other Orkney Tourist Brochure cover that I can remember. Yet we are being told that for the good of the nation we must industrialise this view .... We have to be very careful not to ruin this image of Scotland and its islands. I honestly believed we had for the first time in a long time a Scottish government that was singularly proud of the nation's iconic landscape ... Little did I know that there were forces at work that put political expediency above natural heritage. The last planning guidance that quietly went out to regional authorities I'm told, read like a "developers charter"! It costs money and real time to properly overview planning policy and strategy for the goodof all, and of course it actually costs nothing to keep the obvious wild and beautiful pieces of each regions landscapes as they are and as visitors and locals expect them to be.

It seems that it was the final appeal to the morality of the loss of a kind of "aesthetic" authenticity—both materially and in relation to perceived threats of "cultural change"—if Orkney were to lose its vital tourist industry vis-a-vis the potential loss of World Heritage Status—that helped representatives of the Orkney Islands Council rejected the Merranblo project planning application.

Conclusion

This chapter has engaged with some contemporary ethical and moral questions surrounding how people understand preservation, conservation and the ways in which discourses of "sustainability" are performed and contested amongst varying social groups at a particular WHS. Using the classic concept of "the Commons," to illuminate various elements of how people tend to see and understand "conservation" in relation to both the historic preservation of material heritage for the benefit of "humankind." Specifically, I examined how social groups and political organizations argue for harnessing forms of material "heritage" for their potential economic benefits, and legitimate these stances through articulation of their interests within "official" policy, mass media outlets, and other documented community exchanges. It thus provides a case for examining how different types of philosophical discourses concerning conservation can come into conflict with one another in the context of "managing" "commons" resources like WHSs.

It has also outlined the ways in which ethnographic approaches to the study of World Heritage Sites has been and is integral to gaining an understanding of the impact of heritage management practices on communities who live amongst them, as well as demonstrating that qualitative research can illuminate how conflicts and tensions surrounding WHSs are played out in practice amongst social actors with varying political, economic and cultural interests.

The arguments presented both for and against the Merranblo project all outline overtly humanist and utilitarian moral debates about how the conservation of "living" cultures should be ensured, the well-being of humanity at large in relation to the stewardship of the natural world, as well as the potential "loss" of culture through the loss of history and possible economic degradation in the globalized world. Following these arguments, and employing the concept of "the commons" to analyze them provides further evidence of how heritage sites are integral to the ways in which moral values are judged and articulated in contemporary society. The case of Merranblo is of particular interest from an "heritage ethnography" point of view, as it pits a number of arguments about cultural and natural conservation against one-another, which at first glance seem diametrically opposed, but on closer analysis, are actually deeply similar in terms of the themes through which they are discursively mediated. They appeal to people's sense of morality, duty, community, and the idea of working towards a "common good."

References

Anonymous (2010). *Response to Scottish Land Use Strategy Consultation in Relation to the Proposed Wind Farm at Merranblo, Orkney*. Available at <http://www. scotland.gov.uk/Resource/Doc/341108/0113285.pdf.> (accessed May 2, 2011).

Aull-Davies, C. (2008). *Reflexive Ethnography*, 2nd edn. London: Routledge.

Denyer, S. (2008). *Prerecognition for ICOMOS-UK, Public Local Inquiry into an Application for the Proposed Erection of Three Wind Turbines at Merranblo, Orkney*. Available at <http://www.scribd.com/doc/2055837/Orkney-World-Heritage-Site-Precognition-for-ICOMOSUK.> (accessed May 2, 2011).

Gable, E. and Handler, R. (1996). After Authenticity at an American Heritage Site. *American Anthropologist*, New Series, (98)3: 568–78.

Hardin, G. (1968). The Tragedy of the Commons. *Science*, 162, (3859): 1243–8

Lynn, D. (2007). *Historic Scotland Heart of Neolithic Orkney Management Plan Consultation Response*. Available at <http://www.historic-scotland.gov.uk/ lynn__david.pdf> (accessed May 2, 2011).

Marcus, G. (1998). *Ethnography through Thick and Thin*. Princeton, NJ: Princeton University Press.

McClanahan, A. (2006a). Histories, Identity and Ownership: An Ethnographic Case Study in Archaeological Heritage Management in the Orkney Islands. In: Edgeworth, M. (ed.), *Ethnographies of Archaeological Practice*. California: AltaMira Press, pp. 126–36.

McClanahan, A. (2006b). Monuments in Practice: The Heart of Neolithic Orkney in its Contemporary Contexts. Manchester: University of Manchester, unpublished PhD thesis.

McClanahan, A. (2007). The Cult of Community: Defining 'the Local' in Public Archaeology and Heritage Discourse. In: Grabow, S., Hull, D. and Waterton, E. (eds), *Whose Past, Which Future?: Treatments of the Past at the Start of the 21st Century*. Oxford: British Archaeological Reports, pp. 51–6.

Nonini, D. (2008). *The Global Idea of the Commons*. New York: Berghahn Books.

Orkney Today (2008). Local Concerns Aired at Merranblo Inquiry. *Orkney Today*, 31 January. Available at https://www.orcadian.co.uk/ (accessed September 2011).

The Orcadian (2005). Stromness Wind Farm Development Announced. *The Orcadian*, April 4–10. Available at https://www.orcadian.co.uk/ (accessed September 2011).

The Orcadian (2007). Turbine Plans Under Fire at Public Meeting. *The Orcadian*, October 8–14. Available at https://www.orcadian.co.uk/ (accessed September 2011).

Chapter 17

Old Maps, New Traffics: Political Itineraries around Scattered Heritage of Portuguese Origin

Maria Cardeira da Silva

Introduction

Increasingly closer to the universalistic rhetoric's of Human Rights—and thus, trapped in the same ambivalences—UNESCO promotes local and regional cultures while appealing to feelings and emotions allegedly universal in its search for global ethics. The "international community" is more and more an imagined community of emotions which is displayed through its diverse, although universal, heritage. It is thus only natural that at this stage of globalization there is frequent recourse to UNESCO's powerful instruments to ensure international sanction of political statements and rhetorics of economic development, and this is particularly true of countries with few resources of any other kind. This is a fact, whether we are dealing with countries outside the Western world (Africa, Asia or South America), or countries on the periphery or semi-periphery, such as Portugal, or else regions within these with even less economic resources and a far more muted political voice. A multi-sited (Marcus 1995) and plural ethnography of patrimonialization and touristification processes in places in North and Western Africa with ancient historical interchanges with Portugal within a contemporary and global context is particularly interesting because it throws a light on political relations that emerge between peripheral states and some south-to-south networks, thereby decentralizing a debate that remains far too often shaped by a vertical "UNESCO/ classified sites" axis of analysis.

Despite efforts of many anthropologists (Eriksen 2001; Wright 1998 and others), transnational institutions such as UNESCO and other political entities, such as states themselves, are still frequently perceived in abstract and disembodied and depersonalized manners—which is accentuated by a bureaucratic form-filling, communication and institutional language. Seen from this light, these entities seem disconnected from the social world and as such seem immune to a real flow of emotions. Pursuing networks and emotive experiences that travel between the ordinary every day and the institutional, the local and the transnational, the people and the state, can show how emotions flow in different directions and are negotiated at different levels. This might be an important path to understand both the attraction of some places while others are forgotten, as well as the success of integration in some heritagization processes while others cause social upheavals. I will endeavor to show this by taking you on a journey to some destinations where heritage of Portuguese influence is under process of patrimonialization.[1]

AlJadida (Morocco)

In 2004, AlJadida—by the time of Portuguese presence Mazagan—succeeded on its second attempt in having its application as UNESCO World Heritage accepted after its name was changed for the sake of its application from "Portuguese City of AlJadida (Mazagan)" to the "Portuguese City of Mazagan (AlJadida)" as a result of pressure from the Portuguese delegation. In the criteria presented by UNESCO to justify its final decision what was mostly highlighted was the past of AlJadida connected in some way with Portugal. Although the citadel underwent later occupations, in particular as a *mellah* (Jewish quarter, as it is still commonly known today) until the early twentieth century, and that these remain visible and were taken into consideration in its application dossier, they were not catapulted forward as a validation for its patrimonialization. This type of legitimization obviously serves Portugal's purposes far better seeing that, as it has few recourses for international cooperation, it continues to invest principally in its image as a former first "globalizer" during its Golden Age of Discovery in the sixteenth century. This allows Portugal to maintain a national image both for foreign as well as domestic consumption. However, from an economic point of view, it was very much in Morocco's interest to gain UNESCO's approval given the concomitant development of a tourist project along the coastal area between AlJadida and Azamor, a few kilometers to the north, where another citadel was being restored with the help of the Portuguese. It may have been this that led Morocco to allow this form of territorial alienation of heritage which we could consider dissonant (Tunbridge and Ashworth 1996). This along with the fact that historical distance of Portuguese colonization makes it less threatening in Morocco's memory. The management of heritage of Portuguese origin is in a privileged position in comparison to others, such as the French and Spanish, which have a more recent colonial history and strained political relations with Morocco. Whatever the case may be, Moroccan concessions to Portuguese requests about its heritage are underscored by the possibility of getting another discourse going, an alternative yet corresponding one in Portugal's favor: one that also falls back on the military and architectural magnificence of the

---

1   The following reflections are supported by ethnographies developed in the scope of two research projects funded by the Portuguese Foundation for Science and Technology, which I have been coordinating since 2004: the current edition is called "Castles Abroad II. Heritage, Tourism and Portuguese Cultural Cooperation in African Contexts."

monuments in order not to sing the praises of those who built them but to glorify all the better those who managed to get rid of them.

In AlJadida, as in other sites of Portuguese influence in Morocco (such as Arzila or Essaouira) it is not so much the heritage criteria as advanced by UNESCO that are shown as tourist attractions. In fact, the Portuguese citadels are in themselves, just as walled-in *medinas* are, features that are in line with the contemporary tourist's taste as a whole. First of all, because they are framed and objectified. Then because they allow us to visualize the strata of different occupations as they follow one another through the centuries inside a space that won't consent to large structural and urban changes. Therefore, they are, as a rule, centers of huge historical and cultural density with a very active contemporary social life. This is why in many cases it is easy to apply here a multiculturalist discourse and insist on the notion of conviviality, which really only conceals and aestheticizes a succession of historical events and frequently hides moments of conflict. Churches that became mosques or synagogues reflect the presence of different religious groups at different times, but the synthetic and uncritical argument is that of a timeless fusion of a common heritage. In AlJadida, time is compressed to give the tourist the idea of creative diversity so dear to UNESCO and now equally prized by tourists.

AlJadida is on many levels a good demonstration of heritage as a contemporary and metacultural process. Let us now go to one of its main tourist attractions and a must for all tourists: the cistern. Nobody in the sixteenth century, which is when the Portuguese built this magnificent room, had access to what is today the citadel's visiting room but once was used to store water in case of siege. The supposed lure of the tourist gaze at authenticity is spoilt because the gaze here is subterranean and totally different from that which guided the daily affairs of the men and women who lived on the surface. MacCannel's notions of backstage and frontstage seem to get really dazed here.

Another rhetoric that has been developed in parallel with the citadel heritage has to do with the African diasporization through the Atlantic. In 1769, the Portuguese abandoned Mazagan after bombing it with their own cannons. Within the framework of the Amazonia colonization policy that the ruler of Portugal, the Marques de Pombal, had drawn up, the people who had until then lived in the Moroccan fortress were sent to what is now the State of Amapá in Brazil. Uprooted, they created there a New Mazagan. A brief ethnography (Silva and Tavim 2005) shows how transatlantic contacts and protocols have developed between these two urban agglomerations and how this is being increasingly used in diplomatic relations between Morocco and Brazil. This has set off a root-tourism on the part of some Brazilians from Amapá who now seek their origins in Morocco, tracing their genealogy back to colonial elites and thereby ensuring their present social capital. And then there are the Quilombola. They say they are the descendents of escaped African slaves in Brazil and now trying to claim their origin in the Mazagan as the first moment of the diasporization of the black-african slave community. In these discourses, Morocco is essentialized and referred to as "Africa" in order to justify the origin of negritude. (This reading does not seem, however, to have a great deal of historiographic foundation in that none of the *colonial* uprooted families taken to Amazonia were accompanied by African slaves.) To all effects and purposes, what is important to highlight here is the political eloquence afforded by the visibility given by UNESCO, thereby awarding people a capacity to set up networks and initiating new maps and itineraries of identities.

As in so many other historical centers, these and other gentrification fluxes interfere with the residents' habitat and daily lives. In AlJadida, urban requalification processes sets inflation and real estate speculation soaring. "Like in Palestine," say some young people of AlJadida seated at the entrance to the cistern as they see several houses being bought and restored by foreigners. They repeat here Dennison Nash's models for interpretation of tourism as a new form of imperialism over "leisure peripheries." However, this does not prevent these same young people from displaying in one of their tourist shops a Barcelos rooster—a symbol of popular Portuguese culture as emblematized during Salazar's fascist dictatorship. They call it, ironically, Dom Sebastião, the king who, in Portuguese legends, disappeared one misty morning in Morocco and is to return to save Portugal (but whose tomb is well identified by the Moroccans near Alkasr Kibir, where the Portuguese army was vanquished).

In this imagined community of people who share emotions that UNESCO is striving to create, AlJadida is a stage on which to display various things: Portugal's pride in its history, the viability of creative and peaceful diversity that cultural and touristic industries increasingly produce as an attraction and, finally, a focus for diasporic nostalgia. But, as Kirshemblatt-Gimblett says, "a hallmark of heritage productions—perhaps their defining feature—is precisely the foreignness of the 'tradition' to its context of presentation" (1995: 374). In this case, local inhabitants don't seem to recognize themselves in any of these displays of emotions. Lacking political resources, with the space they circulate in daily regulated tightly by the patrimonialization apparatus and tourist routes, and with their homes appropriated by foreigners, they opt for the economic advantages that result from decisions their government made without consulting them, while making ironic remarks about the political and asymmetric relations that the patrimonialization process reproduces.

I lack the time to examine (which would be needed here for a more complete understanding of the question) the diplomatic relations between the two countries, basically economic investment interests on the part of Portugal (road infrastructures, telecommunications and tourism) and political on the part of Morocco (proximity to the European Union and a common approach to the Atlantic). None of these interests, or any relevant diplomatic relationship, seems, however, to have any influence over the case that I am now going to speak about: the patrimonialization and entry into tourist routes with the help of Portuguese bilateral cooperation of Ouadane, a small oasis in Adrar—a mountainous desert region in north Mauritania.

Ouadane (Mauritania)

Ouadane, a small oasis of some 2,300 inhabitants, has recently entered the touristic routes of the Mauritanian desert. Ouadane belongs to the route of holy libraries—along with Chinguetti, Tichitt and Oualata—and shares with these other towns the symbolic capital of knowledge and religiosity gathered during centuries of pilgrimage flow, coming from the south on their way to Mecca. As a result, UNESCO accepted its application as an "ensemble" in 1996 according to criteria 3 and 4.

In the specific case of Ouadane, something else has contributed to its touristic capitalization and to place it on the tourist route: this was the construction of the walls around the ruins of the *ancienne ville* subsidized under the scope of a bilateral cooperation agreement signed by the Portuguese and the Mauritanian governments in 1998. Such cooperation was warranted by the idea that the Portuguese had built a trading post there in the fifteenth century in order to intercept the caravans of Saharan merchants (something which is still to be archeologicaly confirmed). The construction of the walls has played an important role in the touristic promotion of Ouadane, since it permitted a new reading of the landscape: something which used to be a pile of stones became "ruins" and earned a symbolic density that enabled it to be transformed into a touristic attraction. A touristic attraction that appeals to the preservationist rationale, the salvage impulse (Butcher 2003), which leads most tourists to Ouadane. Those ruins are the leftovers of a past that deserves all efforts to preserve it since it supports the identity of cultures: remains of culture. What most tourist are not aware of is that, although Ouadane has obviously its own history that it strives to save—and now to display as merchandise for tourists—the type of construction that the walls signal and preserve—a *ksour*—was not necessarily enclosed by walls (see Cheikh, Lamarche, Vernet and Durou 2002). This type of urban gathering was adapted to the seasonal rhythms and flows of its inhabitants who lived mostly from long-distance trade and goat grazing and, therefore, a *ksour* was made of perishable material, since its population was relatively mobile. Constructions and ruins were intertwined. In any given moment, the ruins were part of the present of the town, whose inhabitants did not waste much effort rebuilding what time or the unpredictable force of the river destroyed every year. Moreover, the several drought periods (in the 1960s and 1980s) and subsequent urban migration, the war between Mauritania and Senegal in 1989 and, with more direct effects over Ouadane, the Sahara War, all contributed to its *natural* urban decadence (at that time, Ouadane had hardly little more than 100 inhabitants). And when, at the beginning of the 1990s, some of the country's more distinguished patricians returned, in part attracted by the cultural capitalization of their homeland, they were more committed to developing the new part of the town than repopulating the ancient nucleus. Consequently, preservationist worries that today are part of daily ideology and practices in Ouadane seem relatively recent and imported. The ruins (*ghariba*), nowadays circumscribed by the walls built with the help of Portuguese funding—testify to a much more recent past (and therefore, from a semantic point of view, much more insignificant) than tourists can imagine. They possess, nonetheless, a fundamental value—rightly accrued by the circumscription that has improved its display—since, in the eyes of the visitor, they claim the need to preserve, or shall I say, to salvage local heritage. In the eyes of the tourist, ruins are the witnesses to a marked out authenticity that you need to preserve at all cost.

The ethnographies that we managed to carry out on emerging tourism in Ouadane—and which we published in other places (Silva 2006, 2010)—show that in Ouadane, what attracts most tourists is this sense of frailty and urgency expressed in the monumental enframing of the ruins and other areas of local touristified life and culture. The UNESCO highlighted motive of safeguarding turns into a tourist attraction itself. The emotion that moves many tourists who visit Ouadane, and most of them are supportive and engaged with local development, is the appeal of preserving an endangered culture and ethnicity. Inadvertedly, Portuguese cultural cooperation appears to have actually contributed towards local development. Part of the local population—frequently the youngest members and those with less symbolic capital and thus less social constrictions—has joined the process: not only because they have found economic recourses in it, but also because they view it as a way to join "modernity." In this case, and more significantly than what seems to be happening in AlJadida where the government has had a greater presence in the whole process, at least part of the local population here has re-appropriated in an informal and creative manner the dramaturgy of safeguarding heritage as inspired by the capitalization of UNESCO. This is evident, among many things, in the proliferation of spontaneous museums that come in the aftermath of the process. In Ouadane, as well as in neighboring Chinguetti, the foreignness of the "tradition" to its context of presentation has been reincorporated in "culture." This is also visible, on a broader Atlantic scale, in the last case that I want to present to you.

Gorée Island (Senegal)

In 1994, UNESCO launched the Slave Route Project, a program that supports among other things the setting up of structures to develop "places of memory tourism." African countries involved in similar patrimonialization processes have undertaken to set up networks and to lobby at UNESCO committee meetings with the aim of getting African monuments accepted as World Heritage. It was within this framework that the classification of Cidade Velha of Ribeira Grande in Cape Verde as World Heritage was proposed to UNESCO in 2009. In June 2009 I attended a seminar in Gorée (Senegal) that dealt with this application dossier and with the importance of south–to–south cooperation and the role that the heritagization of slavery could have in challenging tangible—thus eminently colonial—heritage allegedly hypervalued by UNESCO in Africa. At the same seminar, concomitant discussions regarding the twinning of the towns of Gorée and Cidade Velha were using kinship vocabulary, as is common in this type of political procedure, with Cape Verde (represented by a delegate of the mayor of Cidade Velha) calling Gorée its elder sister (as UNESCO's classification of Gorée dates back to the end of the 1970s). The final debate at the seminar, also attended by students from the Dakar School of Architecture, was lively even rather heated, and mainly revolved around the fact that heritage rehabilitation in Africa was in the interest of its "financers." It was further inflamed when notions of debt and reparation were brought to the arena of debate as one of the young students suggested that it should really be colonizing countries that had to pay Gorée for the rehabilitation of this type of heritage, which was in remembrance of the oppression that local people had endured for centuries.

But along with these south-to-south cooperation networks, Gorée has also been twinned, in 2008 with Lagos (Algarve, Portugal), the birthplace of the first European navigator to reach Gorée (then called Ilha da Palma). I felt that both the mayor of Gorée and the team from Lagos were friendly and genuinely committed to developing joint activities under the formal umbrella of town twinning. This was made evident in the words both sides proffered at the official ceremonies. But, at the same time, the "Seven Portuguese Wonders of the World" contest was launched with the support of the Portuguese government and was to perturb the sleep as well as the dreams of Luso–tropicalism in Portugal.[2] An online petition against this contest circulated among academics and eventually triggered public debate about slavery. The petition drew attention to the fact that "when describing these sites (of slavery), the organization of the contest omitted the history of these places and the use they had during the period of the Atlantic slave trade."[3] The petition signers requested "all those concerned by the research on the Atlantic slave trade to disagree with the attempt to diminish and erase the history of this commerce, in order to exalt a glorious Portuguese past expressed in the architectural 'beauty' of these sites of death and tragedy." I do not intend to pursue this debate here, one that Portugal has evaded officially until now. But these discursive fragments illustrate how nations connect with each other, within the 'international community' framework, by means of a kinship language (or, in others cases, one of neighbors) while displaying emotions such as hurt, revolt, shame and pride. Emotional contradictions and paradoxes are being sublimated through multiculturalist conceptions consonant with the "creative diversity" proposed by UNESCO, either sustained in the present or projected in the past, even when this diversity is the result of a traumatic history.

---

2 Luso-tropicalism, which actually was a concept proposed by Gilberto Freire—a well-known Brazilian ideologist—to glorify the virtues of Brazilian hybridism and support multiculturalism, refers to a distinctive Portuguese soft way of colonialism that promoted race and culture miscegenation. According to Freire, the historical roots of luso-tropicalism were to be found in the multicultural stratigraphy of Portuguese own National History. It was this legacy of genuine tolerance that later on softened Portuguese colonialism and produce what he entitled as *luso-tropicalism*. There is an underlying rhetoric of Portuguese colonialism which still persists in the official documents.

3 http://www.petitiononline.com/port2009/petition.html (accessed May 2, 2011).

In 1992, at the House of Slaves in Gorée Island, the Pope, John Paul II, apologized publicly for the role played by the Catholic Church in the period of the Atlantic slave trade. Visiting Africa, Bill Clinton, George W. Bush and the Brazilian President, Lula da Silva also condemned the wrongs of the slave past. It was in this setting of condemnation and celebration of the memory of slavery that Barack Obama also spoke to the world on the spectacular stage that is one of the Ghanaian castles. Obama's speech was not very fervent and this was perhaps deliberate. Nor did it have to be: his negritude and his nationality were strong enough factors to arouse the required emotion in a bellicose landscape where, from behind the cannons, one can imagine the dramatic voyage that Gilroy places at the heart of the formation of the African diasporic identity and cultural history (1992). Other presidents have provided more spectacular performances than Obama did. Lula da Silva, as the Pope and Mandela are said to have done, cried at the "door of no return" of the Slave House in Gorée. Although Edward Bruner in his short essay on the Ghana Castle (1996) attests to animosity between white and black tourists, Lula's visit to Gorée emphasized the experience of negritude, which included himself, who the Senegalese president called the first "black" president of Brazil. In the House of Slaves, Lula held a metal ball that had once been tied to a slave's ankle and tried on an iron chain. "The pain of slavery is like a kidney stone. There's no point in talking about it, it has to be felt. It's only by standing here that we understand the enormity of what these people felt during those three hundred years," he said.

This is what many tourists say, and perform, in different ways when they highlight and display the experience of pain these sites arouse. These emotions are shared publicly, as in the case of many videos on *YouTube* showing people crying convulsively in Gorée. Records of the same emotions can also be found in the Visitors' Book at the House of Slaves.

These expressions and sort of commoditization of the memory doesn't end in Gorée. Many Afro-American diasporic artists, whether they have Senegalese roots or not, have turned the island into an icon of *negritude* to export in a variety of performative formats, such as music, dance and film, converting the emotions experienced there into inspiring and artistic material. We cannot examine here this profusion and diversity that regularly returns to the island even if only at the time of the great Gorée Diaspora Festival that the government promotes every year.

This whole paraphernalia of means, forms and circuits raises an awareness of the wide range of emotions that converge onto and emerge from the island, which are made authentic by the experience of being there. On their return to Gorée, some of these transnationalized performances have greater effect than others on the locals, especially the youth. The world famous Daraa J. Rap group have retained in their repertoire a long speech that the old charismatic curator of the Slave House—Joseph N'Diaye—often mentioned in the international media made about slavery, and which they present at the start of their international concerts. I found it on mobile phones and Mp3s belonging to many young people in Gorée.

In this case, it seems that it is the transnational voyage of the Daraa J. tours that transform Joseph N'Diaye's message into an authoritative one for local young people.

But there are other forms of incorporating memory and emotion currently taking place in Gorée. Unlike roots tourism to Elmina Castle (of Portuguese origin as well) in Ghana, the number of Afro-American visitors to Gorée has declined (due to air traffic, amongst other things). Educational tourism for students, and not just Senegalese students, is what Gorée nowadays seems to be investing in. Every Wednesday the island receives students from different grades and of different ages. The House of No Return is then transformed into a classroom for lessons on the history of Africa and the rest of the world. In the current class that the present curator performs (in French) every week, the most repeated words regarding slavery are "Pour pardonner mais non pas oublier" (To forgive but not forget).

As Kirshenblatt-Gimblett says "the power of heritage is that it is curated, which is why heritage is more easily harmonized with human rights and democratic values than is culture" (2004: 1). The patrimonialization of slavery in Gorée followed this path and transformed the island into a pedagogic setting where pain, regret and pardon are displayed. This, perhaps even better than the other examples I have given you, shows why UNESCO can be examined in the light of Bennet's assumptions about what he called the "exhibitionary complexes"—museums, galleries, national and international exhibitions in the nineteenth century (Bennet 1988). Just as they historically opened up objects to more public contexts of inspection and visibility, forming new public and inscribing them in new relations of sight and vision, UNESCO seems to continue fulfilling, on another scale, the same regulating function that nation states undertook in modernity: the creation of an imaginary community of feelings with a global ethic by means of a set of cultural technologies that organize a voluntary self-regulating global citizenry.

References

Bennett, T. (1988). The Exhibitionary Complex. *New Formations*, 4(Spring): 73–102.

Bruner, E.M. (1996). Tourism in Ghana. The Representation of Slavery and the Return of the Black Diaspora. *American Anthropologist*, 2(98): 290–304.

Butcher, T. (2003). *The Moralization of Tourism. Sun, Sand and … Saving the World*. London and New York: Routledge.

Cheikh, A.W.O., Estibal, S., Lamarche, B. and Vernet, V. (2002). *Sahara. L'Adrar de Mauritanie sur les traces de Théodore Monod*. Paris: Vents de Sable.

Clifford, J. (1997). *Routes: Travel and Translation in the Late Twentieth Century*. Cambridge, MA: Harvard University Press.

Eriksen, T.H. (2001). Between Universalism and Relativism: A Critique of the UNESCO Concept of Culture. In: Cowan, J.K., Dembour, M.-B. and Wilson, R.A. (eds), *Culture and Rights. Anthropological Perspectives*. Cambridge: Cambridge University Press, pp. 127–48.

Gilroy, P. (1992). *The Black Atlantic: Modernity and Double Consciousness.* Cambridge, MA: Harvard University Press.

Kirshenblatt-Gimblett, B. (1995). Theorizing Heritage. *Ethnomusicology*, 3(39): 367–80.

Kirshenblatt-Gimblett, B. (2004). From Ethnology to Heritage: The Role of the Museum. *SIEF Keynote*, Marseilles, April 28. Available at <http://www.nyu. edu/classes/bkg/web/SIEF.pdf> (accessed May 2, 2011).

Marcus, G.E. (1995). Ethnography in/of the World System: The Emergence of Multi-Sited Ethnography. *Annual Review of Anthropology*, 24(1): 95–117.

Pratt, M.L. (1992). *Imperial Eyes: Travel Writing and Transculturation.* London; New York: Routledge.

Silva, M.C. (2006). Hospedaria Vasque. Cultura, raça, género e expediente num oásis da Mauritânia. *Etnográfica*, November 2(10): 355–81.

Silva, M.C. (2010). Mauritanian Guestbooks. In: Palmer, C.A., Lester, J.-A.M. and Burns, P.M. (eds), *Tourism and Visual Culture, Volume 1: Theories and Concepts.* Oxfordshire: CAB International, pp. 181–91.

Silva, M. and Tavim, J.A. (2005). Marrocos no Brasil: Mazagão (Velho) do Amapá em festa—a festa de São Tiago. *Actas do Congresso Internacional 'Espaço Atlântico de Antigo Regime: poderes e sociedades'.* Lisbon: Conhecer, Biblioteca Digital Camões.

Tunbridge, J.E. and Ashworth, G.J. (1996). *Dissonant Heritage: The Management of the Past as a Resource in Conflict.* Chichester: Wiley.

Wright, S. (1998). The Politization of Culture. *Anthropology Today*, (14)1: 7–15.

Chapter 18

World Heritage and Sustainable Tourism: Shared Values?

Jane Brantom

World Heritage, sustainable tourism and values-based management are concepts that have developed since the 1970s. In the words of De la Torre and Mason (2002: 3): "It is self-evident that no society makes an effort to conserve what it does not value." But considering what society does value, and in particular the relationship between World Heritage and values-based management, on which much has been published (De la Torre 2005), little has been published on links between World Heritage and sustainable tourism values and the implications this has for policymakers and practitioners. The question of whether shared values exist between World Heritage and sustainable tourism and, if so, the implications of this for both World Heritage and tourism management will be explored at a theoretical level in the following pages. Values are mapped and critical comparisons made, themes are identified and conclusions drawn about the World Heritage and sustainable tourism interface. A model derived from the analysis suggests an approach for improved understanding of the World Heritage and sustainable tourism interface that could be applied to policy and practice.

Values and Value-Based Management

Values have been described as "… priorities, internal compasses or springboards for action—moral imperatives. In this way, values or mores are implicit or explicit guides for action" (Oyserman 2001: 16, 150). There are many other definitions and dimensions of values (Smelser and Baltes 2001: 16, 138–57), but the concept of values as "guides for action" is the interpretation used in the following discussion and is fundamental to the concept of values-based management.

Values-based management has been described as an approach "in which the main management goal is the preservation of the significance and values of a place" (De la Torre 2005: 5). While values-based management is being explicitly developed in the areas of culture and heritage management, its application for sustainable tourism is more implicit. For example, the growth in attention to branding and tourism destination management in the UK is based on identifying core values of an area and using these values as "guides for action" for all associated activity. It is about preservation and presentation of the significance and values of a place, in this case for tourism development.

Socio-cultural values:

Historical value: *connection with the past*
Cultural/symbolic value: *objects or sites as repositories or conveyors of meaning*
Social value: *connections with others, a sense of identity*
Aesthetic value: *beauty, harmony*
Spiritual/religious value: *understanding, enlightenment, insight*

Economic values:

Use (market) value
Non-use (non market) values:

- Existence value: *(people value the existence of a cultural facility or heritage item regardless of whether they wish to take part in it or use it themselves)*
- Option value: *(people want to keep open the possibility of using or enjoying something in the future, even though they don't use it today)*
- Bequest value: *(people value leaving something to future generations)*

Figure 18.1   Mason's typology of heritage values (De la Torre 2002) with descriptors from Throsby

Source: Clark 2006: 43.

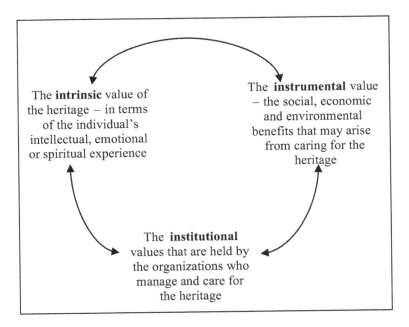

Figure 18.2   Cultural values

Source: Hewison and Holden 2006.

Values are clearly important to both heritage and tourism management. But what type of values are these? Prior to the 1990s, heritage management values were dominated by historic values. The more recent inclusion of socio-cultural values reflect the post-modern turn towards broader interpretations and definitions of heritage (Graham 2000). Figure 18.1 illustrates a typology of heritage values that identifies "socio-cultural" and "economic" categories of values. Figure 18.2 describes "intrinsic," "instrumental" and "institutional" cultural values based on work in the UK (Hewison and Holden 2006). Both typologies will be referred to in the following pages.

World Heritage Values

The following section analyzes values of world heritage at a number of levels; the United Nations (UN), the United Nations Educational, Scientific and Cultural Organisation (UNESCO), the World Heritage Convention and site inscription (Table 18.1). Ultimately, World Heritage values are derived from the UN, established in 1945 "to promote international cooperation and to achieve peace and security" (UN 2008). UNESCO was founded in 1945 as a specialized agency of the UN responsible for "promoting international understanding through education, social and natural science, culture and communications" (UNESCO 1945). The UNESCO aim is now summarized as, "Building peace in the minds of men and women" (UNESCO 2011).

At the levels of the UN and UNESCO, values of intercultural respect and understanding, tolerance, mutual assistance, fundamental freedoms for all are evident (UN 2008; UNESCO 1945). More emphasis on education, the free exchange of knowledge and ideas and protection of heritage is unsurprisingly evident within UNESCO (ibid.). The overarching aim of both is international peace.

The next level considered is the *Convention Concerning the Protection of the World Cultural and Natural Heritage*, known as the World Heritage Convention. The convention was adopted in 1972 and its values derive from both UN and UNESCO values but also reflect its history. The convention grew from international movements, largely led by Europe and America after World War Two, concerned with preserving and protecting cultural and natural sites of "Outstanding Universal Value" (OUV) (UNESCO 1972). The World Heritage Convention's guidelines define OUV as

> ... cultural and/or natural significance which is so exceptional as to transcend national boundaries and to be of common importance for present and future generations of all humanity. As such, the permanent protection of this heritage is of the highest importance to the international community as a whole. (UNESCO WH Centre 2008: para. 49)

The emphasis is clearly on valuing exceptional places that are considered to be of universal importance.

Table 18.1 World Heritage values

Common values: UN; UNESCO; World Heritage Convention; World Heritage Sites						
Universal—important to all humanity; collective responsibility; transcend national boundaries; mutual respect and understanding						
UN values						
International peace	Common welfare of mankind	Intercultural respect and understanding	Mutual assistance	Fundamental freedoms for all	Human Rights	Tolerance
UNESCO values *"Building peace in the minds of men and women"*						
Peaceful and equitable sustainable human development through education, social and natural science, culture, communications	Free exchange of knowledge and ideas	Equality of educational opportunities for all	Protection of cultural heritage			
UN World Heritage Convention values						
Identification, protection, conservation, preservation and transmission to future generations of cultural and natural heritage of outstanding universal value	Universal ownership and collective responsibility	International collaboration	Intercultural respect and understanding			
World Heritage Site inscription—core values (Outstanding Universal Value)						
Exceptional examples of value to all humanity	Historical cultural, symbolic, social, aesthetic, spiritual, religious significance	Authenticity and integrity				

As well as being able to demonstrate integrity and authenticity, sites must meet criteria set out in the guidelines to the convention (UNESCO WH Centre 2008: paras 77, 78). These criteria include descriptors such as "exceptional, outstanding, unique, superlative ..." (UNESCO WH Centre 2008), and values expressed largely reflect the socio-cultural values referred to in Figure 18.1. They tend towards a material interpretation of these values and also favor traditional historic, scientific and aesthetic values (Table 18.1).

This tendency towards material values combined with the concept of universality has, it has been argued, led to over-emphasis on the inscription of monumental and architectural sites in the early years of the Convention (UNESCO 2007). The core concept of universalism as it relates to World Heritage has been contested by many as a eurocentric concept (Labadi 2007; Titchen 1996). The term does, after all, stem from the enlightenment philosophy that has its roots firmly planted in Europe. The issue of the need for greater representation was, and remains, a constant theme within discourse on World Heritage (UNESCO 2002, 2007: 25). Research suggests that one of the barriers to greater representation was lack of understanding of the World Heritage Convention (Labadi 2007). The debates, discussion and reports both from within UNESCO and by academics and others about the nature, values and processes of the World Heritage List continue (Harrison and Hitchcock 2005; Leask and Fyall 2006, 2007) but underpinning most of these, it is suggested, is the issue of improved understanding of the values of World Heritage.

Moving on to individual values, each world heritage site is required to produce a Statement of Significance (SoS) which includes a description of the site's OUV as well as assessments of integrity and authenticity and requirements for protection and management (UNESCO WH Centre 2008: para. 155). The SoS includes the World Heritage criteria values for which the site is inscribed and, in theory, guides all work around the World Heritage Site. However, there are many other values that can be attributed to heritage sites not covered by world heritage criteria. These tend to be instrumental or economic values (Figures 18.1 and 1892), and include socio-economic values often associated with tourism. In site management, all values attributed to it need to be taken into account. The caveat is that they should all contribute to, or enhance, the values (or OUV) of the site otherwise the World Heritage status of the site may be under threat. This is one of the challenges for World Heritage management and one that needs to be understood by all stakeholders.

The volume of debate and frequency of use of the word *value* in World Heritage documentation show how values and values-based management is central to world heritage management, at least at a theoretical level. It can be argued that values of world heritage go back to the UN and UNESCO values of aiming for peace, intercultural respect and understanding as well as the historic and socio-cultural values reflected in WH inscription. The analysis now goes on to look at values of sustainable tourism.

Sustainable Tourism Values

Searching for global definitions and values of sustainable tourism is more complex than for World Heritage. World Heritage definitions and values are enshrined in the World Heritage Convention and its operational guidelines (UNESCO WH Centre 2008). Sustainable tourism on the other hand is a concept that like heritage, has been developed over the last 20–30 years, has no single global definition and is constantly evolving.

It was the *Brundtland Report* that really began to articulate and emphasize the need for holistic approaches to development and the interrelationship of economic, social and environmental impacts (World Commission on Environment and Development 1987). The report defined sustainable development as "a process to meet the needs of the present without compromising the ability of future generations to meet their own needs" (ibid.). During the 1980s and 1990s the phenomenon of tourism grew more and more, and there were many debates, academic and otherwise about its impacts (MacCannell 1999; Urry 1990). The concept of sustainable tourism began to emerge based on principles from the *Brundtland Report*.

In 1990, the UN established the World Tourism Organisation (UNWTO) as a specialist agency serving as a "global forum for tourism policy issues and a practical source of tourism know-how" (UNWTO 2008a). UNWTO "promotes the development of responsible, sustainable and universally accessible tourism, with particular attention to interests of developing countries" and has a membership of 161 countries and over 390 private and public sector affiliate members (ibid.). The UNWTO's conceptual definition for the sustainable development of tourism (Figure 18.3) was agreed in 2004 (UNWTO 2008b) and is used as the baseline in the following comparative analysis. In 2008, UNWTO also launched global sustainable tourism criteria in collaboration with the UN Foundation, the Rainforest Alliance and the UN Environment Programme (Partnership for Global Sustainable Tourism Criteria 2008). UNWTO is clearly a significant player in global sustainable tourism.

The UNWTO is however just one of several international industry networks and NGOs actively campaigning for sustainable tourism and other types of responsible tourism. The analysis continues with examining how far the sustainable tourism values described by these networks and groups reflect those for the UNWTO. The sustainable tourism values of nine industry groups, one government body and three NGOs as expressed in publications and web sites were compared against sustainable tourism values of the UNWTO (Tables 18.2 and 18.3). Organizations were selected through internet searches of tourism industry groupings and available sustainable and responsible tourism codes and policies.

"**Sustainable tourism development guidelines and management practices are applicable to all forms of tourism in all types of destinations**, including mass tourism and the various niche tourism segments. Sustainability principles refer to the **environmental, economic and socio-cultural aspects** of tourism development, and a **suitable balance must be established** between these three dimensions to guarantee its long-term sustainability.

Thus, sustainable tourism should:

1) **Make optimal use of environmental resources** that constitute a key element in tourism development, maintaining essential ecological processes and helping to conserve natural heritage and biodiversity.

2) **Respect the socio-cultural authenticity of host communities**, conserve their built and living cultural heritage and traditional values, and contribute to inter-cultural understanding and tolerance.

3) Ensure viable, long-term economic operations, **providing socio-economic benefits to all stakeholders** that are fairly distributed, including stable employment and income-earning opportunities and social services to host communities, and contributing to poverty alleviation.

Sustainable tourism development requires the **informed participation of all relevant stakeholders, as well as strong political leadership** to ensure wide participation and consensus building. Achieving sustainable tourism is a **continuous process** and it requires **constant monitoring of impacts**, introducing the necessary preventive and/or corrective measures whenever necessary.

Sustainable tourism should also maintain a **high level of tourist satisfaction** and ensure a meaningful experience to the tourists, raising their awareness about sustainability issues and promoting sustainable tourism practices amongst them."

Figure 18.3   United Nations World Tourism Organisation definition of sustainable tourism
Source: UNWTO 2008c.

Values were grouped into socio-cultural, environmental, economic and institutional values for the purposes of analysis. Comparisons between UNWTO and industry network values revealed greatest divergence on socio-cultural values, especially "helping intercultural understanding." There was a closer fit with environmental values, especially those to do with effective use of resources and a close correlation on economic values (except for "poverty alleviation and equity"). Values categorized as "institutional values" for this analysis showed a mixed response. Areas such as collaboration and long-term view showed greatest synergy here.

Table 18.2 Comparison of sustainable tourism values: UNWTO and industry groups

	UNWTO	CAST [1]	ITP [2]	PATA [3]	ResponsibleTravel [4]	TOI [5]	WTTC [6]	Travel Foundation [7]	Green Globe [8]	AITO [9]	VisitBritain [10]
1. Socio-Cultural Values											
Local social benefits	***	*	*	**	**	***		***	**	**	*
Help intercultural understanding	***	*	*	**	*	*	**	*			
Respect others' places and lives	***			***	***	***		**	*	**	**
2. Environmental Values											
Protect & conserve environment & heritage	***	*	*	***	***	***	**	**	***	***	**
Minimize resource use/pollution	***	***	***	***	***	***	**	***	***	***	***
3. Economic Values											
Local economic benefits	***	*	**	**	**	***		***	***	***	**
Viable long-term operations	***		***		**	***	***	***	**	**	***
Maintain tourist satisfaction	***	***	**	***	***	***	*	***	**	**	***
Poverty alleviation & equity	***					*		*			
4. Institutional Values											
Policy integration	***			***	**	***		**		***	**
Long-term global view	***		***		**	**	*	**	***	*	*
Long-term sustainability through balance	***		**	**	***	***		**	***	**	**
Inclusive of stakeholders	***			***	***	***		**	*	*	**

	[1]	[2]	[3]	[4]	[5]	[6]	[7]	[8]	[9]	[10]
Share knowledge	***		***	***	***	***	***	***	**	**
International collaboration	***	*	***	***	***	***	***	***	**	*
Universal—all tourism, everywhere	***			***	*	*	***	***	*	***
Collective responsibility	***			**	**	**	**	**	*	**

Sources: [1] CAST (2008). *Sustainable Tourism Certification.* Available at www.cha-cast.com (accessed April 11, 2008). [2] ITP (2008). *International Tourism Partnership.* Available at www.tourismpartnership.org (accessed April 11, 2008). [3] PATA (2008). *About PATA.* Available at www.pata.org/patasite/index (accessed April 11, 2008). [4] Responsible Travel (2008). Available at www.responsibletravel.com (accessed April 11, 2008). [5] TOI (2008). *Tour Operators Initiative for Sustainable Tourism Development.* Available at www.toinitiative.org (accessed April 11, 2008). [6] WTTC (2008). Available at www.wttc.travel (accessed April 11, 2008). [7] The Travel Foundation (2008). Available at www.thetravelfoundation.org.uk (accessed April 11, 2008). [8] Globe, G. (2008). *Green Globe.* Available at www.ec3global.com/about/why-be-sustainable (accessed April 11, 2008). [9] AITO (2008). *Responsible Tourism.* Available at www.aito.co.uk/corporate Responsible-Tourism.asp (accessed April 11, 2008). [10] VisitBritain (2008). *The Importance of Sustainable Tourism.* Available at www.visitbritain.com/en/campaigns/green/why-sustainability-important.aspx (accessed June 25, 2008).

Notes: *** close match, * weak match.

Table 18.3   Comparison of sustainable tourism values: UNWTO and NGOs

	UNWTO	IIPTT [1]	Tourism Concern [2]	WWF [3]
1. Socio-Cultural Values				
Local social benefits	***	***	***	*
Help intercultural understanding	***	***	***	*
Respect others' places and lives	***	***	***	*
2. Environmental Values				
Protect and conserve environment and heritage	***	**	***	***
Minimize resource use/pollution	***		***	***
3. Economic Values				
Local economic benefits	***		***	
Viable long-term operations	***			
Maintain tourist satisfaction	***			
Equity/poverty alleviation	***	***	***	
4. Institutional Values				
Policy integration	***		**	**
Long-term global view	***	***	***	***
Long-term sustainability through balance	***	**	***	***
Inclusive of stakeholders	***		***	**
Share knowledge/education	***	***	***	**
International collaboration	***	***	***	***
Universal, all tourism, everywhere	***	***	***	
Collective responsibility	***	***	***	**

Sources: [1] IIPT (2008). *International Institute for Peace through Tourism*. Available at www.iipt.org/media/transitions%20abroad.html (accessed April 11, 2008). [2] Concern, T. (2008). Available at www.tourismconcern.org.uk (accessed April 11, 2008). [3] WWF (2008). Available at http://www.wwf.org.uk/researcher/issues/Tourism/index.asp (accessed April 11, 2008).
Notes: *** close match, * weak match.

The closest correlation with UNWTO and industry values is with the Tour Operators Initiative for sustainable development (TOI). TOI is a partnership launched in 2000 supported by UNWTO, UNEP and UNESCO and represents 19 global tour operators (TOI 2008). The initiative appears to be well organized, highly articulate with a clear statement of commitment, mission and objectives and reflects many of the UNWTO values.

In the non-commercial sector, NGO comparisons with UNWTO values, unlike the industry comparisons, all show good correlation with institutional values particularly between the values of sharing knowledge; international collaboration; long-term global view and respect for others' places and lives. The matches with socio-cultural and environmental values on the other hand, vary by organization reflecting the NGOs' priorities. The World Wildlife Fund for nature (WWF), for example, emphasizes environmental, and the International Institute for Peace Through Tourism (IIPTT), social and humanitarian values. Economic values are largely absent.

At an international level, it can be seen, unsurprisingly, that the private sector led initiatives favor the economic instrumental values over the other values of the UNWTO sustainable tourism conceptual definition. However, they all include some socio-cultural as well as environmental values. A similar analysis even 10 years ago would probably have revealed more dominant economic values. There is a considerable degree of correlation with the UNWTO for some of the international industry networks and NGOS.

To conclude this section, it can be seen that definitions of sustainable tourism can vary significantly from one organization to another and in discussing sustainable tourism it is important to note the wide divergence in interpretations. All however include a balance between environmental, social, cultural and economic values in order to ensure that the place is there for future generations. When sustainable tourism is being discussed in the world heritage context, it is suggested that the UNWTO definition is applied as a reference point as both concepts derive from the UN.

The World Heritage and Sustainable Tourism Interface

Having made generalized conclusions about sustainable tourism values, the interface between world heritage and sustainable tourism will now be examined. This will be done firstly on a theoretical level and secondly by briefly looking at work of the World Heritage Centre and world heritage policy. The theoretical interface between UNWTO sustainable tourism and world heritage values is illustrated in Tables 18.4 and 18.5. Table 18.4 compares UNESCO, world heritage and UNWTO values. As all stem from the UN, values of collective responsibility, international collaboration, intercultural respect and understanding and long-term vision are apparent throughout. Differences emerge in the focus on economic values. Table 18.5 compares the UNWTO sustainable tourism principles first with world heritage values as expressed in the *World Heritage Convention* and its operational guidelines and then with the wider set of values that can be associated with World heritage site management. Once again, divergence is apparent in the economic sphere. It is recognized that economic values play an important part in world heritage management but, as discussed earlier, they do not relate to world heritage inscription. Protection (of the built and natural environment) on the other hand, does feature in both UNWTO principles and the *World Heritage Convention* and it is the tension between this and the economic dimension that not only goes back to the roots of the *World Heritage Convention* but also features in aspects of world heritage and tourism management today.

Table 18.4   Comparison of UN agency values

	UNESCO	**WH Convention**	**UNWTO sustainable tourism**
Universal ownership and responsibility	Yes	Yes	Yes
International collaboration and sharing knowledge	Yes	Yes	Yes
Intercultural respect and understanding	Yes	Yes	Yes
Protection of cultural and natural heritage of outstanding value	No	Yes	Yes
Authenticity and integrity	Yes	Yes	Yes
International peace	Yes	Yes	Yes
Economic development and prosperity	No	No	Yes

Table 18.5   UNWTO sustainable tourism and WH interface

UNWTO sustainable tourism principles	**Fit with WH values**	**Fit with wider WHS management values**
Long-term sustainability through balanced development	Yes	Yes
Optimal use of environmental resources … conserve natural heritage	Yes	Yes
Conserve built and living cultural heritage and traditional values	Yes	Yes
Ensure viable, long-term economic operations, providing socio-economic benefits	No	Depends on the site
Informed participation of all relevant stakeholders	Yes	Yes
High level of visitor satisfaction, raising awareness about sustainable issues	No	Yes

Part of the UNESCO World Heritage Centre's work is to deal with these tensions. To help address this and to help the Committee and those responsible for world heritage site management make better use of tourism; a world heritage tourism program was established in 2001. The stated mission was "to aid the World Heritage Committee and site management using tourism as a positive force to retain World Heritage site values and to help mitigate site threats" (Unesco World Heritage Centre 2008). Manuals guiding tourism management at world heritage sites were produced (Pedersen 2002) together with the creation of new linkages and programmes between key players in the tourism and conservation sectors (UNESCO 2007: 190). The program was coordinated by the World Heritage Centre which also conducts missions to examine impacts of tourism development projects on world heritage and organizes workshops for world heritage site managers. Raising awareness of world heritage among tour operators and the public was an important part of the work and the program established partnerships with other intergovernmental agencies, NGOs, the UNWTO and the tourism industry. In 2007, greater emphasis was put on sustainable tourism and the sustainable tourism initiative was established as part of the program.

The world heritage tourism program has now ended and ways of taking the work forward are being considered. Recommendations are that these should include the following elements:

- adopt and disseminate standards and principles relating to sustainable tourism at world heritage sites;
- support the incorporation of appropriate tourism management into the workings of the Convention;
- collation of evidence to support sustainable tourism program design and to support targeting;
- contribution of a world heritage perspective to cross agency sustainable tourism policy initiatives. (Martin Jenkins & Associates Ltd 2010)

This move by the World Heritage Centre to address the world heritage and tourism interface reflects wider recognition by UNESCO of the relationship between world heritage and economic and other development. The *Budapest Declaration* of 2002 for example, states the intention to "seek to ensure an appropriate and equitable balance between conservation, sustainability and development, so that world heritage properties can be protected through appropriate activities contributing to the social and economic development and quality of life of our communities" (UNESCO 2002). Sustainable tourism development, it is suggested, is logically classified as such an "appropriate activity" in this context. The *World Heritage Convention's* operational guidelines also refer to World heritage sites supporting, "a variety of ongoing and proposed uses that are ecologically and culturally sustainable" (UNESCO WH Centre 2008: para. 119).

Discussion and Conclusion

Comparison of World Heritage and sustainable tourism values shows many areas in common, first and foremost the need to ensure that the place is there for future generations and that it maintains its authenticity and integrity. Other common values at a global level include universal responsibility, intercultural respect and understanding, long-term sustainability through holistic management, protection of the environment, involvement of stakeholders and international collaboration. The main difference of emphasis is the World Heritage focus on protection and preservation (of OUV) of the built and natural heritage and the sustainable tourism concern with appropriate socio-economic development. The history of both movements reveals differences. Sustainable tourism development as a recognized concept has been implemented now for nearly 30 years and the *World Heritage Convention* for even longer. World Heritage stemmed largely from potential threats to the built heritage from conflict and economic development. Sustainable tourism started largely from concerns about the impact of tourism on the environment and communities.

The values analysis also reveals that although there is a greater emphasis on values-based management in the field of World Heritage, values also appear to be core to sustainable tourism work, at least in theory and especially at an international level. The analysis shows World Heritage generally having more humanitarian values than most sustainable tourism definitions, with the UNWTO definition of sustainable tourism arguably most closely reflecting world heritage values. Whilst the UNWTO does not have a convention to rely on, it is suggested that encouragement of more industry groups to adopt the UNWTO conceptual definition of sustainable tourism could be a positive move.

Moving on to World Heritage site values-based management, Figure 18.4 shows a suggested theoretical values-based framework for' linking world heritage management and sustainable tourism work in policy and practice. The SoS described earlier is core to this model and can be described as the "filter" for guiding work around a world heritage site. The model describes how World Heritage values should not just be a fundamental part of World Heritage Site management but also recognized in tourism management of the area, region or "destination" in which the site is located.

The theoretical model shows how well-managed tourism focusing on the intrinsic World Heritage site values could contribute to the preservation of OUV at a World Heritage Site. The approach could bring other benefits too. From the tourism management point of view, acknowledgment of the broadest interpretation of World Heritage values brings recognition that the World Heritage Site is an international, not just a national asset and responsibility. It can bring opportunities for introducing sustainable tourism concepts into areas where this is not yet practiced through using the World Heritage Site as an exemplar regional or national project. The sustainable tourism approach can also help contribute to wider climate change and development agendas.

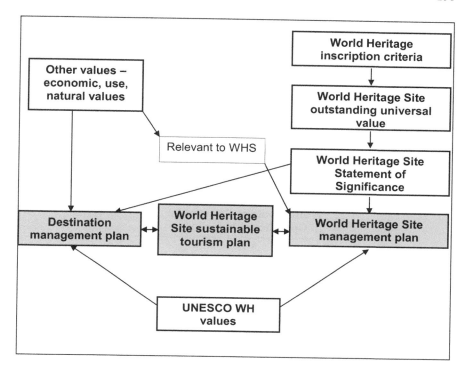

Figure 18.4   Values-based WHS and sustainable tourism management

From the World Heritage management point of view, adopting such an approach can give opportunities to influence tourism planning, to introduce sustainable tourism principles where they do not exist and develop and support them where they do. This can include encouraging others in the area, and suppliers to the World Heritage Site, for example, to adopt sustainable principles.

Good understanding of World Heritage and OUV as well as sustainable tourism by all stakeholders is critical to success of such an approach and significant education programmes are, arguably, needed. The lead bodies for developing and delivering work may be very different. For example, the lead body for tourism may be the regional tourism agency whereas for World Heritage it will be the site owner and, possibly, a world heritage management plan committee including tourism expertise. As has been shown, developing better understanding of all stakeholder values and common agendas can help avoid conflicts between competing economic and conservation values (De la Torre 2005).

In considering implementation of this model, one point that may be considered is the historic difference between cultural heritage and tourism management.

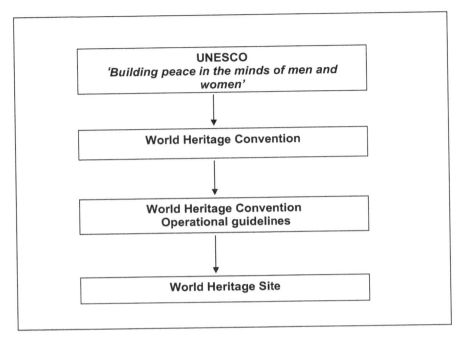

Figure 18.5 The roots of world heritage

The former has tended to be monocentric whereas tourism management considers wider linkages (McKercher and du Cros 2002). Encouraging those involved in World Heritage management to take a broader view and improve understanding of destination management and tourism work is beginning to feature in the World Heritage Centre's work and is a good example of developing mutual understanding of values (WH Centre 2008). An extension of this is to look at branding in tourism. It can be argued that the OUV defines the "essence" of the World Heritage Site. Similarly, work on branding a tourist destination identifies core values of that place and the principle is that all activity, marketing or development, associated with the place must reflect this "brand essence." In communicating the OUV of World Heritage to tourism stakeholders it may help to draw on these parallels and explain OUV in terms of "brand essence." The OUV may then be communicated to visitors and reflected in supporting tourism development in ways that should bring long-term benefit to both the World Heritage Site and the tourism industry. A challenge in this is to explain OUV in simple, non-academic terms to non-world heritage experts and the visiting public. It is suggested that further research on the role of tourism in contributing to, and communicating the significance of, World Heritage could be useful.

A final point is that lack of understanding of the *World Heritage Convention* has been identified as an issue of all aspects of world heritage, not solely tourism, policy and management (UNESCO 2007; WH Centre 2008). In considering World Heritage, the usual focus is the *World Heritage Convention*. It is suggested that more explicit inclusion of the UNESCO goal of "Building peace in the minds of men and women" (Figure 18.5) in World Heritage work could contribute to UNESCO aims of better understanding of World Heritage and improved communication and capacity building in World Heritage management (UNESCO 2002, 2007). This could also contribute to the concept of World Heritage Sites as places of intercultural dialogue (Hitchcock 2005: 185, Robinson and Picard 2006: 57). Greater understanding of both UNESCO goals and OUV could also help in the UK, where the gap between UK sustainable tourism, and global World Heritage values was identified through an extension of this research as more apparent than that between UK World Heritage policy and the UNWTO.

The question of whether or not there are shared values between World Heritage and sustainable tourism and implications of this for World Heritage Site management was posed earlier. The above analysis demonstrates that while definitions of sustainable tourism may vary considerably, there are many common values. From this it can be concluded that values-based sustainable tourism development that adheres to UNWTO values would appear to be an invaluable tool to aid implementation of the *World Heritage Convention*. Values-based sustainable tourism can, in theory, help present and preserve the significance and values of World Heritage. There will always be tension between access and protection but developing greater understanding of World Heritage values by the tourism industry and policy makers and of the tools and values of sustainable tourism by World Heritage management could make a significant contribution to the long-term future for both World Heritage and tourism.

References

Clark, K. (2006). *Capturing the Public Value of Heritage*. London: English Heritage.

De la Torre, M. (ed.) (2002). *Assessing the Values of Cultural Heritage: Research Report*. Los Angeles: Getty Conservation Institute.

De la Torre, M. (ed.) (2005). *Heritage Values in Site Management, Four Case Studies*. Los Angeles: Getty Publications.

Graham, B., Ashworth, G.J. and Tunbridge, J.E. (2000). *A Geography of Heritage: Power, Culture and Economy*. London: Arnold.

Harrison, D. and Hitchcock, M. (eds) (2005). *The Politics of World Heritage: Negotiating Tourism and Conservation*. Clevedon: Channel View Publications.

Hewison, R. and Holden, J. (2006). *Capturing the Public Value of Heritage Conference*. London: English Heritage.

Hitchcock, M. (2005). Afterword. In: Harrison, D. and Hitchcock, M. (eds), *The Politics of World Heritage: Negotiating Tourism and Conservation*. Clevedon: Channel View Publications, pp. 251–63.

Labadi, S. (2007). Representations of the Nation and Cultural Diversity in Discourses on World Heritage. *Journal of Social Archaeology*, 7(147): 148–70.

Leask, A. and Fyall, A. (eds) (2006). *Managing WHS*. Oxford: Elsevier.

Leask, A. and Fyall, A. (2007). Managing WHS. *Journal of Heritage Tourism*, 3(2): 131–237.

MacCannell, D. (1999). *The Tourist: A New Theory of the Leisure Class*. Berkeley, Los Angeles and London: University of California Press.

Martin Jenkins & Associates Ltd (2010). *Draft Final Report of the UNESCO World Heritage Tourism Programme Evaluation*. Available at <http://whc. unesco.org/en/sessions/34COM/documents/> (accessed August 22, 2008).

McKercher, B. and du Cros, H. (2002). *Cultural Tourism: The Partnership between Tourism and Cultural Heritage Management*. New York: Haworth Hospitality Press.

Oyserman, D. (2001). Values: Psychological Perspectives. In: Smelser, N.J., Wright, J. and Baltes, B. (eds), *International Encyclopedia of the Social and Behavioural Sciences*. Oxford: Pergammon.

Partnership for Global Sustainable Tourism Criteria (2008). *Sustainable Tourism Criteria*. Available at <www.sustainabletourismcriteria.org> (accessed October 28, 2008).

Pedersen, A. (2002). *Managing Tourism at World Heritage Sites*. Paris: WH Centre.

Robinson, M. and Picard, D. (2006). *Tourism, Culture and Sustainable Development*. Paris: UNESCO.

Smelser, N. and Baltes, P. (eds) (2001). *International Encyclopedia of the Social and Behavioural Sciences*. Oxford: Elsevier.

Titchen, S. (1996). On the Construction of "Outstanding Universal Value." *Conservation and Management of Archaeological Sites*, 1(4): 235–42.

TOI (2008). *Tour Operorators Initiative for Sustainable Tourism Development*. Available at <www.toinitiative.org> (accessed April 11, 2008).

UN (2008). *History and Charter*. Available at <http://www.un.org/aboutun/> (accessed June 23, 2008).

UNESCO (1945). *Unesco Constitution*. Available at <http://portal.unesco.org/en/ev.php-URL_ID=15244&URL_DO=DO_TOPIC&URL_SECTION=201.html> (accessed June 23, 2008).

UNESCO (1972). *Convention Concerning the Protection of the World Cultural and Natural Heritage*. Paris: UNESCO.

UNESCO (2002). *The Budapest Declaration*. Paris: UNESCO.

UNESCO (2007). *World Heritage: Challenges for the Millenium*. Paris: UNESCO World Heritage Centre.

UNESCO (2011). *Homepage*. Available at <http://www.unesco.org/new/en/unesco/> (accessed March 21, 2011).

UNESCO WH Centre (2008). *Operational Guidelines for the Implementation of the World Heritage Convention*. Available at <http://whc.unesco.org/en/guidelines> (accessed June 23, 2008).

Unesco World Heritage Centre (2008). *Sustainable Tourism Programme.* Available at <http://whc.unesco.org/en/sustainabletourism> (accessed November 3, 2008).

UNWTO (2008a). *About UNWTO.* Available at <http://www.unwto.org/aboutwto/index.php> (accessed April 11, 2008).

UNWTO (2008b). *Sustainable Development of Tourism.* Available at <http://www.unwto.org/sdt/mission.php> (accessed April 11, 2008).

UNWTO (2008c). *Sustainable Development of Tourism.* Available at <http://www.unwto.org/sdt/mission/en/mission.php> (accessed August 27, 2009).

Urry, J. (1990). *The Tourist Gaze.* London: Sage Publications.

UNESCO (2008). *Managing Public Use at WHS.* Paris: UNESCO World Heritage Centre.

World Commission on Environment and Development (1987). *Our Common Future (The Brundtland Report).* Oxford: Oxford University Press.

Index

For Product Safety Concerns and Information please contact our EU
representative GPSR@taylorandfrancis.com Taylor & Francis Verlag GmbH,
Kaufingerstraße 24, 80331 München, Germany

Printed and bound by CPI Group (UK) Ltd, Croydon, CR0 4YY
08/05/2025
01864530-0001